HITLER'S
Siegfried Line

Neil Short

SUTTON PUBLISHING

First published in 2002 by
Sutton Publishing Limited · Phoenix Mill
Thrupp · Stroud · Gloucestershire · GL5 2BU

British Library Cataloguing in Publication Data
A catalogue record for this book is available from the British Library

ISBN 0 7509 2762 3

Typeset in 10.5/13.5 pt Times.
Typesetting and origination by
Sutton Publishing Limited.
Printed and bound in England by
J.H. Haynes & Co. Ltd, Sparkford.

Contents

Mother, dear, I'm writing you from somewhere in France,
Hoping this finds you well,
Sergeant says I'm doing fine 'A soldier and a half'
Here's what we'll all sing,
It'll sure make you laugh:

Chorus

We're gonna hang out the washing on the Siegfried Line,
Have you any dirty washing, Mother dear?
We're gonna hang out the washing on the Siegfried Line,
'Cos the washing day is here.
Whether the weather may be wet or fine,
We'll just rub along without a care,
We're gonna hang out the washing on the Siegfried Line,
If the Siegfried Line's still there.

Second Verse

Everybody's mucking in and doing their job,
Wearing a great big smile,
Everybody's got to keep their spirits up to-day!
If you want to keep in swing,
Here's the song to sing!

Lyrics by Jimmy Kennedy, music by Michael Carr

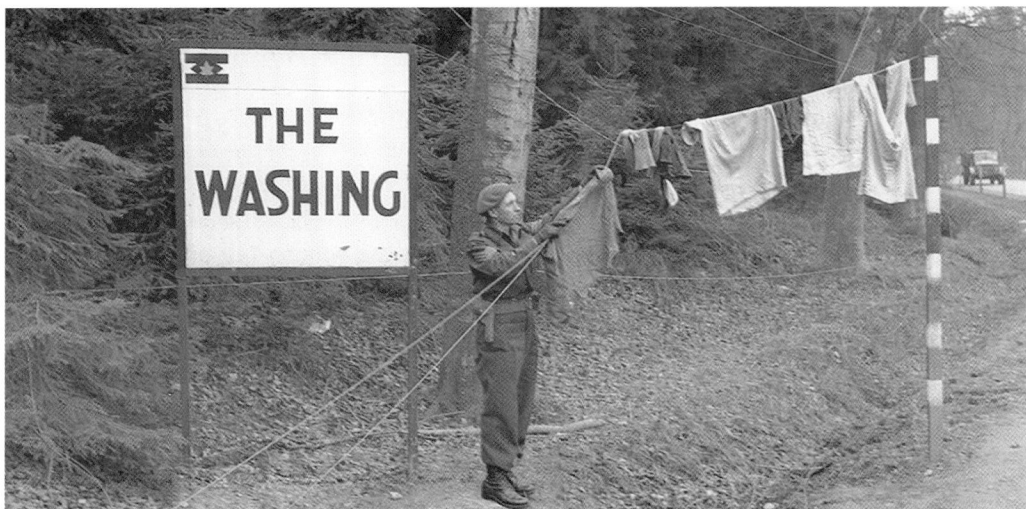

Sergeant L.E. Thompson of the Canadian Army Film and Photo Unit hanging up washing on the Siegfried Line, Kleve, 31 March 1945.

Preface

In the summer of 2000 I was invited by Jonathan Falconer of Sutton Publishing to discuss a proposal for a book that I had. After a short meeting and a very pleasant lunch in a public house in the historic town of Stroud, tucked away in the Cotswolds, I returned to my home in Somerset with a commission, not for a book based on my original idea but a book on the Siegfried Line. Disappointed that my initial idea had been rebuffed, but delighted with the commission, I began to turn over ideas in my mind and the more I considered the subject matter the more I realised that this subject, at least in terms of English language texts, has been very much overlooked.

I should stress at this point that although I did not plan to write a book on the Siegfried Line, and had not specifically researched the subject, I had, over a number of years, carried out a lot of research on different aspects of the defences and the commission by Sutton enabled me to draw a lot of these threads together. As such I am deeply grateful to Sutton Publishing, and in particular Jonathan Falconer, for giving me the opportunity to write this book. Without his vision I would not have considered writing about such a seemingly vast topic.

Clearly, the sheer diversity of the subject necessitated contacting numerous bodies and individuals as I gathered the material to complete my research. In particular, I would like to thank the staff at the Imperial War Museum, especially the Departments responsible for Documents, Printed Books and Photographs. I should also like to thank the staff at the Public Record Office who processed my seemingly endless requests for files. The staff in the photographic department at the Bundesarchiv, Koblenz were also most helpful, especially as they patiently tried to understand my schoolboy German.

Special thanks are also due to a number of veterans I contacted in the course of my research. In particular I would like to thank Bob Kingsbury (94th Division) and Robert Herman (5th Armored Division).

A number of individuals who volunteer their time and energies to the furtherance of knowledge of fortifications also contributed in no small way to the production of this book. Margaret Pinsent of the Fortress Study Group has provided immeasurable assistance in my research over the years, as has Herbert Jäger, who provided many useful contacts and avenues of research. Frank Klar and the other volunteers at the Westwall Museum, Niedersimten, kindly showed me around their museum and allowed me to use material relating to the *Gerstfeldhöhe*.

At this juncture I would also like to thank Mike Yared who provided me with details of a number of pertinent texts and the staff at Nailsea Library who attempted, but sadly could not always trace these rare, specialist publications. Your efforts were nevertheless very much appreciated.

I should also like to express my special thanks to the staff at the Abbey Wood Library, in particular Mr Frank Pritchard, who efficiently processed my numerous requests for texts and politely notified me when they were overdue! I should also like to thank the staff at the MoD Whitehall Library who diligently traced the obscure titles that I ordered from their extensive holdings, many of which had not been borrowed for some considerable time.

Finally, I would like to thank my family. During my formative years my parents and sister tolerated the unusual interest I had in things military and subsequently supported me during my time at university. More recently my wife has not only helped me to draft and translate numerous letters and documents but has also kept everyday interruptions to a minimum so that I could concentrate on my writing and research – so important when trying to write and keep down a full-time job. She also showed immense patience and forbearance when we were on holiday; for, while the average family enjoys a beach holiday in Spain or Greece, I have dragged her around the battlefields, museums and archives of Europe and beyond. I hope the sacrifice was worthwhile!

> This book is dedicated to the memory of Elizabeth Annie Bastin (15 May 1899 – 17 November 2000), who witnessed the monumental events of the twentieth century from its dawn to its close.

Introduction

The voice of his fate was stronger than the supplications of his parents: 'Stay with us, please. One day you will inherit the royal crown!' But he was not to live long enough. The father lived longer than the son. However, on the other hand, glorious splendour still surrounds the name of the young hero.

From the Rhine Saga 'Siegfried and Kriemhilde'

It may seem somewhat strange in a factual work such as this to admit at the outset that the title of the book is 'technically' incorrect. That is, the fortifications constructed on Germany's western border were officially called *Der Westwall* or the West Wall, rather than the Siegfried Line. The anglicised version was adopted by the western powers soon after work began on the defences and was derived from the name given to a German defensive line of the First World War that ran along a similar axis.[1] However, it is unclear whether it was renamed because of a genuine belief in the similarities of the two or whether it was an attempt to belittle Hitler's 'impregnable' defences, the predecessor being a much shorter and less impressive position. Whatever the reasoning behind the name it stuck, helped in no small part by a song penned in the early days of the war – 'We're gonna hang out the washing on the Siegfried Line'. The song was written by the British songwriters Jimmy Kennedy and Michael Carr and was popularised in London by Ambrose and his orchestra. Ubiquitous during the Phoney War, the song lost a little of its appeal after the defeat of France when Hitler largely abandoned the West Wall and concentrated his efforts on the construction of fortifications along the coast. This confused the matter of names still further with the coastal defences being referred to as the 'New West Wall'. However, this name was rarely used and instead the more widely accepted title – 'The Atlantic Wall' – was adopted. After the war English language texts on the subject generally referred to the Siegfried Line, while in Germany the reverse was true with references to the original, official nomenclature. For the purposes of this book, however, the two terms are used synonymously.

Original 78 of Arthur Askey's version of 'We're gonna hang out the washing on the Siegfried Line'. (Author)

In the First World War the Allies had similarly renamed the *Siegfriedstellung* as the Hindenburg Line as a mark of respect to the

A concrete machine-gun shelter of the Siegfriedstellung *at Le Pave, summer 1917. The inscription reads: 'In greatest need was this built here, for a hero's death I greatly fear, 23.4.17 M.K., 19'. (Imperial War Museum)*

man attributed with its design and construction. In fact the Chief of Staff of the German First Army, Colonel Fritz von Lossberg, was the principal architect. He was concerned about the ability of the *Siegfriedstellung*, as envisaged, to defeat the anticipated Allied offensive. Although undoubtedly strong – the defences were to include forward and rear trenches, reinforced with concrete pillboxes sited to cover the approaches and barbed wire laid in front of the defences in such a way as to channel the attacking troops into pre-prepared killing zones – they were only to be constructed in a relatively narrow band. Von Lossberg planned to create a defensive system that would consist of numerous zones each stronger than the last which would gradually slow and ultimately stop the enemy attack. By building the defences in depth the attacking infantry would soon outreach its supporting artillery, making further progress all but impossible. Moreover, the attackers would become increasingly isolated from their own forces and thus vulnerable to counter-attack by reserves held in the rear, safe from the preliminary bombardment, and earmarked for the purpose.

The practical application of von Lossberg's ideas saw the construction of a series of defences in front of the main position. Forward of the first trench was the outpost zone which was designed to slow the enemy attack. If the enemy pierced this first line of defence it would enter the battle zone which was chequered with little forts, machine gun nests and strong points. These positions were all mutually supporting providing fire for their own defence and cover for the flanks and rear of the adjacent units in the so-called 'Hedgehog' (Igel) pattern of defence. Behind this zone were the defences of the Siegfried Line proper which was now known as the *Siegfried Zwischenstellung* (or to the British as the Hindenburg Support Line). With work on these positions complete, von Lossberg set about creating another line built on the same principles to the rear which was named the *Siegfried II Stellung*. More defensive lines further to the rear were also contemplated. Thus to describe this position as a 'line' was a misnomer; it was a defensive system built in depth (in fact some 6 – 8,000 metres).

The Hindenburg Line was eventually breached, but this was largely the result of German exhaustion and the arrival of fresh American soldiers rather than frailties in the defensive system developed by von Lossberg. In the postwar period as the German High Command sought to understand the reasons for Germany's defeat it would have been easy to overlook this fact, but it did not. The senior staff believed that there was still merit in the defensive strategy and tactics adopted in the war and in particular the idea of defence in depth. However, the Versailles *diktat* meant that it would be difficult to meaningfully employ any of the lessons learned and the newly formed *Reichswehr*[2] was obliged to bide its time. As the years passed and the restrictions placed on the German military were eased, removed or simply ignored, Germany began to construct a series of fortifications along her western border that utilised many of the principles developed in the First World War. A series of small reinforced concrete shelters, protected by a curtain of anti-tank obstacles, covering almost the whole length of the western border and built in considerable depth, were constructed. Again, the idea was to slow the invader's advance, sucking it into a bloody battle of attrition as the enemy forces fought their way deeper and deeper into the defensive system. As they became weaker and increasingly detached from their own lines they would be vulnerable to a counter-stroke that would be launched at the critical moment.

Nor was this the only similarity between the defensive system of the First World War and the West Wall. Many of the structures were built to standard patterns (although not on the same scale as those in the West Wall) enabling the mass-production and pre-fabrication of many of the parts. Larger strong points, called *werke*,[3] were also built and although less elaborate and not as strong as their successors they were nevertheless the precursor of the later West Wall structures that bore the same name. In addition, civilian contractors were employed to construct the concrete bunkers and pillboxes just as they were to be in the construction of the West Wall. The authorities also made use of forced labour from Belgium and France and used Russian prisoners of war, as was the case in the latter stages of the Second World War.

In marked contrast to its German counterpart, the French High Command drew very different conclusions from the fighting of the First World War. Its thinking was strongly influenced by the bloody battle of Verdun and in particular the crucial role played by the old but immensely strong forts around which the gallant defence of *la patrie* had been organised. Unable to maintain an army of occupation in Germany indefinitely, it was decided to build a series of defences along the border to prevent future German aggression and, not surprisingly, the design of the defences owed much to the perceived strengths of the forts at Verdun.

The Maginot Line, as the defences were christened,[4] was begun in 1929 and over the next seven years a thin line of powerful forts was constructed along France's northeastern frontier. The completed fortifications were undeniably impressive and the ideas and expertise were exported to France's friends and allies, principally Czechoslovakia, but also Belgium and to a lesser degree Holland and Poland, so that eventually a concrete collar ringed Germany. Hitler used the construction of these fortifications, albeit defensive in nature, and the failure of the western powers to disarm

Workers improvise an anti-tank position near Pirmasens, Germany. (Imperial War Museum)

as justification for his flagrant contravention of the terms of the Versailles peace settlement. Firstly, Germany rearmed and then remilitarised the Rhineland. Unchallenged, Hitler was now free to construct his own border defences, but his motives were far from peaceful. Unlike his neighbours, Hitler planned to use the defences as a bulwark to deter the western powers while he sought to extend his Reich eastward.

Work on the West Wall began in 1936 and made slow but steady progress until the first quarter of 1938 when Hitler introduced the first of a series of orders for the acceleration of the building programme that continued until the outbreak of war. The completed defences were immensely strong, but they were not impregnable, as Hitler would have had everyone believe. The western powers had gathered an immense amount of detail on the defences and were well aware of their shortcomings. Equally, the likely casualties that would accrue should they launch an offensive against Germany perturbed them. Unwilling to countenance such an attack they prevaricated and allowed both Czechoslovakia and Poland to be overrun by Hitler's forces. Britain and France now awaited the inevitable German assault confident that the forts of the Maginot Line would stymie any attack, but their confidence was misplaced. When Hitler attacked he circumvented the main defences of the Maginot Line, striking through neutral Belgium. The German *blitzkrieg* unhinged the Allies' defence and forced the British Expeditionary Force to withdraw from the Continent, its tail between its legs, leaving France to fight on alone. Recognising the situation was hopeless the French Government sued for peace.

Its purpose seemingly served, the West Wall was now mothballed. Weapons and equipment were removed and inhabitants who had been evacuated from the war zone returned to their homes and attempted to rebuild their lives as Europe enjoyed a peaceful interlude, albeit an uneasy one. Hitler now concentrated his efforts on extinguishing the Bolshevik menace and, with the cancellation of the planned invasion of Britain, the construction of coastal defences from Norway to the Spanish border which he hoped would act as a deterrent to Britain and later the United States. As it transpired neither of Hitler's aims were realised. Stalin's Russia proved a much more resilient foe and gradually the tide of the war in the east turned. In the west the Anglo-American forces stormed Hitler's 'Fortress Europe' and by September 1944, exceeding even the most ambitious forecasts, the Allies stood on the German border. Abandoned for four years the defences of the West Wall would surely present few problems to the all-conquering Allied armies. Certainly General Eisenhower and his staff thought so. Events were to prove them horribly wrong. Restricted by logistical difficulties and with deteriorating weather making movement on the ground difficult and curtailing air support the Allies spent the final months of 1944 involved in a series of bloody battles as they advanced literally pillbox by pillbox through the line.

In December the optimism of the summer was finally shattered when the Germans launched a massive counter-offensive. The Battle of the Bulge, although finally stopped

A motorcycle patrol passing through a thick belt of barbed wire and dragon's teeth, 27 September 1939. (Imperial War Museum)

well short of its target, saw the Germans recapture many of the Siegfried Line positions that had been so dearly bought in the previous months. The prospect of attacking these positions again filled the Allies with foreboding, although in the end it proved to be a less daunting undertaking than initially envisaged. The German winter offensive turned out to be Hitler's last throw of the dice. With reserves of men, equipment, fuel and ammunition dwindling the once mighty *Wehrmacht* could do little to stem the Allied advance and soon the Siegfried Line was broken and the Americans were across the Rhine. The Allies could at last hang out their washing on the Siegfried Line, but they had paid a terrible price in casualties.

Notes

1. In the First World War the Imperial German Army generally designated their defensive lines after mythical gods and heroes such as Wotan, Hagen and Siegfried. The Siegfried Line or *Siegfriedstellung* was conceived in September 1916 (although not manned until the spring of 1917). It was some 90 miles long and ran from Arras to St Quentin and on to Soissons on the Aisne.

2. The name given to the standing army during the Weimar Republic and the early years of the Third Reich.

3. For example, the Hanseatenwerk.

4. Named after the new Minister for War, André Maginot.

— · —	National border	
XXXXX	Siegfried Line	
● (2)	B-Werke (No. of forts)	
·········	Luftverteidigungszone	
▨▨▨	Lake	

Scale 0 ⬅➡ 50kms

Battery position ⊣ 17cm ⊣⊢ 24cm ⊣⊢⊢ 30.5cm

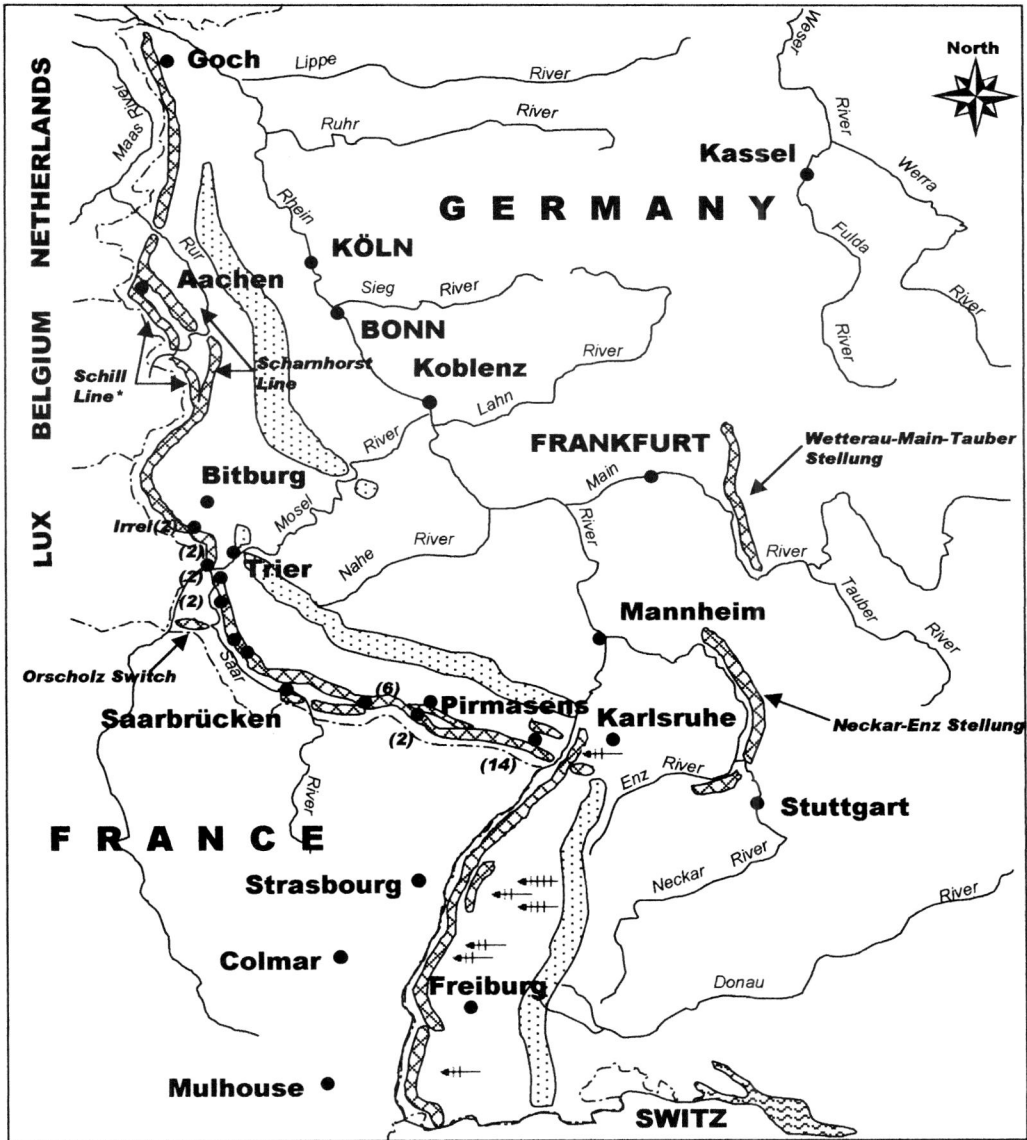

Also known as the Aachener Vorstellung

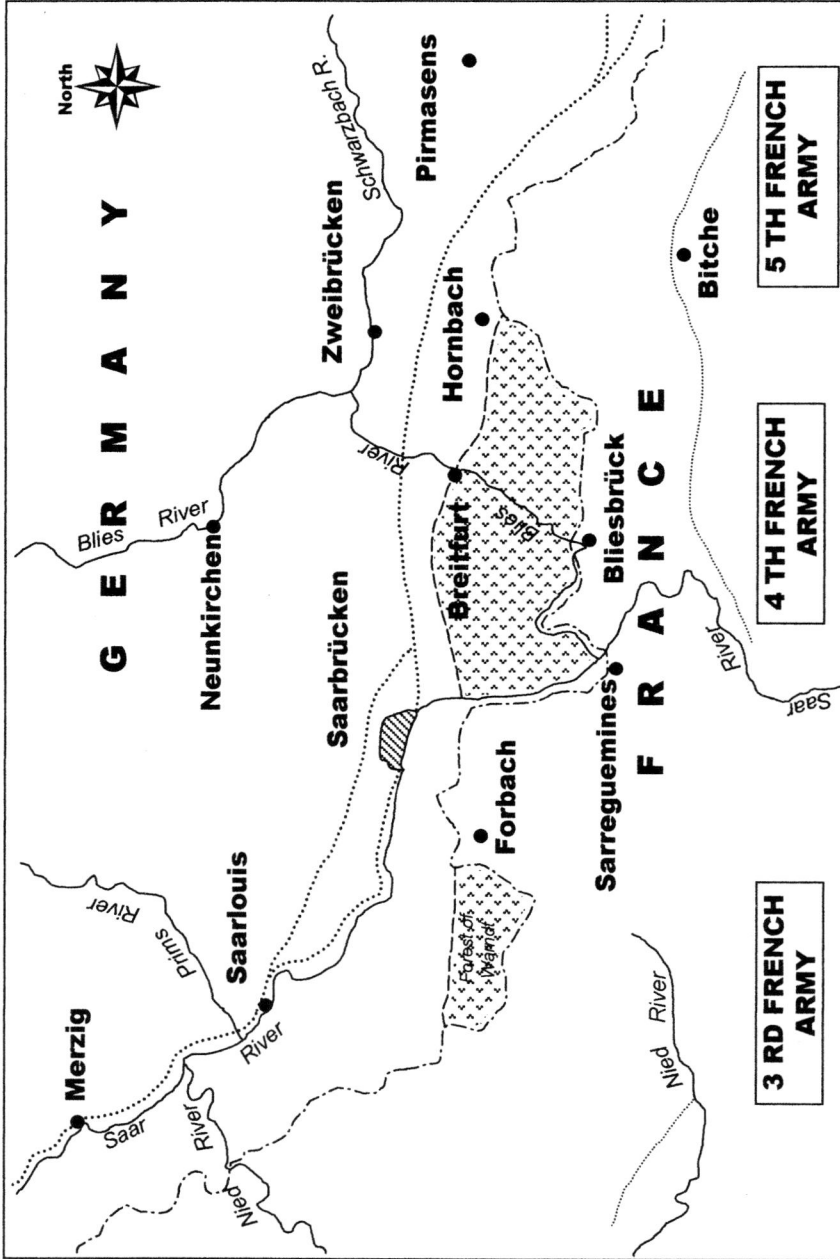

North

G E R M A N Y

Merzig

Prims River

Saar River

Saarlouis

Neunkirchen

Blies River

Saarbrücken

Zweibrücken

Schwarzbach R.

Hornbach

Pirmasens

Forest of Wardt

Forbach

Breitfurt

Bliesbrück

Blies

Sarreguemines

F R A N C E

Saar River

Nied River

Nied River

Bitche

3 RD FRENCH ARMY

4 TH FRENCH ARMY

5 TH FRENCH ARMY

Scale   0   10kms

.... Maginot Line

. . . . . . Siegfried Line

– · · – · · Franco-German border

Territory occupied by French forces

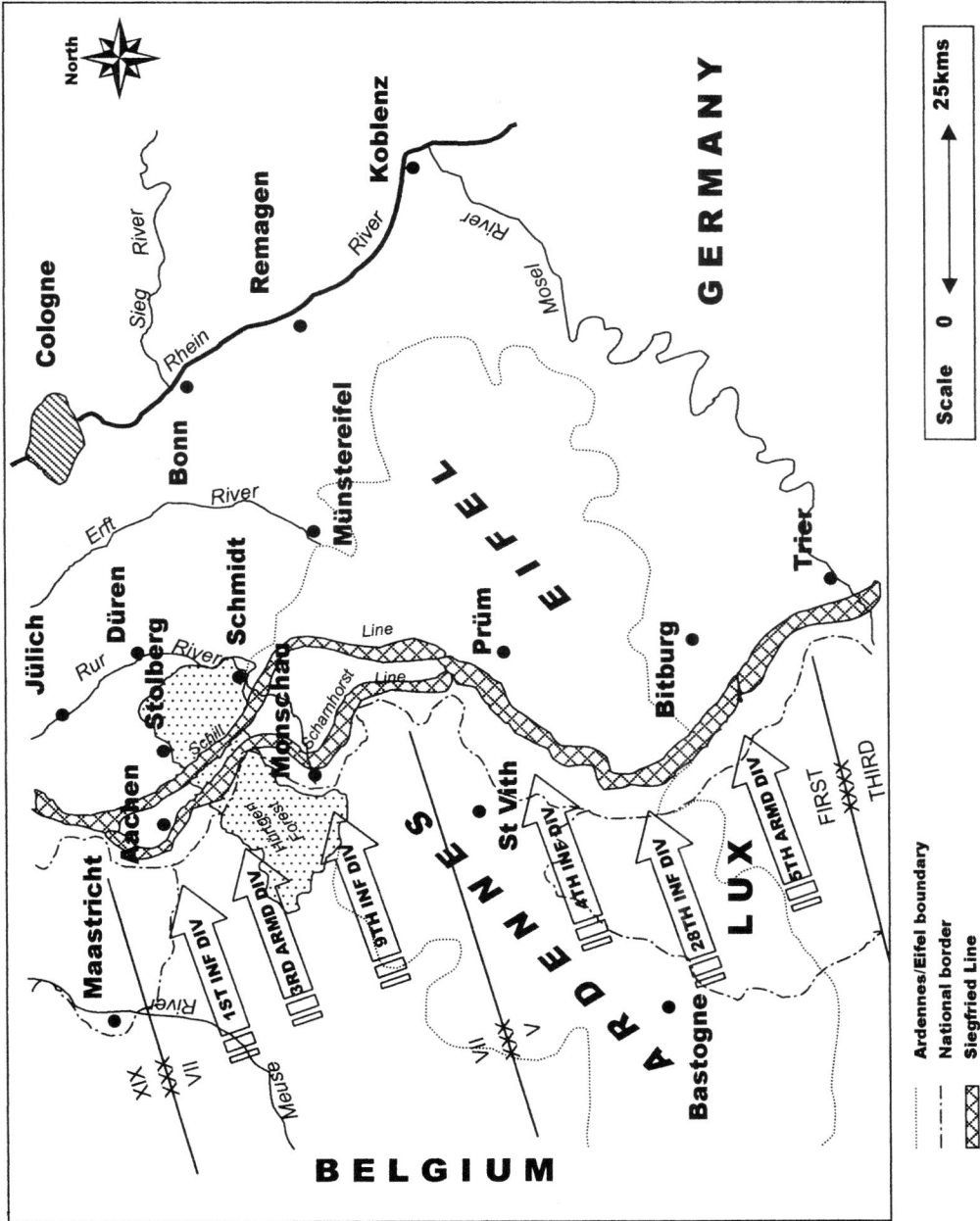

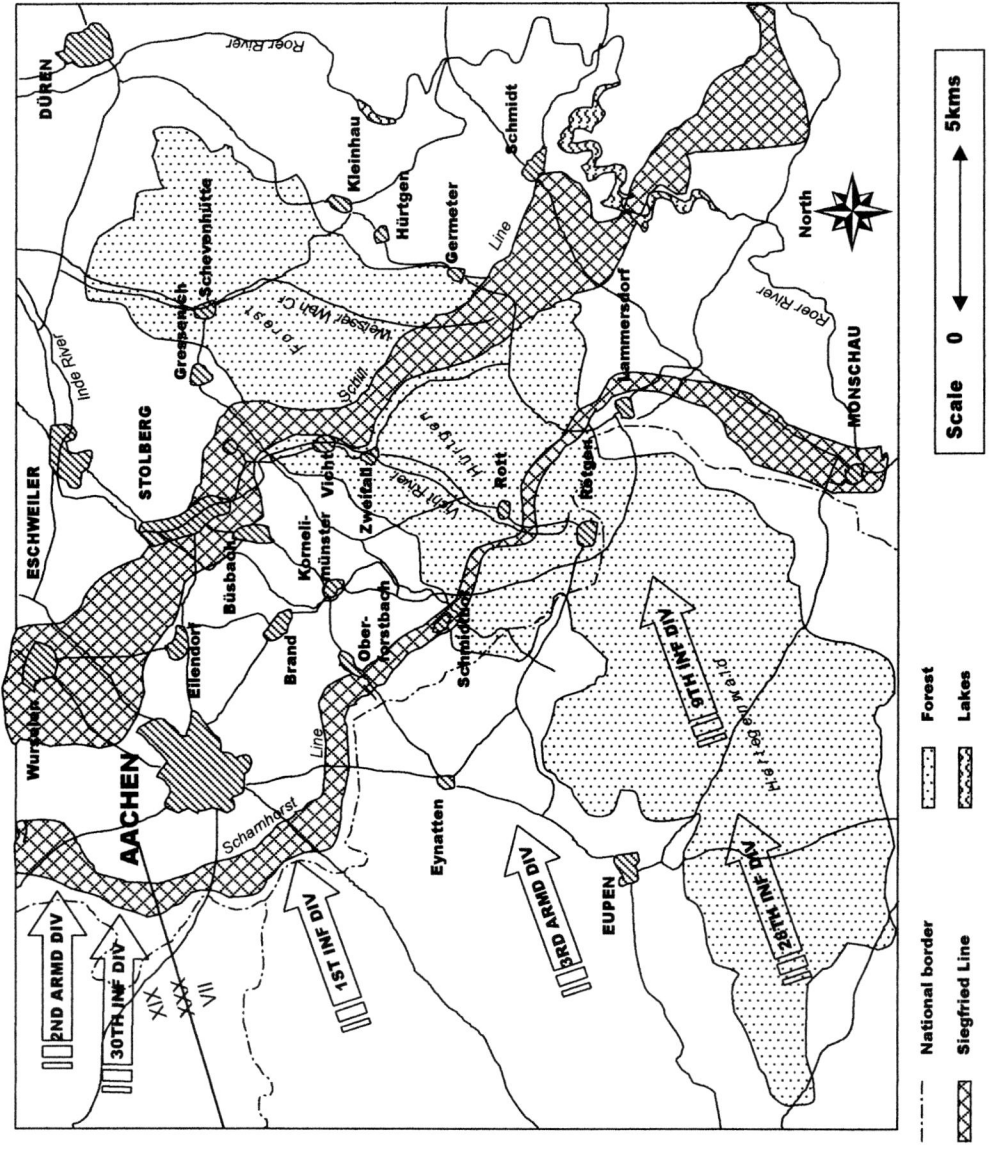

2ND ARMD DIV

30TH INF DIV

XIX
XXX
VII

1ST INF DIV

3RD ARMD DIV

9TH INF DIV

28TH INF DIV

AACHEN

Wurselen

Ellendorf

Brand

Eschweiler

Stolberg

Büsbach

Kornelimünster

Ober-forstbach

Vicht

Zweifall

Schmidthof

Eynatten

Eupen

Rott

Rötgen

Lammersdorf

Greseuich

Schevenhütta

Kleinhau

Hürtgen

Germeter

Schmidt

Düren

Monschau

Roer River

Roer River

Inde River

Vicht River

Scharnhorst

Line

Line

North

Forest Wald C.

Weisser Wald C.

Hürtgen

Scale   0   5kms

National border

Siegfried Line

Forest

Lakes

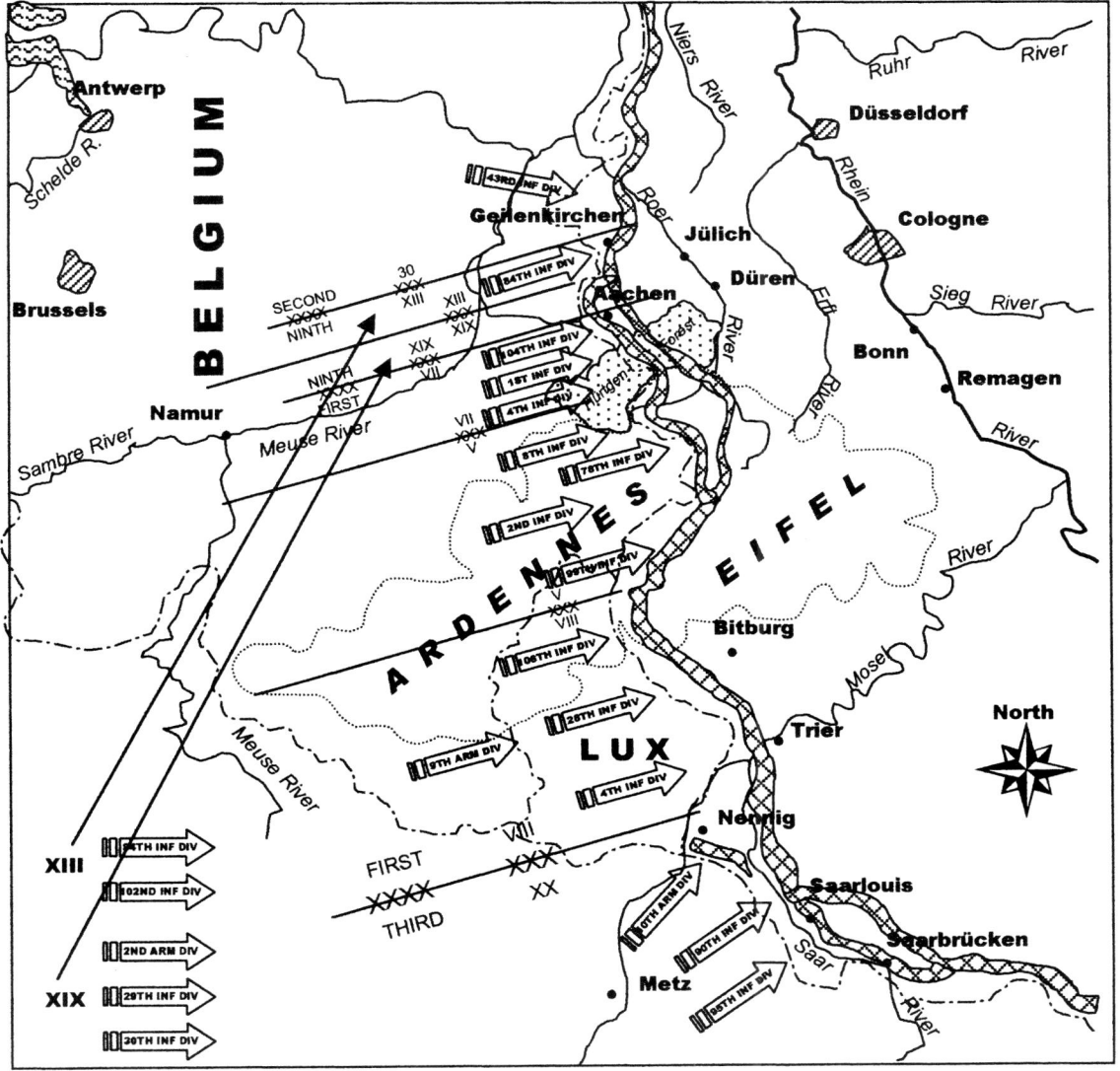

Antwerp

BELGIUM

Schelde R.

Brussels

Sambre River

Namur

Meuse River

Meuse River

XIII

| 4TH INF DIV |

| 102ND INF DIV |

| 2ND ARM DIV |

XIX

| 29TH INF DIV |

| 30TH INF DIV |

Niers River

Ruhr River

River

Düsseldorf

Roer

| 43RD INF DIV |

Geilenkirchen

Jülich

Düren

30

XXX

XIII

SECOND

XXX

NINTH

XIII

XIX

XIX

| 84TH INF DIV |

Aachen

Rhein

Cologne

Sieg River

XIX

VII

| 104TH INF DIV |

| 1ST INF DIV |

| 4TH INF DIV |

Bonn

NINTH

XXX

FIRST

VII

XXX

Hürtgen Forest

Erft River

Remagen

River

| 8TH INF DIV |

| 78TH INF DIV |

| 2ND INF DIV |

A R D E N N E S

| 99TH INF DIV |

E I F E L

River

V

VIII

| 106TH INF DIV |

Bitburg

| 28TH INF DIV |

L U X

| 9TH ARM DIV |

| 4TH INF DIV |

Mosel

Trier

North

Meuse River

VII

FIRST

XXX

THIRD

XX

Nennig

| 10TH ARM DIV |

| 90TH INF DIV |

Saar

Saarlouis

Saarbrücken

Metz

| 95TH INF DIV |

River

Legend:

.... **Ardennes/Eifel boundary**

— - — **National border**

XXXX **Siegfried Line**

| **Scale** | 0 | ← → | **25kms** |

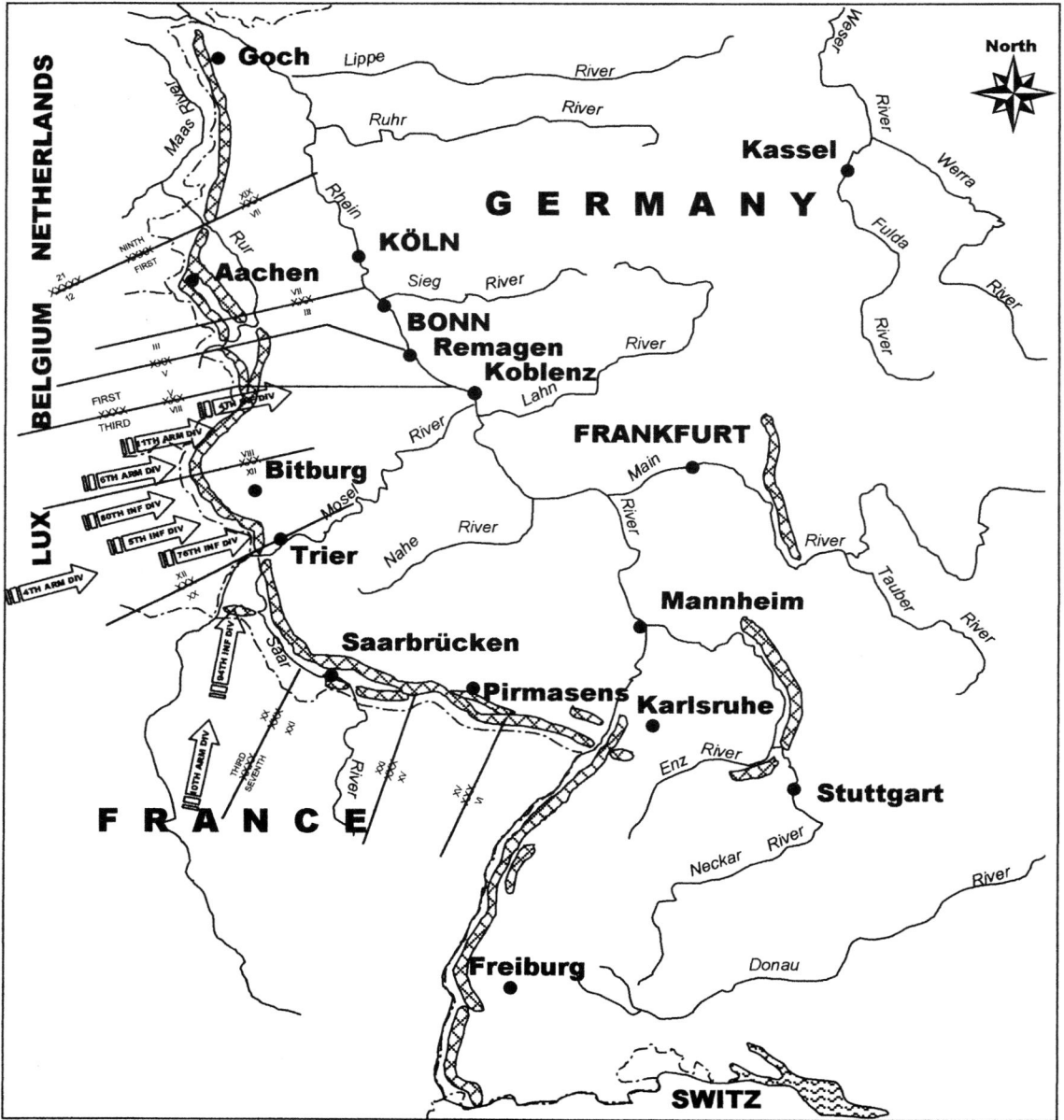

CHAPTER I

Deterrent

JANUARY 1919–SEPTEMBER 1939

After a superhuman fight he had succeeded in killing a dragon on the Drachenfels, a rock where dragons used to live . . . . The blood of the monster immediately congealed, where it came into contact with his body, into an impenetrable, horny skin. Consequently, he took a bath in the blood and became invulnerable.

From the Rhine Saga 'Siegfried and Kriemhilde'

GENESIS

To anyone reading the articles of the peace settlement imposed on Germany at the end of the First World War it would be difficult to comprehend how the Siegfried Line came to be built. Not only was the Rhineland declared a demilitarised zone, which meant that Germany was not allowed to station any troops on her western border, but Germany was also specifically and indefinitely prohibited from building fortifications in the area. Furthermore, the Rhineland was to be occupied by Allied troops for fifteen years and a series of Commissions created which were tasked with ensuring that Germany complied with all the restrictions placed on her. Yet only twenty years after the peace treaty was signed, Germany had constructed a series of fortifications that stretched some 350 miles (560 kilometres) from the Dutch border to the border with Switzerland. To understand how this remarkable turnaround came about it is necessary to take a more detailed look at the terms of the peace settlement agreed at Versailles and the extraordinary series of events thereafter.

In January 1919, the leaders of the victorious nations gathered at Versailles to thrash out the terms of the peace settlement. The issues they faced were many and complex, but one aim was clear – never again should people have to endure the horrors of modern warfare. To this end Germany, who in the eyes of the victorious powers was responsible for the outbreak of hostilities, was to be prevented from waging war in the future. This was to be achieved by imposing on the fledgling democracy a series of conditions, the most significant of which was the emasculation of Germany's armed forces.

The job of formulating the terms of the treaty relating to arms reduction was passed to a military commission under Marshal of France Ferdinand Foch, who in the First World War was Chief of the General Staff and later Supreme Commander on the Western Front. He was deeply affected by the enormous French losses and was keen to impose a 'Carthaginian Peace' on the Germans.[1] This became all too evident in March 1919 when, after only two months of deliberations, the commission finalised the terms of the German disarmament. The army was to be a volunteer army with officers serving for 25 years and other ranks serving for 12 years and it was to be only 100,000 strong. It was prohibited from having tanks, artillery and poison gas and the General Staff, which devised and implemented German strategy in the war, was abolished. The navy was reduced to little more than coastal defence force, with only six obsolete battleships, six light cruisers, twelve destroyers and twelve torpedo boats. It was denied submarines and dreadnoughts. To cap it all the German air force, was scrapped.

Germany was also forced to demilitarise the west bank of the Rhine, and the east bank to a depth of 50 kilometres.[2] This encompassed not only the stationing of soldiers and equipment but also fortifications. These were specifically covered in Article 42 of the Political Clauses for Europe which stated that: 'Germany is forbidden to maintain or construct any fortifications either on the left bank of the Rhine or on the right bank to the west of a line drawn 50 kilometres to the east of the Rhine.'[3] And was expanded in Article 180 of the Military, Naval and Air Clauses which stipulated that: 'All fortified works, fortresses and field works situated in German territory to the west of a line drawn fifty kilometres to the east of the Rhine shall be disarmed and dismantled.'

'Within a period of two months from the coming into force of the present Treaty such of the above fortified works, fortresses and field works as are situated in territory not occupied by Allied and Associated troops shall be disarmed, and within a further period of four months they shall be dismantled. Those which are situated in territory occupied by Allied and Associated troops shall be disarmed and dismantled within such periods as may be fixed by the Allied High Command.

'The construction of any new fortification, whatever its nature and importance, is forbidden in the [demilitarised] zone'.

Significantly, the Allies did not stipulate how long these restrictions should stay in place.[4]

To ensure that Germany complied with the terms of the peace settlement the victorious Allies felt that some kind of leverage was required. It was therefore agreed that the left bank of the Rhine would be occupied and only if Germany met her obligations would this army of occupation be removed; troops from the most northerly zone after five years, those from the middle zone after ten years and those from the most southerly zone after fifteen years.[5]

In spite of this measure, in January 1923, French and Belgian soldiers occupied the Ruhr, the industrial heart of Germany, in order to extract reparations after Germany had defaulted on deliveries of timber.[6] Forbidden from fortifying her border and with no army to speak of the German government could do nothing to stop the French and Belgian troops entering the country let alone forcibly eject them. Instead the German authorities adopted a policy of passive resistance. This not only prevented the French and Belgians from extracting raw materials in lieu of reparations, but also sent the German economy into decline as industrial production ground to a halt. The result was hyperinflation and a rise in political extremism.

France too suffered politically and economically; her actions were criticised by Britain and the French Franc weakened. Under enormous pressure, France (and Belgium) eventually withdrew her troops and thereafter the French government worked to contain Germany using both military and diplomatic measures.

French officers and officials atop a fort of the Maginot Line point towards Germany, c. 1939. (Hulton Getty Images)

Militarily, France decided to construct a series of fortifications along her eastern border; the so-called Maginot Line. To the French the First World War had demonstrated that fortifications still had an important part to play in modern warfare. As such they conducted a number of studies to identify what defences would be most suitable to protect the border with Germany when the army of occupation left the Rhineland. These studies generated a lively debate. Some argued that a continuous line of defences should be constructed while others favoured a series of strong points. Other arguments raged about whether strong defences should be built like those at Verdun, or lighter more flexible defences in depth. In the end it was decided to construct a thin line of strong fortifications all along the border with Germany. Work began in 1929, under the new Minister for War André Maginot, and was expected to be completed by 1935 when the French forces occupying the Rhineland were scheduled to complete their withdrawal. Despite the injection of enormous amounts of money and the increased urgency caused by the decision to withdraw the army of occupation in 1930, the defences were not in a position to be manned until 1936.

Diplomatically, France worked to engineer a political solution to the question of Germany's western border. This culminated in a conference held in Locarno, Italy in September 1925 where a number of agreements were made. One of the key conditions was the pledge by Germany, France and Belgium to uphold existing frontiers and

Germany's acceptance of the demilitarised status of the Rhineland. Moreover, the signatories also pledged not to resort to force to alter the territorial settlement.

Despite the outward signs of acceptance of the peace settlement evinced by the signing of the Treaty of Locarno, there was evidence to suggest that Germany was trying to circumvent or simply not comply with the provisions by which she was bound and particularly the restrictions placed on her armed forces. Tanks or 'tractors' were built and tested overseas (ironically many of them in the Soviet Union). Glider clubs sprang up all over the country which gave potential fighter and bomber pilots' valuable experience. The General Staff, although forbidden, also continued to operate, albeit surreptitiously. The Allies had anticipated such actions and so as to ensure that the Germans complied with the letter rather than simply the spirit of the peace settlement Inter Allied Military (IAMCC), Naval (IANCC) and Aeronautical (IAACC) Control Commissions were established in June 1919. The IAMCC, by far the largest control commission, was further divided into three sub-commissions dealing with 'Effectives' (or military personnel), 'Munitions and Armaments' and 'Fortifications'. Soon thereafter (September 1919) the *Reichswehrministerium* set up the Army, Navy and Air Peace Commissions which exactly mirrored the Allied Control Commissions. These commissions were created to act as a focal point for the Allies when requesting documents or when a visit needed to be organised. Initially, the creation of the Peace Commissions was welcomed by the Allies but it soon became clear that they were designed to obstruct and slow the disarmament programme not expedite it with the most trivial of questions referred to higher authorities for consideration.

This was never truer than with fortifications. A British report written at the time noted that as a result of the peace settlement, 'It was . . . necessary to survey all works affected and to draw up a dossier on each. The German government, as usual, refused to supply detailed plans, so the reconnaissances were a lengthy business. They also had no intention of allowing the system of existing fortifications to exist in the "existing state". They argued that tactical improvements, modernisation and the installation of additional weapons, were all permissible provided the general system was not altered.'

The report continued: 'In the case of fortresses to be dismantled, the Germans sometimes tried to hide them by burying [them] under rocks. A favourite method was to invoke the need for economy. This always worked well when dealing with the Allied governments, who were hoping for large sums in reparations, because anything spent elsewhere would mean less for reparations.'

Visits by inspectors of the Fortifications Sub-commission of the IAMCC were also organised in such a way that, as General der Artillerie Friedrich von Rabenau noted, 'they did not see what they ought not to see'.[7] In spite of all these difficulties, however, the Fortifications Sub-Commission did ensure that no new fortifications were constructed in the west, as per the terms of the peace settlement.

With the signing of the Locarno Pact and Germany's entry into the League of Nations in the autumn of 1926 there was growing pressure for the Control Commissions to be wound up and eventually in January 1927 they were. A number of British and French military experts remained in Germany to ensure that a number of outstanding issues were resolved – including the demolition of fortifications in the east – and these experts were finally withdrawn in April 1930. The main task of verification now fell to the League of Nations, but its task was never going to be easy and Colonel Gosset, one of the British military experts, noted before his recall that the only safeguard against German rearmament was 'to maintain in power a government in Germany depending in the main on the republican parties.'[8] But this was not to be. Only three years after the last Allied military expert was brought home Hitler came to power and he was determined to restore German military might, righting the wrongs of the diktat agreed at Versailles.

For years the German government had argued, with some justification, that since the victorious powers were not taking steps to disarm, as had been intimated in the terms of the peace settlement, Germany was justified in rearming.[9] Matters came to a head with the inability of the major European powers to implement measures of arms limitation at the Disarmament Conference that had been in session on and off since 1932. This precipitated Germany's exit from the Conference in October 1933[10] and set Hitler on a collision course with the western powers. He demanded the right to rearm and made it clear that if this demand was not met through a negotiated settlement then Germany would build up her armed forces anyway, in direct contravention of the provisions of the Versailles peace settlement. In 1934 the Disarmament Conference broke up without agreement and gave Hitler a golden opportunity to challenge the resolve of the western powers. In true Machiavellian style he made a series of revelations that took London and Paris by surprise. In March 1935 Hitler declared that Germany had an air force. In the same month he also announced the introduction of conscription, which saw the size of the German Army swell to 500,000 men, and the creation of three armoured divisions.

The western powers condemned these actions, but no direct action was taken for, although still poorly equipped, trained and organised, the German armed forces proved to be a powerful deterrent to nations still haunted by images of the First World War.[11] Buoyed by his success, Hitler now planned a major challenge to one of the main pillars of the peace settlement. With France, Britain and Italy, the three major powers who had until this point worked in concert to check German action, embroiled in the Abyssinian crisis and under the pretext that the Locarno Treaty was rendered null and void by the Franco-Soviet Treaty of May 1935, Hitler ordered German forces into the Rhineland in March 1936.

Britain and France had been expecting Germany to raise the issue of the Rhineland as a topic for negotiation, but were surprised by Hitler's brazen act. As such, they had not developed a common approach to meet this emergency. France had the means to challenge the German move, but would not do so without British backing. Britain for her part felt that Hitler's action was regrettable but was not threatening in substance. This was, after all, Germany's 'backyard' and consequently the British government indicated that it would not support French military action if it precipitated the possibility of war with Germany. Consequently, the German remilitarisation of the Rhineland went unchallenged save for a few token measures by the French as they cancelled leave and moved some units to the frontier to man positions of the Maginot Line.

Hitler later admitted that if France had taken action to challenge the German move 'we would have had to withdraw with our tail between our legs, for the military resources at our disposal would have been wholly inadequate for even moderate resistance.'[12] But France did not act. Hitler had gambled and had won and he was now in a position to mount a genuine challenge to Articles 42 and 180 of the peace treaty.

CHRONOLOGY

In 1934, only a year after Hitler had become Chancellor of Germany, the first tentative steps had been taken to fortify the German border in the west. Still wary of the possible French reaction to any German attempt to bend or break the terms of the peace settlement agreed at Versailles, design work began on two lines of fortifications which were to be built outside of the 50km exclusion zone east of the Rhine – the Wetterau – Main – Tauber – Stellung and the Neckar – Enz – Stellung. In 1936 work on the defences was started but was subsequently abandoned following the remilitarisation of the Rhineland. The focus of fortification construction now transferred to the western border proper. But disagreements emerged, as they had done in France, over the shape that any fortifications should take. Generals Blomberg (Supreme Commander of the new Wehrmacht), Keitel and Manstein believed that Germany would be best protected by a linear defence system that stretched along the German border. Generals Fritsch (Commander in Chief of the Army), Beck (Chief of the General Staff) and Förster, who was from 1933 to 1938 the Chief of the Army Inspectorate of Fortifications and Engineers, favored the construction of fortifications in depth in those areas where the enemy was most likely to attack. Initially the view of Blomberg, the Supreme Commander, held sway. Thus, in 1936 Phase 2 of the West Wall began with construction of a thin line of obstacles – *sperrlinien* – all along the French border from Switzerland to Luxembourg. This line consisted primarily of small bunkers and cloches which were only suitable for machine guns or observation.

In February 1938 revelations about Blomberg's new bride were made public and he was forced to resign. Hitler now made himself Supreme Commander of the Armed Forces and almost immediately sought to fashion the defences to reflect his own ideas.

Hitler's motorcade of open-topped Mercedes cars drives along an empty autobahn in high summer, c. 1938. (Bundesarchiv)

He favoured the fortified area concept and although in March 1938 he gave his permission for the linear defences to be extended further north along the border with Belgium and part of the Dutch border he also ordered construction work to begin on a series of much stronger lines of defence, or *stellungen*, especially around Aachen.

Progress on the West Wall was slow with little money or raw materials available due to the massive public works programme instigated by Hitler; principally the construction of the *Autobahnen*. Indeed, so grim was the situation that Westphal, in his memoirs, deemed it important enough to quote a note to Beck in 1937 which stated, 'The Führer has determined the distribution of the steel consignment. The fortifications were not mentioned.' Further delays stemmed from the need for the Army to complete a series of preparatory tasks before work on the fortifications could begin in earnest. These tasks included the construction of accommodation for workers and the supply of food and materials. Thus by the spring of 1938 only 640 structures had been completed with a further 1,360 planned.

When Hitler was informed of the pedestrian progress he was less than impressed, and was further incensed when he was told the defences would not be complete until 'about 1948'.[13] Determined to accelerate the building programme, on 27 May Hitler issued new construction targets to the army. The existing schedule of work was to be speeded up, but additionally a further 1,800 pillboxes and 10,000 bunkers were to be completed by 1 October 1938 to coincide with his planned invasion of Czechoslovakia.

The new accelerated plan of construction – Phase 3 of the West Wall – was called the *Limesprogramm*.[14] This not only encompassed strengthening of the border fortifications but also, at the behest of Göring, the *Luftwaffe* Commander-in-Chief, the building of the *Luftverteidigungszone West* (LDV West). This was a line of anti-aircraft defences behind the West Wall designed to prevent enemy aircraft entering Germany. And this was not Göring's only involvement in the construction of the West Wall.

In light of the disappointing progress reports,[16] in June 1938, Hitler sent Göring to review progress on the defences. Being no expert on fortifications he used the mission from the Führer as an opportunity for self-aggrandizement, to throw his (considerable) weight around and to undermine the army. His report was scathing, '. . . virtually nothing had been done, what had been done was inadequate and there was hardly the most primitive defence system.'[17] Hitler needed no more evidence of the army's incompetence. The completion of the fortifications was critical to the success of Operation Green, the codename for the invasion of Czechoslovakia, and on this evidence they would not be completed in time. Hitler needed someone in charge of the construction programme that he could trust. Responsibility for the construction of the West Wall was therefore now passed to Fritz Todt, whose Organisation Todt had built the miles of *Autobahnen* that criss-crossed Germany.

By August 1938 almost 150,000 workers were employed on the project, with a further 50,000 army engineers providing technical support. These men were supplied with construction materials by 100 trains a day with 8,800 lorries transporting these materials from the railhead to the construction site. This enormous effort ensured that an average of 70 new positions were completed every day and that by the time of the Munich crisis of September 1938 the majority of the defences had been finished. But despite the exertions of the Organisation Todt to complete the defences in time for the invasion, and only two weeks after the Munich Agreement,[18] Hitler announced the beginning of the *Aachen-Saar programm* – Phase 4 of the West Wall. Cleverly portraying the British political system and individuals like Churchill as the main threat to European peace he stated in a speech in Saarbrücken on 9 October that:

'The statesmen who are opposed to us wish for peace . . . but they govern in countries whose domestic organisation makes it possible that at any time they may lose their position to make way for others [like Churchill] who are not anxious for peace . . . I have therefore decided, as I announced in my speech at Nuremberg, to continue the construction of our fortifications in the West with increased energy. I shall now also bring within the line of these fortifications the two large areas which up to the present lay in front of our fortifications – the district of Aachen and the district of Saarbrücken.' [19]

On 17 October 1938 Hitler telephoned Todt and outlined the new construction targets. Todt explained the difficulties that he was experiencing with transport increasingly being monopolised by the harvest and the problems of inclement weather, but Hitler was not swayed and Todt yielded.

In February 1939, a month before the rump of Czechoslovakia was occupied, a further review of the fortifications was undertaken and a decision was made to construct stronger bunkers with walls up to 3.5m thick.

The fifth and final phase of the West Wall came in the autumn of 1939 and the spring of 1940 with the decision to extend the fortifications further north along the Dutch border to the point where the Rhine crossed into the Netherlands.

Workers on the West Wall collecting steel reinforcing rods which were used to strengthen bunkers, pillboxes and dragon's teeth, October 1938. (Bundesarchiv)

Table A – Bunker classification

Type	Concrete thickness (metre)	Steel thickness – cloches (cm)	Steel thickness – armour plate (cm)	Bunker types	Phase
A	Exterior 3.5 Interior 1.0 Ceiling 3.5	60	25–52	30, 30a, 36, some types over 100, A-Werken	4 and 5
A1	Exterior 2.5 Interior 1.0 Ceiling 2.2	42	25–35	35, A1-Werken (concept only?)	
B alt (until 23/12/38)	Exterior 1.5 Interior 0.8 Ceiling 1.5	25	20	1 to 36, B-Werken	2 – B-Werken and 3
B neu (from 23/12/38)	Exterior 2.0 Interior 0.8 Ceiling 2.0	25	20	96, 100-, 500- and 700 series	4 and 5
B1	Exterior 1.0 Interior 0.5	12–16	10	B1–1 to B1–29 (and separate arms rooms coupled to the types 10, 10a and 11	1 and 2 (also 3 by way of the separate arms rooms for 10, 10a and 11)
C	Exterior 0.6 Interior 0.3 Ceiling 0.5	6	6–7	C-1 to C-8	2
D	0.3	5	2–5	D-1 to D-5	2

Phases:

1 *Wetterau-Main-Tauber Stellung* and *Neckar-Enz Stellung* 1934
2 *Pioneerprogramm* 1936 – 1938
3 *Limesprogramm* May 1938
4 *Aachen-Saar Programm* October 1938
5 Autumn 1939 – Spring 1940

COMPOSITION OF THE DEFENCES

In 1936 at the start of the construction work on what was later to become the West Wall, designs that had been established for the Neckar-Enz and Wetterau-Main-Tauber lines were adopted. By the end of the year new improved standard construction models had been developed. These were utilised well into 1938 and the implementation of the *Limesprogramm* which saw the introduction of a further tranche of standard models. The

Army Inspectorate of Fortifications developed these standard models in order to realise a number of benefits: it enabled them to better plan the supply of raw materials; to produce large quantities of standardised components; and allowed better supervision of costs. It also enabled engineers, when reconnoitring prospective sites, to envisage a suitable design for optimal defence purposes. Where no standard building model was deemed appropriate special adaptations or special constructions could be suggested. If the idea was accepted and was successful it might be classified as a standard model. Unfortunately, this led to an ever-increasing number of standard models, which conflicted with the original concept.

PIONEERPROGRAMM

These standard models saw their first widespread use in the so-called *Pioneerprogramm*. This saw the development of three different categories of shelter reflecting the differing construction strengths of each (B1 old, C and D)[20] and no less than 53 different models.

Generally, structures built at this time were designed to deploy the maximum number of weapons possible and to ensure that they enjoyed extensive fields of fire. However, this preoccupation with firepower meant that compromises had to be made. Protection for the crew was reduced – rooms up to 5.0m across only had ceilings of 0.8m – which

A field gun emplaced in a bunker of the Siegfried Line, September 1939. (Hulton Getty Images)

was hopelessly inadequate against sustained heavy artillery fire. In addition, maximising the field of fire meant that bunkers often had to be sited on higher ground leaving them exposed to enemy observation and fire.

Type B1

The Bunker B1 was by far the most numerous, both in terms of designs (38) and the actual number of shelters constructed. The exterior walls were 1.0m thick and the ceiling 0.8m while the interior walls and floor were 0.5m (although exceptionally the wall between the combat room and the living quarters was 1.0m). The entrance was located at the rear of the shelter and was covered by a machine gun mounted in the living quarters. Both the door and the machine gun aperture were protected from artillery and mortar fire by an overhanging diagonal canopy. The door itself was constructed from armoured plate that was made gas-tight. It was covered internally by a small aperture set into the rear of the combat room that allowed the use of a machine pistol. The exterior door led into the entrance area which was built in the form of chicane and was sealed at the far end by a gas-tight sheet metal door.[21]

The interior of the bunker was divided into a series of separate rooms which varied according to the different designs. However, it is possible to make a number of generalisations. The stand-to area, which was reached from the entrance area, served as the crew's sleeping quarters and rest area. It was fitted with beds in groups of three on top of each other and was often the location for the small emergency exit. A small anteroom linked the crew's quarters with the combat room(s). This housed the main weapon, a water-cooled MG 08 mounted on a carriage which enabled it to be moved into place. When not in use it could be withdrawn and the aperture in the thick armoured embrasure plate closed.[22] Some of the shelters were fitted with small steel cloches for observation. Bunkers with special functions such as artillery observation positions, battle headquarters or medical posts, were built with additional facilities such as planning, telephone, command or first aid rooms.

Once building work was complete the front and sides of the bunker were covered with earth which helped to camouflage the structure and meant that although it was 3.4m in height only half of the structure was above the ground at the front (1.75m) and little over half (2.25m) at the rear.

Early pillboxes were fitted with thick armoured steel plates which mounted an MG08 or MG34. This example was removed and is now on display at the Werhrtechnische Studiensammlung, Koblenz. It has clearly been used for firing practice, having been pierced at least ten times. (Author)

Type C

The Type C shelter was derived from the Type B1, the principal difference being that the Type C had considerably thinner walls and armour and was less elaborate.[23] As such the shelters required fewer raw materials and less time to construct. But these savings came at a price; the shelter could only withstand bombardment from smaller artillery pieces (a calibre of 105mm or less) and could not withstand a direct hit from a bomb.

Although classified into eight different models, twelve versions were in fact produced in this category. These included variants fitted with six and three loophole armoured turrets, standard shelters to mount one or two machine guns, an anti-tank gun or a combination of these. The machine gun fitted in the armoured turret, as was the case for all versions, was mounted in such a way that it could be swivelled from loophole to loophole. The shelters designed to mount anti-tank guns could accommodate the 3.7cm Pak 35/36 which together with the general-purpose machine guns could be removed from the shelter and used outside adding flexibility to the defences.

Type D

The Type D construction was the weakest of the three types. They were built to provide protection against machine gun and small arms fire and with walls only 30cm thick they were not able to withstand bombs and artillery shells. The design of the various shelters was very simple and with limited space they were not fitted with a ventilation system, beds or stoves. Because they needed few raw materials they were relatively cheap and quick to build. They were also perfect for a more mobile style of warfare because only light weapons were mounted inside which could easily be removed and used outside. Five versions of the Type D were developed (D1–D5) – with a further unnamed shelter designed to house the 3.7cm Pak anti-tank gun.[24]

The Type C and D shelters were only used in stage 2 of the West Wall construction. In August 1938 the Inspectorate of Fortifications in the West prohibited the use of these designs because they were considered to be too weak. In total 716 Type C and D bunkers were built.

B-Werke

One of the most interesting features of the *Pioneerprogramm* was the so-called B-Werke.[25] Thirty-two bunkers of this type were started in the period 1937–38. Each one was different although they did share common features. The entrance was secured with an armoured door behind which, in a throwback to medieval castles, was a 3.5–metre deep pitfall. The shelter consisted of approximately forty rooms spread over two or three storeys. As well as the fighting compartments there was a machine room for generating electricity and providing ventilation, a room with a water well, a kitchen, first-aid room, washroom and toilets and storerooms for food, oil, water and ammunition. The latter were capable of holding sufficient stores to enable the crew to survive independently for thirty days.

A hand-operated ventilator used in many West Wall bunkers. This example can be found in the Katzenkopf. (Author)

Within the Katzenkopf a loophole covered the length of the tunnel. (Author)

One of the tunnels below the main block of the Katzenkopf that led to one of the six loophole armoured turrets. (Author)

The sleeping quarters in the Katzenkopf as it is today with the three-tier bunk beds still in situ. (Author)

Sink, taps and tiled wall at the Katzenkopf all still in remarkably good condition despite the best efforts of French engineers and the passage of time. (Author)

The trap that protected the entrance to the Katzenkopf. It was heavily damaged as a result of French attempts to demolish the structure. (Author)

On average the bunkers had a crew of ninety men, the majority of whom were specially trained to operate the technical equipment and weaponry. This included two machine-guns in each of the six-loophole turrets, a 5cm M19 automatic mortar which could fire 120 rounds per minute and which had a maximum range of 600 metres, and a flamethrower which could be rotated 360 deg. A small cloche was also fitted for observation and target guidance.

One fort worthy of note, not least because it is now a museum, is the *Katzenkopf* or 'Cat's Head' which is situated on the southwest slope of the Katzenkopf Hill overlooking the town of Irrel. The main body of the structure consists of a two-storey construction which accommodated the crew living quarters, sanitary facilities and munitions storage as well as the fighting compartments. These housed an automatic mortar mounted in an armoured turret, a six loophole armoured turret fitted with a machine gun, and a flame-thrower. From the main body of the structure a stairway descends to two tunnels. The smaller but longer tunnel is linked to a further armoured turret some 75 metres away, while the other larger tunnel leads to a well (although it is believed that it was originally intended as an access tunnel).

During the fighting for the Siegfried Line it was captured intact by the Americans but after the war was demolished by the French. In 1977 the local fire brigade began excavating the site and although impossible to return to its original state it is open to visitors.

LIMESPROGRAMM

Hitler's displeasure at the speed of the construction programme and his decision in May 1938 to order the construction of some 11,000 bunkers which were to be completed by the autumn caused immense problems for all concerned. For the designers it meant returning to the drawing board because the standard construction models used up to that point were too complicated and costly for what was now a programme of mass production. The need for simplified designs was also dictated by the fact that the workers who were to construct the bunkers were often inexperienced.

The expanded programme also placed an increased burden on resources. Not only did Hitler demand greater numbers of shelters but he also insisted that the front and side walls and the ceiling should be strengthened, each was now to be 1.5m. This necessitated the provision of larger quantities of both concrete and reinforcing rods. These increased demands could be met, but German industry was unable to supply the armoured plates and cupolas that would be required and certainly not in the time scale envisaged. This compelled the authorities to develop concrete alternatives for the former which they did and which took the shape of an open-mouthed embrasure and a crenellated embrasure. However, tests on these expedients showed that they were far less effective and attempts to strengthen them were not entirely successful.

A completed bunker is readied for use, October 1938. (Bundesarchiv)

A bunker being constructed on the West Wall clearly showing one of the concrete mixers, October 1938. (Bundesarchiv)

The most widely constructed model (3,471 were built) of the *Limesprogramm* was the Regelbau 10 (standard construction 10). The shelter could be accessed via two gas-proof entrance areas which were bisected by a crenellated embrasure that covered both doors. Both entrances led to the stand-to area which acted as living and sleeping quarters for both the crew and the resident rifle squad.[26] There were fifteen beds in five tiers of three. The shelter also included a separate combat room which could only be accessed by the crew if they left the confines of the main bunker. Once there communication with their compatriots was via a speaking tube. Access to the combat room was secured with a wooden access door which was not gas-tight. A diagonal wall behind the door had a small aperture to cover the entrance. In the combat room itself was an open-mouthed embrasure with cement pedestal for mounting the machine-gun as well as a smaller crenellated embrasure with shutter (although most of these shutters were fitted after construction was complete).

Luftverteidigungszone West[27]

A unique element of the *Limesprogramm* was the so-called *Luftverteidigungszone West* (LDV West) which was commissioned by Göring as commander-in-chief of the Luftwaffe. The threat of aerial bombardment against heavily populated conurbations had gripped the public's imagination, fomented by films and newsreel footage of the bombing of Guernica in the Spanish Civil War in April 1937.[28] Göring was determined to ensure that German cities would not suffer the same fate. He therefore ordered the construction of a series of standard concrete structures to house anti-aircraft weapons, their crews and munitions. It was built some way to the rear of the West Wall proper in a zone some 10–30km in depth. In fact the zone had a dual purpose. As well as preventing enemy aircraft attacking the Reich it was also to act as a fallback position with pillboxes to mount machine-guns, anti-tank guns as well as dragon's teeth and water obstacles. In all some 1,544 structures were built.

An anti-aircraft position which formed part of the Luftverteidigungszone West, *c. 1939. (Hulton Getty Images)*

The structures used were often exact duplicates of those developed for the *Limesprogramm* or were slightly modified. For example, the MG Pillbox (LVZ B) was effectively a copy a standard construction model 1 with a number of slight alterations; the Führer shelter (LVZ F) equated to standard construction 10a; the battle headquarters (LVZ K) to standard model 31 and the double infantry section dugout (LVZ U) was to all intents and purposes standard model 11. The munitions room (LVZ M) was a unique design, while the anti-tank shelter (LVZ Pz) used fittings, for example the cupola, which had been captured when Czechoslovakia was overrun.[29]

AACHEN-SAAR PROGRAMM

Although the enormous effort invested in the West Wall as a result of the *Limesprogramm* undoubtedly increased the strength of Hitler's border defences they still suffered from a number of shortcomings. One of the main criticisms was that for a system of defences designed to delay an enemy attack relatively little space had been provided for the storage of ammunition or provisions which might allow the defenders to fight an extended campaign. A further criticism was that the main fighting compartment often doubled up as the garrison's accommodation, or was separate to the main bunker.

The *Aachen-Saar Programm* sought to rectify these problems and more. One of the key improvements of the programme was the increased thickness of the walls and ceilings. The bunkers were now built to medium (B) and heavy construction (A)[30] thicknesses – 2 and 3.5m respectively. The new designs were also far roomier. The stand-to area was extended so that each person was permitted 1.3–1.4sq m rather than 1sq m as had previously been the case. New storage areas for food and ammunition were introduced, as was a special room for an observer equipped with either a periscope or an observation cupola. The interior of the stand-to area was also improved with the addition of plywood cladding. This not only made the shelter more homely

'Day and night the concrete mixers run at full speed', or so German propaganda would have us believe. Concrete mixers mounted on a timber framework mix concrete that is poured into the shuttered framework to produce a new bunker on the West Wall, March 1940. (Bundesarchiv)

and allowed personal effects to be affixed, but, more importantly, significantly reduced the choking dust and splinters produced when the bunker suffered a direct hit. Importantly, separate fighting compartments were also dispensed with.

The *Limesprogramm* also saw the development of a bewildering range of models with seemingly little synergy as all concerned endeavoured to meet the Führer's challenging targets. Improvisations and amendments to designs added to the haphazard nature of the programme which was far removed from the continuity that existed in the period prior to May 1938. A series of standard constructions were therefore developed that followed on from the *Pioneerprogramm* but which also drew on the lessons learned from the later *Limesprogramm*. The reforms were encapsulated in guidelines which were published on 23 December 1938.

The new standard construction models were initially numbered 1–17 but to avoid any confusion they were renumbered 101–130 in February 1939 and later the series was extended to 139.[31] Four variations were developed – with or without a flanking structure or small cloche and all combinations thereof. Moreover, with the exception of those features that were specific to the design, e.g. command posts or medical aid stations, a system of 'building blocks' was developed. This meant that each shelter had, for example, an identical entrance area. If conditions dictated, it was also possible to construct a mirror image of the standard construction. In the period to July 1940 some 3,828 bunkers were constructed as part of this programme.

ANTI-TANK OBSTACLES

In many places the West Wall relied for its anti-tank protection not on concrete and steel but natural obstacles such as rivers, lakes, forests and hills, as well as a man-made features such as rail cuttings and banks and canals. Where such features were absent or less pronounced anti-tank obstacles were erected, the most numerous being the so-called dragon's teeth or *Höckerhindernisse*, which can still be seen in many places today and

Workers dig the foundations for dragon's teeth. In the foreground is a trägersperre *with the crenellations for the H-beams clearly visible, October 1938. (Bundesarchiv)*

Experienced craftsmen work on the dragon's teeth of the West Wall. The shuttering forms a mould for pouring the concrete, January 1940. (Bundesarchiv)

which the official United States historian likened to 'canted headstones in a strange cemetery'.[32] These were reinforced concrete pyramids poured in rows with the smallest teeth at the front and the largest at the back and with a concrete foundation to maintain the structural integrity of the whole. Initially, they were constructed with four rows of teeth increasing in height from 0.4m in the front (from where the enemy would approach) to1.0m at the back.[33] The intention being to either stop the enemy tank completely or to expose the soft underbelly of the tank to the defenders anti-tank guns. Almost 100km of these teeth were constructed, with each kilometre requiring 2000m³ of concrete and 104 tons of reinforcing iron rods. This anti-tank defence was considered suitable to repel vehicles of up to 20 tons, but already by 1939 it was clear that an obstacle capable of defeating heavier tanks would be needed so a new design was developed consisting of 5–6 rows of teeth with the final row some 1.5m in height. This was now capable of blocking the passage of tanks up to 36 tons in weight. A further 76km of the new model dragon's teeth were built, but for each kilometre it was now necessary to use 5,450m³ of concrete and 193 tons of reinforcing iron rods.[34] Often the dragon's teeth would be reinforced with metal stakes which would be criss-crossed with barbed wire to act as an obstacle to the infantry. All dragon's teeth were painted green to blend in with the background.

Of course it was not practical to seal the whole of the German border; vehicles still needed to use the roads, so a number of different roadblocks were used. One was a simple gate made of horizontal steel beams which pivoted on a reinforced concrete pillar. As the enemy approached the gate could be swung shut and either locked or bolted to another pillar on the far side of the road. More rudimentary was the *Trägersperre*. These

A trägersperre *without its H-beams straddles a road. Dragon's teeth can clearly be seen either side. (Bundesarchiv)*

Newly constructed dragon's teeth stretch into the distance, November 1938. (Bundesarchiv)

Construction work progresses on a huge tank trap that stretches across the mouth of a valley, October 1938. (Bundesarchiv)

were concrete structures at an angle of approximately 45 degrees which were constructed on either side of the road. In each structure there was a series of recesses into which were slotted 12-in steel H beams. These could easily be removed and as such relied on covering fire from nearby pillboxes and fieldworks. Where lack of time or materials prevented construction of a recognised roadblock mines were used, or, at a pinch, craters blown in the road.

Other anti-tank obstacles were also used including the traditional *Panzergraben* or anti-tank ditch, the *Hemmkurvenhindernis* – a steel curve, also used in the Atlantic Wall, and the *Pfahlhindernis*, simply wooden stakes knocked into the ground.

ANOTHER MAGINOT LINE?

German fortress engineers, no doubt envious of their counterparts in France who with the wealth of resources placed at their disposal had constructed a labyrinth of subterranean passages linking the *ouvrages* of the Maginot Line, intended to link all structures of the West Wall by means of an underground system whether it be a simple tunnel providing access and egress to the rear lines or a complete tunnel system linking fighting positions

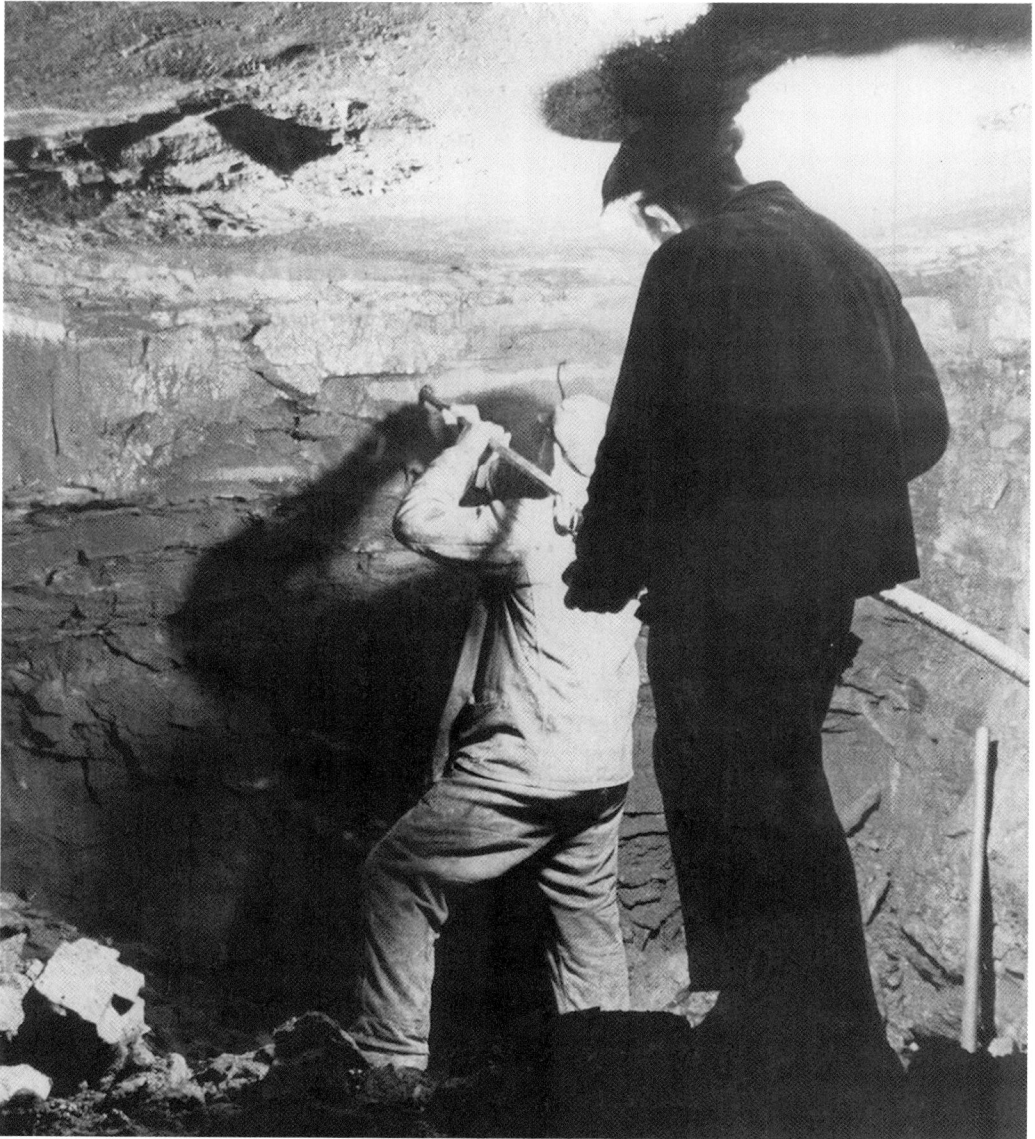

Workers drilling a hole into solid rock as they excavate a chamber, October 1938. (Bundesarchiv)

with stores, living quarters and medical aid posts – in the more complex and extensive systems utilising miniature electric trains.

Short tunnels, used as connections between individual structures, were started in the *Pioneerprogramm* but progress was halted by the introduction of the *Limesprogramm* and its emphasis on pillbox construction. In February 1939 work to connect a series of large structures began in the Trier and Saarpfalz sectors. Hitler inspected the work in May 1939 and although initially sceptical of the value of such tunnels, gave his assent for the work to be extended. Work continued on the tunnels until the outbreak of war, but few were finished and even fewer were declared usable. Many were simply filled in, particularly where no link up had been established with buildings on the surface.

One of the roughly hewn tunnels of the Gerstfeldhöhe. *(Author)*

One of the completed tunnels of the Gerstfeldhöhe *now used to house exhibits. (Author)*

The Gerstfeldhöhe *was constructed on two levels which were to be linked by a lift. The shaft was completed, but work was halted before the lift was installed. (Author)*

The tunnels of the Gerstfeldhöhe *were large enough to house a narrow gauge railway. A small diesel engine provided the motive power. (Author)*

The railway was used to transport men, or material and spoil, in small trucks. (Author)

One tunnel system that was not finished but which warrants a mention is the *Gerstfeldhöhe* at Niedersimten. This was planned to be a key defensive installation in the West Wall around the city of Pirmasens. A series of inter-connected bunkers and pillboxes were to be constructed that dominated the Trulben valley. The plan was to construct a series of tunnels on two levels. The lower level was to act as a bombproof shelter that provided a safe haven for both the personnel and ammunition. A light railway was planned to run from the entrance at Niedersimten to a 68m-high elevator shaft that linked the lower and upper levels. The upper level, again served by a light railway, consisted of a further series of tunnels which linked up the various fighting positions.

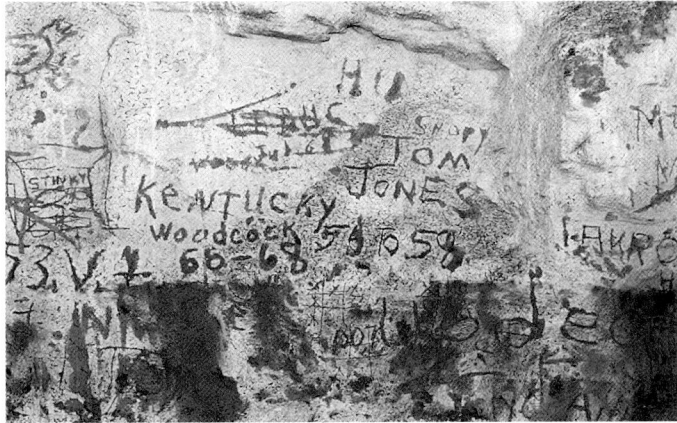

Some of the graffiti that adorn the tunnel walls of the Gerstfeldhöhe *left by American servicemen who worked there when the facility was a US store after the war. (Author)*

One of the chambers in the Gerstfeldhöhe *was transformed into a small church by the local population, who used the tunnels as an air-raid shelter. (Author)*

By the time construction work was suspended following the defeat of France around 3 million Reichsmark had been spent. Work was restarted in 1944 but only a very limited scale. Its main wartime contribution was to act as an air raid shelter for local residents and after the war served as a depot for US Army stores.[34]

The failure of the tunnel building programme was not surprising in light of the initial scepticism of the political leadership and the shortness of time. But it was also undermined by a lack of organisation. Concrete shelters were planned and built according to standard models so that even unskilled workers could be employed. This central control was missing in respect of tunnelling. Projects were undertaken at the behest of individual staff members with no consideration given to the men or materials available to complete the project. In addition, there was a widespread failure to seek expert geological advice which resulted in delays and, on occasions, tunnels being totally unsafe to use.

CONSTRUCTION OF THE WEST WALL

Initially, sole responsibility for the construction of the West Wall lay with the army. The Army Inspectorate of Fortifications was responsible for designing the bunkers and pillboxes with civilian construction companies contracted to undertake the actual building work. Progress was steady, but did not harmonise with Hitler's plans for *lebensraum* in the east and in June 1938 the Organisation Todt was placed in charge of construction with army engineers responsible for the siting of the structures and other tactical input.

The Organisation Todt was a paramilitary organisation created in 1933 under Dr Fritz Todt and was established to carry out major public works programmes, principally the construction of the *Autobahnen*. Although Organisation Todt workers wore uniforms they did not form part of the *Wehrmacht*, nor were they an organ of the party, despite the fact that members wore a swastika armband. Todt was nominally responsible to Göring as author of the Four Year Plan, but he enjoyed a close working relationship with the Führer which meant that in reality Göring was often omitted from discussions. Following Todt's untimely death in an air crash in February 1942 the OT was taken over by his able deputy, Albert Speer, another of Hitler's personal favourites.

Many of the workers from the newly built *Autobahnen* were drafted in to construct the West Wall. Their numbers were swollen by *Wehrmacht* construction battalions and labour battalions from the Reich Labour Service or *Reichsarbeitdienst* (RAD). Hitler created this organisation in 1935 as an attempt to reduce unemployment. Jobless young men between the ages of 19 and 25 were required to work in labour battalions. So successful was this scheme that by September 1936 the Führer was able to report that unemployment had been slashed from six million to one million. At the same time it gave Hitler a large, cheap pool of labourers which he ultimately put to work on the West Wall.

From the outset the building of the West Wall was beset by difficulties. In books and newspapers printed at the time it was alleged that private companies contracted to do much of the work were fleecing the state by substituting state supplied cement for inferior quality. Rumours also abounded that government furnished equipment was being sold to local farmers at knockdown prices. Labourers forced to work on the construction of the defences in one of the RAD Labour Battalions were also less than happy. They were forced to work long hours, often in poor conditions and often undertaking dangerous

Reichsminister Dr Fritz Todt, the leader of the Todt Organisation, and architect of the West Wall. (Imperial War Museum)

Workers on the West Wall march back to their camp, October 1938. (Bundesarchiv)

Temporary accommodation erected for workers constructing the West Wall, November 1938. (Bundesarchiv)

Labourers on the West Wall enjoy lunch at a workers' camp. (Bundesarchiv)

tasks for very little pay. They also had to live in temporary accommodation and had to survive on meagre rations. Not surprisingly there was little motivation amongst the workforce to construct defences of the highest standard.

As a consequence, the completed fortifications began to exhibit signs of serious flaws and these were also reported. 'Partly as a result of the extreme haste with which the fortifications were being built, partly because of the "unintentional sabotage", the Siegfried Line soon began to show defects. The floods, especially of this year [1939], showed up the weaknesses. Whole stretches of the line on the banks of the Rhine had to be reconstructed. There were reports in August that newly constructed forts were blown up to make room for new forts to be built on higher ground out of reach of the Rhine floods. So deep was the water in the vicinity of Kehl that many series of casemates had to be evacuated.'[36]

These difficulties were exacerbated when, in June 1938, responsibility for the construction of the West Wall was split between the Organisation Todt and the Army. General Adam,[37] Commander in Chief Second Army Group, commanding the western front was, unsurprisingly, less than happy with the army's relegation. Never a man to mince his words, he made a number of disparaging comments about the Organisation Todt and the RAD which were rebuked by Hitler 'Todt is the right man – for him the word impossible does not exist!'[38] Todt was somewhat bemused by the attitude of the army towards him and his organisation, but the origins of this ire should not have been difficult to comprehend; the army was criticised for all the delays and shortcomings of the defences

Occasionally the defences had to be constructed around natural features. Here dragon's teeth near Lammersdorf have been built to accommodate a small stream. (Author)

while Todt received all the plaudits, in spite of the fact that much of the foundation work had been completed by the army. This was never more clearly exemplified than at the Nuremberg Rally in September 1938. Despite the fact the OT had only been responsible for the West Wall defences since June, Hitler awarded Todt the hundred thousand Reichsmark National Prize, much to the chagrin of the army generals in attendance.

By generating friction between the Army and the Organisation Todt and other major power blocs in the Third Reich, Hitler ensured that any potential challengers to his crown were too busy with their internecine fighting to threaten his pre-eminence. But Hitler's attitude towards the Army was symptomatic of a deeper enmity and mistrust. The Army High Command questioned Hitler's every move, especially his designs for living space in the east and represented the only real threat to Hitler's autocracy. As such he took every opportunity to undermine its position. Evidence of this was apparent in Hitler's assessment of the fortifications completed by the Army. Hitler was critical of the army engineers, and in particular the Inspector of Engineers and Fortifications, General Otto Förster, who he believed was less than competent in bunker design. As an example he outlined the shortcomings of the huge works that the Army was constructing at Istein and Irrel. These fortifications cost millions of Reichsmarks to construct and could accommodate up to 140 men, but only deployed two machine-guns with a further machine-gun covering the entrance. Such designs, Hitler believed, were the progeny of theory rather than experience.

Hitler, by contrast, had spent a considerable amount of time in rudimentary blockhouses and shelters in the First World War. Drawing on this experience he insisted that the shelters should be clad with wood to reduce the impact of concussion when the position was under bombardment and that simple facilities should be provided where possible including latrines, stoves and air filters,[39] essential if the soldiers in the west were to fight a successful defensive battle.[40]

But Hitler's interest in fortifications went much deeper than this. Hitler was a great believer in permanent fortifications[41] and the construction of the West Wall interested him enormously, so much so that he became intimately involved in designing bunkers himself, drawing on his undoubted artistic skills. He would sketch out bunker designs which included details of concrete thickness, the amount of steel reinforcing and even where girders should be positioned. His thoughts were detailed in a memorandum dated 1 July 1938, which although never formalised into an official order, added to the already confused situation.

Hitler also took it upon himself during the four visits he made to the West Wall to deliver detailed instructions for further improvements to the defences. On a visit to the front in August 1938 he insisted on the construction of defences to the west as well as the east of Saarbrücken which Adam described as 'tactical nonsense'. Hitler also favoured a linear approach with defences following the border. To Hitler every inch of the Fatherland was sacrosanct and should be defended – a strategy that was to prove disastrous later in the war. To General Adam political boundaries were not significant. He believed that the fortified area was better suited to the modern battlefield so as to use the terrain to the best advantage of the defender. Such fundamental differences invariably added to the strained relationship between the Army and Hitler and exacerbated the

Hitler addresses workers on the Siegfried Line during one of the four visits he made while the defences were being constructed. (Imperial War Museum)

already confused position for those involved in the construction of the West Wall and contributed further to the heterogeneity of the defences.

The state of the West Wall greatly worried many in the German High Command. In September 1938 a number of senior German officers[42] drafted a memorial, which was subsequently published in France,[43] detailing their concerns about shortcomings in the German military. This included details of deficiencies in the West Wall due to its hasty construction.[44] Other senior officers echoed this critical view. General Siegfried Westphal, at that time working in the Operations Section of the Army General Staff, wrote in his memoirs that, '. . . what was constructed did not amount to an impenetrable wall of fortifications as our propaganda called it . . . The majority of the emplacements had concrete roofs of only eighty centimetres thickness which afforded no protection against heavy shells. Many of the positions only had loopholes at the front and were thus at a tactical disadvantage . . . Because of the short time available it had been impossible to fit the emplacements into the terrain as well as the tacticians desired. Many of them lay not on the more favourable rear slopes but on the front slopes of the hills. Anti-tank obstacles were only present in comparatively few places. One particularly worrying feature was that some of the emplacements possessed no loopholes at all and could therefore only be used as shelters.'[45] It was quicker to build shelters without loopholes and as such it was possible to report a greater rate of construction.[46]

AIM

But why did Hitler decide to embark on a programme to fortify Germany's western border? It was clear from the French and British reaction to the remilitarisation of the

A very ornate entrance to a West Wall bunker. Above the door is a stylised swastika. Needless to say the majority of bunkers were not decorated so ornately. On top is an armoured machine-gun turret. (Bundesarchiv)

Rhineland that they had no plans to use the military to enforce the terms of the Paris peace agreement and, moreover, France had made her defensive intentions clear with the construction of the Maginot Line.

Certainly there is some strength in the argument that this was a further attempt to goad the victorious Allies. Hitler's biggest gamble, sending troops into the Rhineland, had been a success and he now wanted to challenge another tenet of the Versailles diktat that Germany must not fortify her border. But the Allies had already accepted that Germany had rearmed and had stationed troops in the Rhineland. If they had conceded this much and not acted then it was unlikely that building fortifications along the Rhine would stir Britain and France to take up arms.

Challenging the terms of the settlement enforced on Germany at Versailles was, then, only a minor consideration in the construction of the West Wall. Some cynics claimed that Hitler ordered the construction of the Wall because France had built the Maginot Line.[47] However, Hitler was not driven by envy or one-up-manship. If that had been the case he would simply have built a more impressive series of forts than the French, but he did not. The West Wall was very different to the Maginot Line. Unlike its French counterpart the West Wall covered the entire length of the German western border, including the common borders with neutral Belgium and the Netherlands.[48] Rather than huge fortifications Hitler planned to build thousands of small pillboxes in depth all along the border. These pillboxes would be built to standard design to simplify and therefore speed construction. Also Hitler included in his defences an air defence zone (the LDV West), designed to prevent enemy aircraft reaching Germany. The differences in the two lines clearly demonstrated that Hitler did not want to simply produce a carbon copy of the impressive line of French fortifications.

Nor was the West Wall built simply to protect Germany's western frontier. It is true that Hitler was determined to prevent a repeat of 1923 when the French and Belgian armies marched into Germany unopposed and occupied the country's industrial heartland. But although the West Wall undoubtedly served this purpose, the same end could have been achieved simply through rearmament and the stationing of troops along the border. What fortifications did was reduce the need for a large standing force in the west to protect the border leaving the bulk of the *Wehrmacht* free for Hitler to use in the east; the West Wall was, in short, a deterrent.

One of the first people to recognise the more sinister reason for the construction of the West Wall was Winston Churchill. In April 1936 Churchill predicted that the Siegfried Line, still only in its infancy, would: 'enable the German troops to be economised on that line, and will enable the main forces to swing round through Belgium and Holland. Then look east. There the consequences of the Rhineland fortifications may be more

A concrete bunker covered with earth and loose stones. The gun is just visible and when not in use a camouflaged screen, visible at the front, would be erected to cover the aperture, October 1938. (Bundesarchiv)

immediate . . . Poland and Czechoslovakia, with which must be associated Yugoslavia, Roumania, Austria and some other countries are all affected very decisively the moment that this great work of construction has been completed.'[49]

Churchill's prescience was uncanny. In German Foreign Office papers written before Operation Green the prerequisites for the operation were described: 'When Germany has achieved complete preparedness for war in all spheres, then the military conditions will have been created for carrying out an offensive war against Czechoslovakia, so that the solution of the German problem of living space can be carried to a victorious conclusion even if one or another of the Great Powers intervene against us.

Apart from many other considerations, there is in the first place the defensive capacity of our western fortifications, which will permit the western frontier of the German Reich to be held with weak forces for a long time against greatly superior strength.'[50]

Indeed, the operation was delayed to allow more time for the defences to be strengthened '. . . to deter intervention by the western powers he [Hitler] ordered a crash programme to build the so-called "West Wall" fortifications along the French frontier, delaying the date for the attack on Czechoslovakia until 1 October [1938], the last feasible moment before the onset of autumn reduced the impact of German armour and air superiority, both crucial to the Blitzkrieg concept.'[51]

MISSION ACCOMPLISHED – OPERATION GREEN (FALL GRÜN)

In July 1938 Hitler informed Todt that the West Wall was to have priority over all civil construction projects,[52] and, in spite of Todt's reservations about delays precipitated by the demands placed on road and rail transport by the harvest, the targets set by Hitler were largely met. By September 1938 9,660 of the bunkers and pillboxes ordered by Hitler as part of the *Limesprogramm* had been built.[53] Nevertheless, there was still considerable unease amongst senior officers of the German High Command.

During a visit to the West Wall by Hitler in late August 1938 General Adam, outlined his concerns about the state of the defences along the borders with France, Luxembourg, Belgium and Holland. He believed that delays in the delivery of materials meant that only about a third of the West Wall would be completed before the winter weather brought construction to a halt. Hitler was sceptical and brought the conversation to a close.[54] Later in the tour Adam returned to the subject, this time detailing his concerns about the insufficient number of troops he would have to man the defences should Germany go to war with Czechoslovakia and the lack of any reserves. Hitler, now clearly annoyed at the general's pessimism, insisted that the attack on Czechoslovakia would go ahead and in a final address to the generals in attendance (Brauchitsch, Keitel, Jodl and Adam) he delivered a stinging rebuke which was clearly aimed at Adam. 'Only a scoundrel', he announced, 'could not hold this front!' Keitel noted in his memoirs that it was obvious Adam's days were numbered – and they were.[55]

But Adam was not alone in having reservations about the strength of the West Wall during the tense period of the Munich crisis. Beck, the Chief of the General Staff, concurred. He believed that realistically it would take at least three weeks to defeat Czechoslovakia, which was longer, in his estimation, than it would take for the French to break through the West Wall, especially since the only troops that could be spared to man the defences were reservists and labourers pressed into service.[56]

And even Hitler, despite his public protestations to the contrary, recognised that the West Wall was far from perfect. In a meeting prior to the Munich conference on 29 September 'Hitler . . . made a clean breast of the fact [to Mussolini] that the western front was "completely exposed". There had been some fortification between the Rhine and the Moselle, but only weak forces were deployed there. On the Belgian and Dutch frontiers there was virtually nothing, and the situation on the upper Rhine was "not much better."'[57]

Despite these reservations, Hitler pressed ahead with Operation Green convinced that the French would not act. And he was right. The enormous effort that went into the construction programme leading up to Munich undoubtedly worked to influence the French government in its deliberations over what action to take in respect of its commitments to Czechoslovakia. After the remilitarisation of the Rhineland General Gamelin[58] concluded that if the Germans fortified the border the German army would be able 'to contain the French Army with reduced strength, and thus to attack Czechoslovakia and Poland.'[59] Now that this doomsday scenario had come to pass the French High Command reasoned that a kind of stalemate had been established in Europe.

France was balked by the West Wall but equally Germany could not invade France because of the impregnable Maginot Line. Following this argument to its logical conclusion it was decided that nothing could be done militarily to help Czechoslovakia, despite the fact that the West Wall was seemingly incomplete and the fact that only four regular German divisions, reinforced by 300,000 poorly armed and trained RAD workers, were stationed in the West Wall against a potential French strength of some 80 divisions at the time of the crisis. This belief was reinforced by an overweening desire to avoid war and so it was decided to sacrifice Czechoslovakia's independence, just as Hitler believed France would. The considerable resources and immense effort that had been channelled into the construction of the western fortifications over the previous four months had paid dividends; the West Wall had realised its primary aim and France yielded.

MISSION ACCOMPLISHED – OPERATION WHITE (FALL WEISS)

Having taken over the whole of Czechoslovakia,[60] Hitler now set his sights on Poland. This, if anything, was a trickier proposition because invading Poland would mean a potential conflict with the Soviet Union. This threat, however, was soon removed with the audacious signing of the Nazi-Soviet Pact on 23 August 1939. But if the possibility of a challenge to Hitler's plans had been removed in the east, he still faced a dilemma in the west; would the western powers resort to military force if Germany invaded Poland?

In spite of the concessions made by Britain and France at Munich, it became increasingly clear that Hitler's ambitions had not been sated by the absorption of the Czech Sudetenland. The worst fears of the two governments were realised in the spring

Garrison troops pose for a picture outside a bunker entrance near Pirmasens. (Imperial War Museum)

of 1939 when Hitler marched into Prague. Britain and France now realised that Hitler could not be appeased and made a resolution to act should Poland's independence be threatened. The substance of such a guarantee, however, was more than a little suspect, because the sheer distance that separated the respective countries would limit the amount of direct military support that could be offered by the western powers. Indeed, it was only really feasible to provide indirect assistance in the shape of a naval blockade, bombing German targets, or, most beneficially, by means of a direct assault on Germany itself through the Siegfried Line. But did the governments in London and Paris feel sufficiently strongly about Polish independence to send another generation of young men to their deaths and perhaps start another World War? Hitler did not think so and took steps to ensure that that this would be the case.

In the months after Munich the West Wall had been considerably strengthened and Hitler was now supremely confident that the western powers would not attempt to breach the defences unless provoked. Thus, on 31 August 1939 Hitler issued War Directive 1. This stipulated that the neutrality of Holland, Belgium, Luxembourg and Switzerland was to be respected and that the western frontier of Germany was not to be crossed by German forces without the express permission of the Führer. The army was also ordered to occupy the West Wall and to take up positions along the border with Belgium and Holland in order to prevent the defences being outflanked should the Allies violate Dutch and Belgian neutrality. In the event that Britain and France did act these troops were to contain the threat so that operations against Poland could be successfully completed.[61] But

Hitler did not seriously expect the western democracies to attack after their spineless capitulation at Munich. He therefore took a huge gamble by manning the section of the West Wall running from Aachen to the Swiss border with only eight regular divisions and 25 reserve divisions, with only enough ammunition for three days fighting.[62] As for tanks, these were all committed to the Polish campaign which was now imminent.

On 1 September Hitler launched Operation White (Fall Weiss), the codename for the invasion of Poland. More than 60 divisions, supported by planes of the *Luftwaffe*, poured across the border. The reaction of Britain and France to this flagrant act of aggression was nervously awaited in Warsaw and Berlin. They did not have long to wait. Last-minute shuttle diplomacy failed to secure an acceptable diplomatic solution, so on 3 September Britain and France declared war on Germany. Not surprisingly, this announcement generated starkly contrasting reactions. In Poland there was elation, not least among the military planners who recognised that the Polish armed forces could not win the war without allies. For the German High Command the announcement engendered a feeling of deep foreboding. They had expected the western powers to act every time Hitler had flouted the terms of the Versailles settlement and subsequent undertakings, but had been proved wrong each time. Now their worst fears had been realised and their concern became almost palpable when, on 7 September, France went on the offensive.

German infantry enter an underground bunker of the Siegfried Line, September 1939. (Imperial War Museum)

In accordance with an agreement made between General Gamelin and his Polish counterpart in May 1939 France was obliged to launch an offensive against Germany 'with the bulk of her forces' within sixteen days of mobilization. France had seemingly honoured this agreement and indeed had taken offensive action before she was bound to do. The Polish High Command therefore put into action the strategy that had been developed on the basis of this agreement and fought a series of delaying actions with a view to holding a line along the Vistula and San Rivers. This would buy time and enable France to bring to bear the full weight of her forces against Germany and smash the much vaunted Siegfried Line. This, as the Polish Foreign Minister, Jósef Beck, wrote, 'would destroy the myth that this is impossible, and that the line is, in itself sufficient protection against France'.[63]

The French attack was launched on a fifteen mile front opposite Saarbrücken – the most heavily fortified section of the West Wall. Initial progress was good as the French troops advanced into the territory that lay in front of the main defences and that had been evacuated by the German authorities. Communiqués from the front talked about brilliant attacks and the conquest of German territory, reports that were seized upon by the British press. On 9 September, the Daily Express pronounced that 'France last night began the first big attack on the Siegfried Line'. These stories percolated through to Poland where Polish newspapers reported that the French Army had actually broken through the Siegfried Line. But this was little more than wishful thinking. Gradually the truth emerged and the limited nature of the attack became apparent. In one portion of the front a single German machine gun held up the French attack for an entire day as French commanders sought to minimise casualties, a concept alien to veterans of the First World War who greeted such stories with amazement. Communiqués from the front now spoke of strengthening German resistance and enemy counter-attacks. The press in France and Britain adopted a more sombre and less sensational approach to the reporting of the fighting. Fears in Poland grew about the commitment of her western allies. Fears that were well founded for it soon became clear that French perceptions of the May agreement were very different to those held by the Poles. At a meeting of the Anglo-French Supreme War Council on 12 September,[64] Gamelin made it clear that he intended to begin to 'lean against' the Siegfried Line, but at the same time he dismissed the idea of a full-scale assault.[65] This feint, he argued, would not only fulfil his commitment to Poland but would also be sufficient to distract the Germans while at the same time minimising French casualties and giving the western powers time to fully mobilise. This conservative approach was welcomed in London[66] and Paris (and no doubt Berlin) where the respective governments believed a long war would sap German morale and ultimately lead to the collapse of Hitler's totalitarian regime, but the lack of urgency was greeted with dismay in Warsaw.

The strategy adopted by the French High Command was born out of the unease that permeated all quarters of French society at this time. Families who had lost close relatives in the war were not prepared to countenance an attack on the vaunted West Wall. The casualties of such an action would surely be at least as high as those suffered in the First World War. And for what? A people that shared little in common with the French and who were seemingly fighting a valiant but hopeless rearguard action against the mighty

Wehrmacht. Better then to adopt a defensive strategy and meet any possible German attack from the safety of the Maginot Line. Thus, after advancing only five miles and capturing only 21 square miles of enemy territory the French advance was halted and the troops dug in.[67] France had fulfilled her promise to Poland, but had done so in sentiment rather than deed. Taking refuge in the fact that the French and Polish governments had not formally ratified the May agreement, the High Command did not order 'the majority of its forces' forward; rather a paltry nine divisions were committed to the so-called 'Saar Offensive'.

Clearly however it was pure folly to leave these troops exposed to enemy fire, especially since it was evident that the campaign in Poland was going so well that German units were being transferred from the east to man the defences. Either a full-scale offensive should be launched against the Siegfried Line, or the troops should be withdrawn to the safety of the Maginot Line. With the last organised Polish resistance ending on 5 October and concerned that he might dent the confidence of the French troops by ordering an ill-prepared offensive, Gamelin chose the latter option and the troops were withdrawn.[68] Thus ended France's only offensive of the war and with it perhaps the Allies' greatest chance of an early victory. The West Wall had done its job without a single bunker or pillbox being attacked.

The German High Command breathed a huge sigh of relief with the news that the French had withdrawn, because Germany was far from prepared for war in the west. General von

German officers discussing the situation in front of a Siegfried Line bunker, October 1939. (Imperial War Museum)

Mellenthin, corps commander, inspecting the West Wall defences opposite the Maginot Line, was appalled by the quality of the German troops holding the line and the state of the defences. The troops, he said, were 'second-class, badly equipped and inadequately trained, and the defences were far from being the impregnable fortifications pictured by our propaganda. The more I looked at our defences, the less I could understand the completely passive outlook of the French.' Many senior German officers agreed with him – von Rundstedt is said to have laughed when he inspected the defences – and were of the opinion that the French could have breached the West Wall and reached the Rhine inside a fortnight and might conceivably have won the war before it had even started. Field Marshal von Manstein concluded that, 'The risks which the German leadership ran . . . were undoubtedly very great indeed. Because of the unexpected brevity of the Polish campaign . . . and, above all, as a result of a complete inaction of Poland's western allies at the time of her defeat these risks have hardly ever been properly appreciated.'[70]

But Britain and France did not attack. They recoiled from the possibility of a costly attack on the West Wall and in so doing the West Wall had achieved what Hitler hoped it would; it deterred the French and the British from acting in support of their allies in the east. Westphal sums it up thus:

> Hitler's goal in building the West Wall was without doubt achieved. The sprouting-up of these fortifications along several hundred kilometres of frontier made a deep impression on the French and British politicians in the autumn of 1938 and certainly had some influence in the terms of the Munich agreement which were so favourable to Germany. At the outbreak of the war, also, the West Wall probably bore a very frightening aspect and strengthened the French decision to go slow. Thus Hitler was able to begin and complete the Polish campaign with almost the whole of the active army, while a small number of divisions . . . the majority of which were not ready to fight, held the 'Watch in the West' from behind fortifications which were by no means impenetrable and only partly finished. Once again he [Hitler] had brought off a gigantic bluff, a military feint of the first rank. The West Wall fulfilled the . . . task which Hitler had assigned to it without having to stand any test of its real strength.[71]

With the West Wall protecting Germany's western frontier, Hitler had conquered Czechoslovakia and Poland, and, with the eastern front secure, he was in a prime position to invade France and the Low Countries. The eternal problem of war on two fronts that had vexed the minds of German military strategists was finally solved.[72] Those individuals who had criticised or mocked the idea of a line of concrete and steel defences were silenced. The West Wall had triumphed.

Notes

1. He was, for example, strongly in favour of the Allies retaining military control of the Rhine; a stance which brought him into conflict with both his political superiors and the allies of the French.

2. France initially hoped that the River Rhine would become the new border between France and Germany, or that an independent Rhineland State would be created to act as a buffer between the two nations. However, the British Prime Minister Lloyd George and the United States President Woodrow Wilson would not yield to the French demand arguing that such a solution would lead to future conflict, just as the German annexation of Alsace Lorraine in 1871 had been a contributory factor in the origins of the First World War. For the same reason the Saar was administered by the League of Nations rather than being ceded to France.

3. Germany was allowed to retain her frontier fortifications in the south and in the east.

4. This later caused friction between Britain and France. France was keen to maintain the demilitarised zone, whereas Britain was keen to appease Germany and allow her to do what she wanted to on her own territory.

5. If Germany did not fulfil her obligations (and France secretly hoped that this would be the case) then the Allies would retain their presence.

6. Although the pretext for the French and Belgian invasion was the default in reparation payments it has been argued that the two nations had an ulterior motive and that in fact they hoped to fan the flames of Rhineland separatism.

7. Public Record Office, WO216/970 (Study of German evasions of military provisions of the Treaty of Versailles 1944), p.20.

8. D. G. Williamson, *The British in Germany, 1918–1930: The Reluctant Occupiers*, p.323.

9. Wilson had stated in the preamble to the military section of the Treaty of Versailles that Germany was to be disarmed 'in order to render possible the initiation of a general limitation of the armaments of all nations'.

10. At the same time Germany also left the League of Nations.

11. The western powers' apathy toward German disarmament and later flagrant breaches of the peace settlement can be put down not only to a desire to avoid a repeat of the First World War, but also contrition for the severe terms imposed on Germany at Paris; the desire for a strong Germany as a bulwark against the Soviet Union; and self deception – German lies and untruths were believed because they were more palatable than the alternative.

12. The ten divisions of the Wehrmacht had been broken up to form the basis of the new army and were in no state to challenge the superior might of the French army.

13. S. Westphal, *The German Army in the West*, p.43.

14. In the first century AD the Roman legions built *Limes* or 'threshold' fortifications to safeguard the frontiers of their territories in Germany and Hitler also adopted the term.

15. The decision to proceed with the *Limesprogramm* essentially meant that Hitler had revised his position over the shape of the fortifications in the west; the fortified area concept had been dismissed in favour of a linear defence, albeit that the line was to be constructed in depth.

16. In point of fact, the crisis was very much of Hitler's own making. He had paid little attention to the West Wall prior to May 1938, but having decided to invade Czechoslovakia before the end of the year and fearing a French attack in the west, he needed work on the defences to be expedited.

17. T. Taylor, *Munich: The Price of Peace*, p.687.

18. At Munich Britain and France acceded to Hitler's demand for the Sudetenland to become part of the Third Reich.

19. T. Taylor, *op.cit*, p.294.

20. The East Wall was to provide valuable lessons for the building of the West Wall and during its construction a classification system for defensive works was established based on concrete thickness. Four main categories of construction were established: Type A (the thickest), B, C and D (the thinnest). See Table A.

21. Where a rifle section was housed the shelters were fitted with two entrances.

22. Lack of steel meant that these embrasure plates were later dispensed with and replaced with concrete crenels. These suffered from a number of shortcomings. In particular the outer opening of the armoured embrasure could be kept very small whereas the crenel was large and tended to funnel enemy fire to the weakest point of the shelter.

23. For example, in the MG *Schartenstand*, the intermediate passage to the fighting compartment was omitted.

24. Rather than the 20mm steel door on the other versions the Pak *Unterstellraum* was only fitted with a wooden door.

25. The name originates from the construction thickness 'B'.

26. When a shelter was under attack the rifle squad would take up positions outside.

27. Air defence zone West.

28. Ironically, German bombers of the Condor Legion carried out this raid.

29. The Czechs had constructed an extensive series of fortifications on the French model but they were rendered useless after the Munich agreement of September 1938.

30. It was initially envisaged that resistance type A constructions would only be used in 'fortress constructions' but this restriction was now lifted.

31. After the outbreak of war the 100 series was supplemented by shelters of the 500 series.

32. C.B. MacDonald, *United States Army in World War II. The European Theater of Operations: The Siegfried Line Campaign*, p.34.

33. An alternative version was also built with a high concrete wall at the front which formed an additional obstacle.

34. The old dragon's teeth were reinforced with a further 3–4 rows of teeth added behind.

35. Today the Gerstfeldhöhe is home to the Westwall Museum. One thousand metres of tunnels are open to the public with write-ups and exhibits.

36. J. Eastwood, *Topics of the Moment. The Maginot and Siegfried Lines*, p.50.

37. General Adam had replaced General Ritter von Leeb on 1 April 1938.

38. T. Taylor, *op.cit,* p.688.

39. Hitler had been gassed in the First World War and was therefore well aware of the potential of chemical weapons.

40. Hitler was equally keen to ensure that his men did not enjoy too many home comforts so that they were disinclined to come out of their shelters to fight.

41. A predilection that was to grow stronger as the tide of the war turned against Germany and which manifested itself in the construction of the Atlantic Wall, the Gustav, Hitler and Gothic Lines in Italy and numerous defensive lines on the Eastern Front.

42. General von Hanneken, Ritter von Leeb and Colonel Bodenschatz.

43. By Professor B. Lavergne in *L'Année Politique Française et Etrangère*, November 1938.

44. W. Churchill, *The Gathering Storm, Vol. I, The Second World War*, p.281.

45. S. Westphal, *op.cit,* p.73.

46. Such defects were not surprising considering the fact that in his memorandum of 1 July 1938 Hitler had stated that the emphasis should be on numbers not perfection.

47. Indeed, most of Continental Europe had built some sort of fortifications along their border including Belgium, France and Czechoslovakia.

48. For fear of alienating the Belgians the Maginot Line was not extended along the whole length of the French border.

49. A. Horne, *To Lose a Battle: France 1940*, p.36.

50. J. Noakes and G. Pridham (eds.), *Nazism 1919–1945 3: Foreign Policy, War and Racial Extermination*, p.691.

51. *Ibid*, p.712.

52. Indeed, such was the demand for labour to work on the defences that only a few of the men from the labour service battalions could be spared for the Nuremberg Rally in September 1938.

53. The exertions to complete the West Wall, however, did not come without a price. In the summer of 1939 a Berlin resident noted that there were 'shortages of wool, fats, soap, shoes and meat. Clothes could not be laundered properly because the factories that did such work were

shorthanded – the workers had been sent to build the Siegfried Line.' T. Shachtman, *The Phony War 1939–1940*, p.29.

54. Hitler was already aware of Adam's anxiety. At the beginning of the month Adam's Chief of Staff, Major General Gustav von Wietersheim, had related his concerns about the weakness of the western defences to Hitler when visiting the Berghof. His arguments were challenged by Hitler who reeled off a string of statistics and von Wietersheim was forced to concede.

55. On the grounds of ill health General Adam was removed from his post and subsequently he retired from the Army in November 1938.

56. Beck described the plan to arm Labour Service Battalions and order them to man the West Wall as 'a military impossibility'. D. Irving, *The War Path: Hitler's Germany 1933–9*, p.117.

57. T. Telford, *Munich: The Price of Peace*, p.22.

58. French Chief of the General Staff of National Defence and after the outbreak of war Supreme Commander of all French land forces.

59. *Ibid*, p.142.

60. In September 1938 Germany had taken over the Czech Sudetenland and in March 1939 the rump of Czechoslovakia (Bohemia and Moravia) was absorbed into the Reich.

61. H.R. Trevor Roper (ed.), *Hitler's War Directives 1939–45*, p.3.

62. Numerous figures are quoted for the strength of the German army in the west at this time, but 33 divisions seems to be generally accepted as the true German strength and is the figure used by the official British historian.

63. N. Bethell, *The War Hitler Won: September 1939*, p.92.

64. Attended by Daladier, the French Prime Minister, Chamberlain, the British Prime Minister, Gamelin and General Ironside, British Chief of the Imperial General Staff.

65. It had already been made abundantly clear to Gamelin by General Prételat, the Commander of Second Army Group (tasked with developing the plan of attack against the Siegfried Line), that breaching the Siegfried Line would be all but impossible. Not only was the French mobilisation system cumbersome but also he believed there was insufficient planes to ensure air superiority, there were insufficient shells for use against bunkers and no progress had been made in finding a solution to the problem of the German anti-tank defences. As such a limited three phase operation was developed with the first phase designed to take the French Army to the Siegfried Line, the second phase envisaged some limited penetration of the line and the third phase, dependent on the resistance experienced in phase 2, a full-scale attack.

66. Churchill argued that a more aggressive strategy should be adopted which he believed 'could be done by operations against the Siegfried Line, which was at present thinly held'. Bethell, *op.cit*, p.159. But he later changed his stance, recognising that any French gains could not easily be held if and when the Wehrmacht defeated Poland and was able to concentrate the bulk of its forces in the west.

67. The German authorities had evacuated the vast majority of inhabitants on the border as a precaution prior to the French offensive.

68. During October the German army reoccupied the territory that had been lost and the frontiers reverted to where they had been on 3 September.

69. C. Whiting, *West Wall: The Battle for Hitler's Siegfried Line*, p.14.

70. V. Rowe, *The Great Wall of France: The Triumph of the Maginot Line*, p.103.

71. S. Westphal, *op.cit*, p.74.

72. In the First World War the German General Staff had attempted to overcome this problem by a lightning strike against France in the hope of quickly knocking her out of the war, allowing the Imperial Army to concentrate on Russia. But the Schlieffen Plan was unsuccessful and Germany spent much of the war fighting on two fronts which drained her resources and undoubtedly lessened her chances of victory. Hitler, a veteran of the First World War, was only too aware of this and was determined not to repeat this mistake.

CHAPTER 2

Dilemma

SEPTEMBER 1939–MAY 1940

Günther had not defeated Brunhilde but Siegfried . . . Kriemhilde had mortally offended Brunhilde. Günther was obliged to obtain satisfaction for Brunhilde. This he confided to his armourer, the fierce Hagen. The plan to destroy Siegfried was quickly developed . . . [but] 'Siegfried is invulnerable!'

From the Rhine Saga 'Siegfried and Kriemhilde'

INTRODUCTION

On 17 September Stalin, in accordance with the deal struck by Molotov and Ribbentrop the previous August, sent his troops into Poland. The fate of the Poles was now sealed as the two most powerful states in Europe pitted their overwhelming military might against the brave, but outnumbered and poorly equipped, Polish Army. On 5 October the last vestiges of resistance ended and the independent state of Poland once again disappeared from the political map of Europe.

Reports of Poland's defeat were greeted with despondency and a certain resignation in the west. Britain and France had been able to offer little in the way of direct support to the embattled Poles and their efforts to occupy German forces in the west had been half-hearted and doomed to failure. The upshot of this was that Britain and France were at war with Germany, for an aim that was no longer realisable. This presented the respective governments with something of a dilemma; should their forces massed along the German and Belgian border remain passive in their prepared positions, or should they be ordered to launch a full-scale offensive? The answer to this conundrum was far from straightforward, not least because military strategists had given little thought to an offensive operation. Indeed, the extent of Gamelin's offensive planning had gone no further than an *essai*. This involved an attack by a small force designed to assess the strength of the enemy's dispositions. If this force met significant enemy resistance they were instructed to retreat and await the inevitable German onslaught protected by the tons of concrete and steel of the Maginot Line. And this is exactly what happened in September 1939, except that the Germans did not strike; rather a phoney war, or *sitzkrieg*, developed. This peaceful interlude offered the Imperial General Staff and the French General Staff a chance to reappraise the situation and attempt to answer some fundamental questions. In particular, how strong were the German border defences? Were they impregnable as German propaganda would have them believe, or were they incomplete and riddled with defects as stories leaking out of Germany implied? And what forces did the *Wehrmacht* have to man these defences? The answers to these

The garrison of a West Wall bunker take a well-earned rest after an exercise during the Phoney War, February 1940. (Bundesarchiv)

questions would inform the thinking about any possible offensive operation, particularly where the main thrust should be made, how it should be delivered and, in light of their unpreparedness for an offensive, when any attack could be launched.

In Germany the news of the Polish surrender was received with a mixture of joy and relief. Joy that victory had been secured and relief that France had not launched a full-scale attack in the west. Steps were now taken to minimise the risk of a future attack with the transfer of troops, tanks and aircraft to the western front. Initially, priority was given to strengthening the northern flank along the borders with Belgium and Holland where the West Wall was less well developed, and where the western powers could seemingly strike with ease through the Low Countries and capture the vital industrial region of the Ruhr. It soon became apparent, however, that Britain and France were reluctant to violate the neutrality of Belgium and Holland, but also that they were reluctant to launch an offensive full stop. This passivity perplexed many in the German High Command. To Keitel two alternatives offered themselves. 'Looked at purely from the military point of view this procrastination by the French Army was inexplicable unless – as was hardly probable – they had quite considerably overestimated the strength of our forces in the west;[1] the only alternative was, as Hitler had said, that they were not ready for war.'[2] In fact both of these alternatives contained an element of truth in them. Security measures ensured that details about the fortifications and troop deployments

An expertly camouflaged West Wall bunker which covers the road and tram line into town, November 1939. (Bundesarchiv)

were difficult to come by. The intelligence that was gathered pointed to a number of weaknesses in the Siegfried Line, but there was always the nagging doubt that propaganda peddled by Goebbels's Ministry was in fact true. Even if the West Wall was not impregnable it was still considered to be a substantial obstacle to any attack.

GERMAN STRENGTH, THE ALLIED PERCEPTION

Hitler recognised early on that if his timetable for conquest in the East was to be met, it would not be possible to build a series of defences to match the Maginot Line that had taken ten years to construct. Not only was there insufficient time, there were not enough men, materials or money due to the fact that a large proportion of the country's resources were being channelled into the mechanisation of the army and the expansion and modernization of the navy and air force. But if the West Wall was to act as a powerful deterrent, as Hitler hoped it would, the true strength and scale of the defences could not be exposed to the outside world. Consequently, Hitler recognised the need to draw a veil over the building work on the border, and to allow the outside world only a carefully controlled view of the progress of the West Wall defences. This necessitated not just tight security but also a carefully managed campaign of disinformation. He was a great believer in the 'Big Lie', writing in *Mein Kampf:* 'If you repeat something often enough, with forceful conviction, you can make it seem more truthful than truth itself.'[3]

A warning sign indicating the protected area around the West Wall. It specifically forbids photographs and entry of unauthorised persons. (Bundesarchiv)

Hitler spearheaded the propaganda offensive himself. In August 1938 he stated that 'I can assure you that since May 28th, the most gigantic fortification of all time has been constructed . . . I am the greatest builder of fortifications of all time.'[4] Hitler also used his numerous visits to the West Wall as an opportunity for a stage-managed view of the 'impressive' defences that was captured on newsreel and widely distributed. His boasts were backed up by official statistics. In July 1939 an officially sanctioned publication announced that a third of all cement mixing machines in the Reich had been used on the Wall and had, up to that point, produced six million tons of cement. Also three million rolls of barbed wire had been used. Mixing the cement and uncoiling the wire, it was claimed, was an army of 500,000 workers.[5] Another publication on the West Wall exclaimed that, 'No enemy can approach this bulwark of steel and concrete unpunished. Even an attack with the strongest means will, despite the greatest sacrifice, collapse under the power of the defensive armament.'[6] The book was fully illustrated with pictures of 'West Wall bunkers' and to the untrained eye these fortifications must have looked impressive – as indeed they were, but they were also an impressive distance from the West Wall. In fact many of them formed part of the so-called East Wall.

Troops enter Werkgruppe Scharnhorst Panzerwerk 1238 which formed part of the so-called East Wall. (Imperial War Museum)

Of course the Army was convinced that the western powers had not been deceived by this mixture of exaggeration and untruths. As Blumentritt wrote in his study of von Rundstedt, 'That the so-called 'West Wall' was primarily a propaganda bluff can hardly have been a secret to western intelligence' He continued 'Naturally we assumed that numerous spies had taken part in the construction of the West Wall and that France and England were informed of this bluff.'[7] But intelligence gathering was not easy. At the beginning of 1927 the Inter-Allied Commissions were withdrawn from Germany. This meant that the Allies were now reliant on their small intelligence and espionage services and the information that could be gleaned from aerial reconnaissance, direct observation from France and information gathered through rumour and hearsay.[8] None of them was particularly satisfactory. German counter intelligence and security forces worked to frustrate the covert operations of the western powers while the German use of camouflage and the screening of the construction work restricted more traditional spying methods. Whatever could not be easily disguised was dealt with by deceit and thin cover stories.

With the outbreak of war information gathering became even more difficult. The borders were closed making aerial reconnaissance the only viable source of information. As such the Royal Air Force and their French counterpart were tasked with photographing the Line along its entire length – the RAF from Kleve in the north to Aachen and the French the portion of the line to the south of the city to the Swiss border. But such missions were extremely hazardous, especially for the RAF. The location of

Wherever the enemy could inspect the West Wall, thick mats were erected to obscure the view,
September 1939. (Bundesarchiv)

British airfields and Belgian neutrality meant that it was not possible to provide fighter
cover for the spy planes which left them vulnerable to enemy fighters. This threat,
combined with the danger posed by anti-aircraft fire, meant that the reconnaissance
planes had to operate at altitude. This made photography difficult, especially in the
autumn and winter months when there was likely to be heavy cloud. In light of the
hazardous nature of the mission and with no guarantee of valuable information being
gathered, the RAF was less than convinced of the value of such an exercise. A note
written at the time clearly expressed these misgivings, 'It is hoped . . . that the results
which it is expected to obtain from the photographs are of such importance as to justify
the ordering of such a difficult task.'[9]

From this evidence it might be assumed, as some authors have, that the shroud of
secrecy and the state sponsored propaganda had been extremely effective, in short, that
'the Germans had, by subtle political, military and personal intrigue, succeeded in
deceiving the Allies into believing that the West Wall on Germany's western borders was
impregnable.'[10] But further investigation casts doubt on this assumption.

A report written in June 1939 by the British gives an idea of the intelligence that had
been gathered. It describes the extent of the line, how it line ran from Kleve on the Dutch
border to Basle on the Swiss frontier and identified the section of the line that lay between
Aachen and Saarbrücken as being the most heavily fortified and that work on the line
would be completed by August of that year. The report also pointed out that to describe the
Siegfried Line as a 'line' was incorrect, it was better described as a defensive system
organized in depth – including two and in places three separate lines of fortifications.

The make-up of these defences was also well documented. The report continued,
'These fortifications consist of barbed wire and tank obstacles covered by pillboxes, many

of them connected by trenches and even by underground passages. There are powerful underground works in places where the ground lends itself to their establishment. Field guns, howitzers, A/T guns, machine guns and flamethrowers have been mounted in concrete works.' An approximation had also been made as to the density of pillboxes in different sectors, as well as an appraisal of the strength of the different defences both in terms of design and construction. The report also included photographs and drawings of pillboxes and bunkers and other fortifications, including dragon's teeth.[11]

The British had access to a considerable amount of information on the Siegfried Line from unofficial sources, particularly books and newspaper reports that were written at the time. One such publication stated that, 'No matter what the German Government says to the contrary, it is certain that the Siegfried Line is still far from finished.' It continued with reference to a report despatched by a special correspondent of the Daily Telegraph who made a tour behind the fortifications a fortnight after war had broken out which claimed that '. . . work on the defences was still going forward day and night.'[12] However, British Military Intelligence gave little credence to these reports noting that 'There have been many reports in the press recently of the unsatisfactory work that that has been put into these fortifications, e.g. flooding casemates, crumbling of cement and the like. While it would be unwise to dismiss these reports as being wholly without foundation [but they did anyway], it is considered that the German western defences are on the whole formidable and that each month sees an increase of strength and a greater degree of preparedness. Similarly it is not believed that these defensive lines are tactically badly sited. The Germans had considerable experience of field fortifications in the First World War, e.g. the Hindenburg Line and are fully aware of their importance in military operations.'[13]

French intelligence on the Siegfried Line, unsurprisingly in light of the proximity of the defences, was much more detailed. Because of this the French military was able to make a much more thorough and critical assessment of the fortifications and to assess the validity of information (or more accurately misinformation) passed through official channels. General Bodenschatz, an aide of Göring's, informed Captain Stehlin in the French embassy in June 1938 that Germany was constructing a defensive line along its western border comprising 'a multitude of shelters for men armed with anti-tank guns and concretised so heavily as to give security against the heaviest artillery.'[14] This did not take in Stehlin and the French Air Attaché, Colonel Hubert-Marie-Joseph Geffrier. On 2 August 1938 a report was passed back to Paris based on consular reports and aerial observations, it concluded that the defences were not strong and that, contrary to Hitler's predictions, they could not be completed in the near future.

This was especially true of the defences along the borders with Germany's neutral neighbours. No defences had been built along the border with Switzerland and very few had been built along the borders with the Netherlands and Belgium. It was clear that strenuous efforts were being made to reinforce these weaker sections, but it was also clear that to make the whole western border equally strong would take an inordinate amount of effort. In a report written at the time it was noted that 'It is probable that the defences on the Dutch and Belgian Frontiers will soon be nearly as strong as those now on the Saar, though this would cause a considerable strain on German resources, and the ground is not so suitable for defensive works as is the Saar.'[15]

In addition to the weaknesses observed in certain sections of the line, the French had identified further, arguably more serious, faults from tests they had carried out. At their Experimental Centre at Bourges the French had constructed a series of casemates and dragon's teeth that as accurately as possible replicated the defences of the Siegfried Line. These were then subjected to a series of tests to ascertain the strength of the fortifications and the best method of attack. These tests demonstrated that the pillboxes and bunkers were made of inferior quality concrete and as such were susceptible to heavy artillery fire. Moreover, the embrasures facing the front, following tests on full-scale mock-ups, were found to be vulnerable to anti-tank weapons, while those facing the rear, which were armoured, were vulnerable to heavy concussion.

But whilst these tests highlighted a number of weaknesses in the German defences, they also demonstrated how difficult it would be to successfully neutralise the fortifications. For example, in a demonstration of the impact of French heavy artillery shells it was found that it was necessary, if the bunker was to be destroyed, to a) hit the bunker, which although obvious was, in practice, very difficult, especially if the structure was camouflaged, and b) for the hit to be as near vertical as possible to avoid a ricochet. This made the destruction of enemy bunkers by artillery very difficult, so much so that it was mooted that the artillery, instead of being used directly against the fortifications, would be better employed harassing rear areas, or as a 'curtain' to prevent reinforcements and supplies getting forward.

Greater success was achieved in experiments using direct fire. Both the 47mm anti-tank gun and the 75mm field gun were found to be capable of penetrating 1.5m of concrete, but to achieve this penetration it was necessary to engage the bunker over open sights, which exposed the attacker to enemy fire. A partial solution was the suggestion that high velocity guns of large calibre should be mounted in tanks in order to better protect the crew firing the gun, but it was conceded that the weapon and platform would take time to develop.

Different methods of attacking the dragon's teeth were also demonstrated. Field artillery firing at a range of 4,000 metres successfully blasted a gap in the anti-tank obstacle, but required the expenditure of over 200 rounds of ammunition in order to produce the breach. Tanks mounted with 37mm or 47mm guns were also effective but they had to fire at close range. One hit destroyed a small tooth, two or three a large one. Such results demanded great accuracy from the gunner which was fine in the relative peace and tranquillity of the test ground, but would be far more difficult in the heat of battle when exposed to enemy fire.[16] Small explosive charges were also demonstrated – 5 kg of explosives for a small tooth and 10 kg for a large, but again it was easy for engineers to demonstrate the principle in tests; it would be a completely different scenario when under fire from enemy pillboxes (as the Americans found out in 1944).

The findings from these tests, together with the intelligence that they had gathered clearly demonstrated that the Siegfried Line was very different to their own Maginot Line and, perhaps somewhat conceitedly, was considered in many regards inferior.

Artillery and observation posts were, by and large, constructed as field works[17] leaving them vulnerable to enemy fire. There were few 'major' works as in the Maginot Line, which the French felt would result in a dispersion of garrisons and corresponding difficulty of command (although the bunkers were generally linked by underground telephone cables). The pillboxes also had less elaborate ventilation systems than those in the Maginot Line, which meant that they were more vulnerable to gas attacks. Moreover, the French were convinced that the small, poorly furnished pillboxes and bunkers – it should be remembered that some of the Maginot Line forts had, among other things, gymnasiums, cinemas and sunrooms – would produce a detrimental effect should the enemy soldiers have to man them for any length of time.

HOBSON'S CHOICE

Thus Britain and France were well aware of the deficiencies of the West Wall, but they were also aware that for all its shortcomings it would be exceedingly difficult to breach, particularly the portion of the Wall covering the Saar and Moselle valleys where the attack would have to fall.

During the course of 1935 and 1936 the Belgian government, concerned by Nazi Germany's increasingly bellicose behaviour, renounced the diplomatic and military agreements that had been concluded with the western powers after the First World War and instead adopted a 'policy of independence'; to all intents and purposes Belgium became a neutral state. As the threat of war grew the Netherlands, likewise, adopted a neutral stance. These developments had serious consequences for the western powers and for France in particular. Firstly, Belgian neutrality meant that if Germany was to go to war with the western powers aerial attacks on Germany's industrial heart, the Ruhr, by Britain and France would be severely hampered. Secondly, the agreements signed by Belgium and France after the war meant that the Maginot Line had only been constructed as far as the Belgian border – to construct the line along the border with Belgium would have gravely undermined relations between the two countries.

Belgium's renunciation of these agreements meant that a vast area of the French border was now exposed to a potential German attack.[18] Finally, Belgian and Dutch neutrality practically guaranteed a peaceful frontier for Germany from Luxembourg to the North Sea because of the political implications of any violation. Advancing into Belgium would have had an adverse effect on other neutral countries and would have given Hitler *carte blanche* for further aggression and, more significantly, would undoubtedly disaffect American public opinion. Consequently, as Churchill noted: 'An advance through Belgium without Belgian consent was excluded on grounds of international morality.'[19] This final point had serious implications for French offensive and defensive strategy.

Defensively, Belgian neutrality precluded the development of any plans with the Belgian Army for a collaborative strategy to counter any potential German aggression. The French High Command had always recognised that the best way to defend Northern

France was by advancing into Belgium and stymieing any German attack before it had chance to gain momentum. It also had the added advantage of ensuring that any fighting took place on Belgian rather than French territory. Offensively, the consequences of Belgian neutrality were equally dire. A report written at the time notes, '. . . there would be far more chance of breaking the Siegfried Line if we had the wide choice of objectives which would be offered by the whole German frontier rather than the obvious and only line of approach in the Saar. It may be assumed therefore that the participation of Belgium is a necessary preliminary for a successful offensive against the Siegfried Line.'[20]

It was increasingly clear, however, that Belgian cooperation would not be forthcoming and as such three potential avenues of attack had to be discounted: an attack towards the Ruhr from north of Aachen and an attack through the so-called 'Aachen Gap'. Another alternative, through the Eifel (the German portion of the Ardennes) also had to be dismissed, although in reality this was never a realistic alternative because the terrain here was very difficult and was ideally suited to defence; there were few good roads and only one railway.

This left only two alternatives: an attack through the Vosges, or an advance through the Saar and Moselle valleys. The former was unusual in that the Rhine in the Vosges forms the frontier between France and Germany and the operation of breaking the Siegfried Line would have to come after and not before the crossing of the river. However, it was felt that success in this area would not be easy to exploit because all lines of advance had to pass through the mountainous country of the Black Forest. Nor was there anything of strategic importance in the area; the nearest objective was Stuttgart some 50 miles away, with Munich over a hundred miles further on. As such this option was dismissed.

This left only one alternative; an advance through the Saar and Moselle valleys. If the Allies were successful in getting through the Siegfried Line in this area, and it was a big if, then the prospects for exploitation were considerable. There were good roads and natural approaches to the Rhine and once across this obstacle the Allies would be in a position to advance on Frankfurt and Cassel which were important railway junctions.

Militating against this option, however, was the fact that this was the 'traditional' route for invading Germany and as such the German High Command would be expecting an attack at this point. Moreover, the country was particularly suited to defence and the German engineers had taken full advantage, constructing some of the strongest defences of the Siegfried Line in this area. The British military had calculated that in the forward sections of the line the Germans had constructed 30 to 40 concrete pillboxes to the square kilometre, while to the rear this reduced to 15–20 pillboxes. These defences were reinforced with dragon's teeth (which at the time this report was written were in the process of being doubled), numerous anti-tank weapons protected by concrete and minefields.

Even if the Allies were skilful, or lucky enough, to breach the defences in this section of the line, it was felt that a new and separate operation for the crossing of the Rhine would have to be undertaken. The Rhine in this area was 300–500 yards wide and would require engineers to provide a means of crossing if, as was assumed, the bridges over the Rhine had been destroyed. This was a particularly difficult operation in its own right and would require weeks of preparation before an attack could be launched. But a bridging operation or amphibious assault would be all but impossible following an attritional battle for the Siegfried Line (assuming a traditional attack was launched). Such an attack would devastate the whole area over which they would have to advance and there was also the possibility that French railways near the frontier would have been destroyed in the battle for the line.

STRATEGY

It is worth remembering, however, that France and Britain had not envisaged taking the initiative in any future war, they had anticipated massive bombing of London and Paris, or an attack on the Maginot Line, but not going on the offensive. France, perhaps more than any other nation, had suffered terribly in the First World War. Not only were the casualties she suffered appalling but also the fighting had devastated large swathes of territory. Not surprisingly, France was determined that it should never happen again. To this end the huge fortifications of the Maginot Line had been constructed along the border with Germany. To the French this was the epitome, the apogee of the strategy that had succeeded in the First World War, albeit at enormous cost. In the First World War the immensely strong forts at Verdun had provided the backbone to the valiant French defence. The same successful strategy would be adopted in the next European conflagration, but in the future the defensive battles would be fought around the Maginot Line. Ensconced within the tunnels and casemates the French Army would allow the invading German army to exhaust itself trying to breach the defences. With the enemy seriously weakened by the effort of the futile attacks a powerful offensive would be launched which, it was hoped, would lead to victory as in 1918.

This defensive mentality, however, meant that few resources had been invested in offensive weapons, nor had much thought been given to offensive plans. In the event of war Gamelin planned to launch a limited offensive. French troops would advance until they met serious German resistance at which point the troops would fall back to the fortifications of the Maginot Line. Such a strategy would satisfy the pride of the French army and would hopefully bring Britain and Russia into the war. Thus, when the opportunity to strike at Germany while she was fully occupied in Poland came, France was not in a position to act. The feeble Saar offensive was launched but without any great conviction and was an ignominious failure. France would now have to wait for Germany to attack, or very quickly develop a new strategy to smash the Siegfried Line, which would not be easy in light of the French High Command's conviction that the Maginot Line, and by implication the Siegfried Line, was impregnable.

Nor was Britain prepared for offensive operations on the Continent. Britain was still largely a naval power with commitments of Empire all around the globe. The trade routes to and from these colonies needed to be policed and the colonies themselves garrisoned. This put a tremendous strain on the army which due to financial constraints had already seen its numbers drastically pruned in the years after the war. As such only a small, poorly

British and French officers inspect fortifications of the Maginot Line, November 1939. (Hulton Getty Images)

equipped expeditionary force was available for operations in Europe. In the event of German aggression the British force was to advance into Belgium and stem what was anticipated to be the main enemy thrust, just as their forefathers had in 1914. But that was the extent of the British thinking; a pre-emptive strike was not seriously considered.

The turn of events of 1939 with the German invasion of Poland forced Britain and France to challenge the defensive mentality that had dominated military thinking in the post war period and to contemplate the somewhat unpalatable possibility of launching some sort of military action against Germany. The thinking was muddled and often self-serving. The French identified any number of strategies that would ensure that French losses would be minimised and the chances of fighting on French soil were reduced. The British floated the idea of a naval blockade but this was unlikely to seriously diminish Germany's fighting strength, especially since the River Danube, a vital artery, was under German control. A bombing campaign was also unlikely to cripple the German war machine because, initially, it was deemed unethical to bomb German industry as the factories were privately owned

To make matters worse for the western powers they also had the problem of agreeing a common approach to tackling the Siegfried Line, never easy for two nations that enjoyed good relations and a common language, let alone France and Britain whose relationship had alternated between unease and downright mistrust.

MORALE

In spite of these difficulties, the two countries identified three alternative strategies that it was believed had a reasonable chance of breaching the Siegfried Line. The first of these was loosely described as 'morale'.

Sir Douglas Haig, the commander of the British Expeditionary Force, in his analysis of the reasons for victory in the First World War, insisted that the lowering of the enemy's morale was a significant factor. The strength and tenacity of the earlier attacks, he argued, had worn the enemy down and so undermined the enemy's morale that the soldiers were less inclined to fight on. An example of this, it was claimed, was the operation against the Hindenburg Line in 1917 and 1918. Earlier attacks had made no impression, but with German morale broken the Hindenburg position was captured with far fewer casualties than earlier attacks. And there is some truth in Haig's supposition that lowering of German morale did contribute to Germany's ultimate defeat, but there was dissention as to whether this was due to the effect of earlier battles, or other extraneous factors. Some argued that, even in 1918, morale among German soldiers was still remarkably high and that spirits only declined as they became aware of the deteriorating situation at home; the Allied naval blockade led to serious food shortages which precipitated strikes and general unrest.[21]

Whatever the truth, it was clear that lowering the enemy's morale would render the success of any offensive far more likely.[22] But it was equally clear that undermining morale was not a practicable strategy for defeating the Siegfried Line. These conclusions were accepted in both London and Paris. Only direct military action would lead to the demise of the Siegfried Line and the possibility of ultimate victory, but that was as far as any consensus between the two countries went in respect of a strategy for breaching the Siegfried Line.

DESTRUCTION

The French for their part favoured a strategy of 'destruction', essentially a return to the *modus operandi* adopted by the Allies in the First World War whereby attacks depended for their success on the overwhelming use of matériel. This strategy enjoyed some limited success; single lines or a limited position might be seized, but the Siegfried Line was a different proposition, especially the heavily fortified Saar region. The only defensive line that bore even the slightest resemblance to the Siegfried Line was the Hindenburg Line, and this, as Ironside noted, was little more than a glorified trench. Yet it proved impervious to Allied attacks until the closing stages of the war when the German army was exhausted. It was therefore recognised that in order to rupture the defences it would be necessary to launch a localised attack – which to the French meant attacking along a 40 kilometre front – where men and matériel could be concentrated in the hope of ensuring a sufficiently large numerical advantage over the defenders to ensure success.[23]

An advance post of the Siegfriedstellung *at Honnecourt, August 1917, which seems to bear out Ironside's assertion that the Hindenburg Line was little more than a glorified trench. (Imperial War Museum)*

The attack would commence with a massive preliminary bombardment which, it was hoped, would destroy the enemy works and open the way for the infantry and tanks.[24] To ensure that the enemy's positions had been neutralised all along the front it was calculated that it would be necessary to field as a bare minimum 5,200 pieces of artillery ranging in calibre from 75mm to 400mm.[25] However, the only way of amassing such a concentration of artillery would be to remove weapons from other fronts, notably the borders with Belgium and Italy, and in so doing expose France to attack. Clearly such a bold move would be difficult to countenance, especially since the French Army could almost certainly maintain the status quo by simply holding the strong defensive positions it already occupied. And even if the French High Command was prepared to take such a gamble a bombardment on the scale envisaged would soon exhaust the reserves of ammunition – even if munitions deemed unsuitable for use against reinforced concrete positions were used. The only alternative was to launch an attack on a shortened front of some 20–25 kilometres, but it was felt that a breach on this scale would not provide sufficient scope for further exploitation, particularly any operation to cross the Rhine.

As regards tanks to exploit the breach, the French believed that a battalion of light tanks would be needed for each kilometre of front (circa 40 battalions) and approximately one battalion of heavy tanks every 2 kilometres (circa 15–20 battalions). As with the artillery this was not feasible. The light tanks available would scarcely meet this need and the heavy tanks available clearly would not. The situation was no better in respect of aircraft and anti-aircraft guns to protect the attacking force from the *Luftwaffe* both of which were deemed to be insufficient.

In terms of manpower required, the situation was equally depressing according to the planners. It was calculated that it would be necessary to employ one division for every two kilometres of front followed by another division in second echelon meaning that a minimum of 40 to 50 divisions would be required. But this disguised the true manpower needs of such an operation.

The strategic problem of a French attack in the direction of Mainz was that Germany could counter this move by advancing into neutral Belgium with the object of trying to envelop the French troops engaged in Lorraine.[26] After all, the Germans had violated Belgian neutrality in 1914 and the French High Command was quite right to assume that Hitler, on past form, would be equally unscrupulous. To counter this threat it was calculated that a further 40–50 divisions would need to be stationed along France's northern border. Furthermore, France was aware of the threat posed by Italy and to a lesser extent Spain. Both were fascist states and would be hostile or at least adopt a waiting game necessitating the stationing of troops on the Spanish border and at least 10 divisions in the Alps with a further 6–10 divisions in North Africa (where Italy and Spain had colonies). On top of this already extensive list it was deemed prudent to keep a further 10 to 20 divisions in reserve to meet unforeseen eventualities. The French therefore concluded that to launch an attack on a 40 kilometre front would require as a bare minimum 130–140 divisions and perhaps as many as 150–160, but France only had around 90 divisions on the North Eastern front and was therefore reliant on Britain providing the balance of approximately 60 divisions. But Britain was not in a position to make such a commitment. An annotation to a paper of March 1940 outlining this requirement stated: '. . . it is unlikely that we shall ever have 60, unless we are prepared to accept a drastic cut in scales of equipment. We cannot have it both ways.'[27]

Nor was Britain in a position to provide the necessary armoured support for such an attack. Even assuming that the British were to supply just 40 divisions (the number of divisions initially suggested by the French), of which 20–25 divisions would actually be employed in any offensive, then 20 battalions of light tanks and 10 battalions of heavy tanks would be required, but they simply were not available.

However, the shortages of men and material were not the only factor militating against a traditional set-piece attack. It was clear that the British Imperial General Staff was dubious about the chances of success of this strategy against the Siegfried Line. In a note to General Gamelin on 15 December 1939 General Ironside graphically expressed his concerns:

We have a classical example at Verdun, where their comparatively old-fashioned forts (admittedly built with good material and on a lavish scale) withstood the heaviest of shell fire which the Germans were able to amass . . . In this chapter of the war, both sides expended an astronomical number of munitions and men. The French succeeded in holding their positions, but at such a cost that Falkenhayn was truly right when he said he would hammer the French on the anvil of Verdun.

Today we have, broadly speaking, fortifications, – many of them presumably after the Verdun pattern – stretching not for a few miles, but for hundreds of miles from the sea to Switzerland. Are attacks likely to be any more successful today than they were in 1916? We still have forts, artillery and the normal ancillary services, the one pitted against the other, – admittedly with a new technique and with certain new details, which unfortunately still amount to the old conception of vast military preparation, and then the hoped for breakthrough with other arms.

Admittedly, we have tanks in various sizes, but the effects of these will be very largely cancelled by obstacles, traps and so forth.[28]

Moreover, even if the Allies did succeed in breaking the Siegfried Line using such methods an operation to cross the Rhine would be made considerably more arduous. 'If we attempt to rely on destructive methods, there is no doubt that this will add considerably to the difficulties of an advance beyond the Siegfried Line. The scale of destruction would be such that each stage of the attack would necessitate passing through a completely devastated area, which would necessitate weeks of preparation. The Germans would thus be given ample time to organise new defences and by the time we arrived at the Rhine demolitions and defences would have been completed on what is already a strong natural line.'[29] Ironside had also recognised the implications of any pause in the advance,

. . . it must not be forgotten that even a respite of two or three days would be sufficient for the enemy to put up new concrete defences (always providing he had the material on hand), owing to the fact that many of the new forms of concrete harden within a few days.

Therefore, this fact would appear to completely neutralise any effect which might be produced by the purely local successes. Any attack made must be capable of continual progress through the succession of defended lines which we may expect to meet. The slightest pause and the whole effort would be wasted.[30]

It was also recognised that using this method would necessitate the stockpiling of a massive amount of material, which, even if the Allies could achieve air superiority, could not long remain hidden from the enemy.

SURPRISE

In light of these difficulties the only alternative left was a surprise attack. If it was possible to devise some means of attacking the Siegfried Line without using a massive preliminary bombardment then it should be possible to surprise the enemy. All the more so if the impression could be conveyed that an attack was to be launched in a different sector of the front by the massing of artillery and reserves there. A paper written at the time concludes, 'If the attack is achieved by surprise methods or weapons, it is possible that one or two bridgeheads over the Rhine could be made, which would prevent the Germans organising an effective resistance behind their fortified line . . .' It went on, 'An advance to the Rhine would involve the loss to Germany of many important centres of industry and population and it is possible that German resistance would break without our having to advance further.'[31]

Such an operation was not without its risks. After all, it necessitated the development of new tactics, or new weapons, or both and would be a move away from the methods that had delivered victory in the First World War. But to Ironside it seemed to be the only viable alternative. As he noted in December 1939,

> . . . It appears essential that we should produce a new contrivance for overcoming this obstacle. The Hindenburg Line produced the tank, which was immediately successful, having been specially designed with that sole object. Moreover, it had the great advantage of complete and sustained surprise. This was a weapon which the enemy were unable to successfully counter, or to build for themselves, because they lacked the initial research and the industry to produce it.
>
> We must do the same. We must design a new weapon, a new mode of warfare, contraption, appliance, – call it what you will – to overcome the obstacles which are at present known to us.
>
> It cannot be beyond the wit of man to devise some new thing, some new form of locomotion which will achieve our object. It is not sufficient to be able to batter down a small section of fortified line or obstacles. Our new contrivance must be able to walk through it, jump over it, fly over it as if it were not there. It must be reasonably proof against all the known difficulties which it will have to face. If we were successful enough to devise some new means of attack, it would have not only the advantages inherent in a contrivance specially designed for the job, but all the advantages of complete surprise. Surprise will play a greater and greater part in any successful attack, because once a successful surprise can be effected the corresponding disorganisation within the enemy's lines and staff is so great, on account of the size and complexity of any modern army.
>
> Every weapon admittedly has its antidote, but if one can get a weapon, the antidote for which requires years of planning and vast national industry to produce it, it may well prove to be impossible to produce the antidote in time.[32]

But the 'new contrivance' for defeating the Siegfried Line was seemingly a long way off. As Ironside conceded in the same letter, 'On going through the latest developments which the French have put before us as regards taking concrete emplacements and heavily reinforced concrete forts today, with tank traps and obstacles of every description . . . I am struck by the complete lack of any new ideas which are being brought to bear upon this problem.'[33] And the situation across the Channel was little better with numerous official bodies conducting research and any number of government departments responsible for assessing the merits of new technical discoveries brought to their notice. Communication between the various bodies was almost non-existent and certainly there was little in the way of an exchange of ideas between France and Britain; mutual mistrust as to the intentions of the other saw to that. It was clear that something needed to be done to synthesise and focus these ideas and Ironside, in true British fashion, suggested the creation of a committee. 'It would appear that the question of the offensive against the SIEGFRIED LINE is so specialised that there should be a special committee for the study of this subject and the coordination of training, experiment and invention towards the attempt to breach the line.'[34] This committee was to comprise members drawn from every service and every branch of industry and with the power of co-opting anybody who it was felt would be useful. Training and experiment establishments were set up at Bourges in France and Imber in the United Kingdom and reciprocal visits arranged to review progress.[35] And tangible progress was made. Numerous bridging devices were developed for use against trenches and water obstacles like those on the Siegfried Line. Tanks were designed that could operate over ground that had been heavily shelled and heavier tanks, able to negotiate obstacles, were also developed. They were armed with large calibre high velocity guns capable of engaging and silencing enemy pillboxes. Others were fitted with bulldozer blades to enable them to fill in trenches, or were fitted with searchlights to enable night attacks and to blind the occupants of bunkers.

Wireless-controlled tanks were also developed. These were either in the form of specially designed vehicles or obsolete tanks that were packed with explosives and guided towards the enemy casemate by an operator some distance behind. These showed potential (indeed the idea was adopted by the Germans later in the war) but still needed improvement. One model, for example, could not be stopped! The French had also developed a tank-mounted flamethrower which had a range of some 40 metres, but again this needed further work because much of the flame tended to rise. However, if they could refine the idea they had a powerful weapon that might conceivably, it was thought, disintegrate concrete.

Other less conventional methods were also considered. Both the French and the British carried out trials spraying chemicals from planes and the British also tested various methods for delivering poison gas. In another throwback to the First World War the British also carried out trials using mining machines to enable explosives to be placed under the enemy positions and then detonated.

Aside from designing weapons to tackle the pillboxes and bunkers of the Siegfried Line further counter-measures were developed to neutralise the other defences employed by the Germans. The idea of a pipe filled with explosives was conceived; the so-called Bangalore torpedo. It could be positioned by either infantry or by tank and was designed to blow gaps in wire entanglements, but also worked against Dragon's teeth. Tanks were also fitted with large rollers that deployed a mat which covered the enemy barbed wire and allowed the supporting forces to get forward. Rollers or ploughs were also fitted to the front of tanks which successfully cleared a path through minefields, and a hand held mine detector was also designed and built for the infantry.

As regards tactical developments, the British and French had, if anything, retrogressed. In the closing stages of the First World War the Allies had experimented successfully with infiltration tactics and combined arms operations. And some further, albeit tentative, steps had been taken in the interwar years. But the two armies soon reverted to type with France, for example, employing the tank as an infantry support weapon rather than as a potent weapon in its own right. And the respective High Commands certainly did not see any merit in the tactics that the *Reichswehr* and later the *Wehrmacht* adopted and which were later to play a pivotal role in the success of *Blitzkrieg*. Not surprisingly, therefore, little progress had been made in the development of tactics for use against pillboxes. A memorandum from the British Military Mission in France to the War Office mentioned that the French planned to construct a 'mock-up' section of the Siegfried Line. It was due to be completed by January 1940 and it was hoped that divisions in succession would be sent to the camp where it is being constructed to practice assaults on fortified positions. Curiously, no concrete was to be used in the construction, rather it was to be partly earthworks with concrete works represented by canvas. Damningly, the note that outlined these plans concluded with a desperate plea. 'Have you any ideas on this question of attack on fortified positions? I am sure the French would be interested to have anything you have got.'[36] This tactical naivety and the lack of weapons, both traditional and specialised, did not augur well for an attack in 1940.

AN ATTACK IN 1940?

Even before the outbreak of war concerns had been raised about France's preparedness for war. Raoul Dautry, a talented engineer, who had reorganised the French railways after the war, and who was now placed in charge of rearmament, confided to André Maurois (novelist, essayist and biographer) that he would not be able to supply all the equipment that the armed forces required 'before 1942'.[37] Such a candid confession from one so able and so closely involved in French arms production was particularly damning when looked at in the context of preparations to launch a major offensive, irrespective of which strategy was ultimately chosen. It was recognised that such an operation, especially on the scale needed to breach the Siegfried Line, would require significantly more weapons than a defensive campaign which the French High Command had planned for. In particular, a large number of tanks would be required and more specifically heavy tanks like the French Char 'B' and Char de Fortresse, but heavy tanks were in short supply and the latter was unlikely to reach production in any quantity before the summer of 1943. The British Army was similarly deficient, with only enough tanks for a minor operation in 1941 and a major offensive in the spring of 1942. Moreover, the tanks that the British could field at this time, the Mk II and the Mk III, were only suitable for operations against field fortifications in reasonably good going but would 'fall short of the ideal for the attack on prepared fortifications such as the Siegfried Line'.[38] The more powerful Mk IV and Stern 'Fortress Tank' that might have been suitable for such an operation were still on the drawing board and large-scale production unlikely until late 1941.

The British concluded that this shortage of tanks necessitated the creation of a Tank Board to pool ideas and to get the maximum number of suitable tanks built as rapidly as material resources allowed. This, it was then hoped, would provide a better idea of when it would be possible to launch an offensive in Northeast France.

Not surprisingly, after considering all the evidence, Gamelin concluded that, 'If the very considerable requirements of every kind necessary for the breaching of the Siegfried Line are compared with all the resources on which we can count, it does not seem as if it will be possible to undertake the contemplated breach with prospects of success in the Spring of 1940.'[39] He continued, surmising that the earliest offensive action could be considered was the spring of 1941 and even for that date to be feasible production of the necessary war material would have to begin immediately.

The position in respect of the development and production of 'traditional' weapons was then gloomy and was equally unpromising as regards the development of new weapons to counter the defences of the Siegfried Line. Gamelin in the same study surmised that, 'The discovery of new methods might possibly change the nature of the problem, but we would still have to achieve the mass production of appropriate weapons and it is not prudent to anticipate that this can be realized before the autumn of 1940.'[40] It seemed that an attack on the western front would have to wait; but, unbeknown to the western powers, time was fast running out as Hitler prepared to strike.

Notes

1. The French calculated that in September 1939 the Germans had 43 divisions stationed in the west, which significantly overestimated the actual figure, while British intelligence underestimated the strength of German forces believing they had only 24 divisions. The British, however, overestimated German aerial power. They estimated that the Germans could muster 4,320 aircraft against a British and French total of 3,195. In fact the *Luftwaffe* only had 3,600 aircraft of which approximately 1,000 were available in the west.
2. W. Gorlitz (ed.), *The Memoirs of Field Marshal Keitel*, p.94.
3. I. Werstein, *Betrayal: The Munich Pact of 1938*, p.43.
4. C. Whiting, *The Battle for the German Frontier*, p.12.
5. J. Eastwood, *op. cit*, p.51.
6. Rudolf Kuehne's book quoted in C. Whiting, *West Wall: The Battle for Hitler's Siegfried Line*, p.6.
7. G. Blumentritt, *Von Rundstedt: The Soldier and the Man*, p.56.
8. Early in February 1938 news filtered through from Germany that the Nazi authorities were forcing farmers to sell their property on the banks of the Rhine and rumours circulated that Hitler was beginning to construct an immense system of fortifications on the French model. Later, in July 1938, the mayor of a small French village, many of the inhabitants of which owned valuable land on the right bank of the Rhine, received notice from the Nazi authorities that the land would be expropriated 'because it was required for the purpose of fortification.' J. Eastwood, *op.cit*, p.44–6.
9. PRO, WO197/7, Siegfried Line: photographic reconnaissance by RAF. September–October 1939.
10. C. Partridge, *Hitler's Atlantic Wall*, p.9.
11. WO190/829, The Siegfried Line, 28 June 1939.
12. J. Eastwood, *op.cit*, p.53.
13. *Ibid.*
14. T. Taylor, *Munich: The Price of Peace*, p.689.
15. WO193/157 Siegfried Line: notes on attack on fortified towns. December 1939–May 1940. Answers to Questionnaire, p.5.
16. The British were not convinced that this was by any means the best way of dealing with the dragon's teeth, because it exposed the tanks to enemy fire (even when smoke was used). They preferred the alternative of bridging the obstacle and then allowing the tanks to tackle the pillboxes.

17. Field works were semi-permanent fortifications and were generally built without the use of concrete.
18. Although Belgian neutrality meant that theoretically no country should violate Belgian territory it was widely recognised that although France and Britain would respect her neutrality, Germany, in all likelihood, would not.
19. N. Bethell, *The War Hitler Won: September 1939*, p.171.
20. WO193/157, *op.cit*, Answers to Questionnaire, p.5.
21. The domestic turmoil in Germany at this time later formed the basis for the claim that Germany lost the war because she had been 'stabbed in the back'.
22. Indeed, in August 1939 Gamelin was convinced that German morale would snap the instant France signalled her intention to fight. He opined that 'Hitler will collapse the day war is declared on Germany. Instead of defending the frontiers of the Reich, the German Army will be forced to march on Berlin to suppress the trouble that will immediately break out. The troops manning the Siegfried Line will offer little resistance. We shall go through Germany like a knife through butter.' N. Bethell, *The War Hitler Won: September 1939*, p.6.
23. To contemporary military thinkers this necessitated having three attackers to every defender in order to guarantee a reasonable chance of success.
24. Nivelle and his contemporaries would have been very familiar with this plan of attack – the only difference being the breach in the First World War would have been exploited by infantry and cavalry and not tanks which were too slow and unreliable.
25. In extremis, it was felt that it might be necessary to field 6,120 artillery pieces.
26. The French believed that by the spring of 1940 the Germans would have available 170–175 divisions, less 20 divisions needed to maintain order in Czechoslovakia and Poland. Protected on the frontier with France by the defences of the Siegfried Line, on the flanks by the neutral Netherlands, Belgium and Switzerland, Germany, the French High Command believed, would need no more than 70–80 divisions in the West in order to resist an Allied offensive which would have to be frontal. This would still leave them with 80–90 divisions and therefore in a position to open up other theatres of operation – principally a counter-thrust through Belgium.
27. WO193/157, *op. cit*, Answers to Questionnaire.
28. WO193/157, *op. cit*, Letter from Ironside to Gamelin, 15 December 1939.
29. WO193/157, *op. cit*, Answers to Questionnaire.
30. WO193/157, *op. cit*, Letter from Ironside to Gamelin, 15 December 1939.
31. WO193/157, *op. cit*, Answers to Questionnaire.
32. WO193/157, *op. cit*, Letter from Ironside to Gamelin, 15 December 1939.
33. *Ibid.*
34. *Ibid.*
35. British Army experts were invited to visit the border zone so that they could view the Siegfried Line first hand. They were also provided with the latest information available on the defences.
36. WO193/157, *op. cit*, Letter from the British Military Mission, France to the War Office, 3 December 1939.
37. A. Horne, *To Lose a Battle: France 1940*, p.82.
38. WO193/157, *op. cit*, Letter to the Director of Military Operations and Plans, 3 March 1940.
39. WO193/157, *op. cit*, Annexure to the Study of the Problem of an Offensive between the Rhine and the Moselle.
40. *Ibid.*

CHAPTER 3
Decline
MAY 1940–MAY 1944

'Siegfried took a bath in the blood of the monster, Hagen! That has immensely reinforced his skin – with the exception of a very small place.' And she told him of the Linden tree leaf.[1]

From the Rhine Saga 'Siegfried and Kriemhilde'

In the first months of the war the outcome of the conflict seemingly hinged on the strength of the two great lines of fortifications that faced each other along the Franco-German border. Would the massive *ouvrages* of the Maginot Line with its miles of tunnels be able to stem the German *blitzkrieg*, or would France seize the initiative while the German army was preoccupied in Poland and use its overwhelming military superiority to try and breach the Siegfried Line? As it transpired these predictions failed to materialise. The fortifications that had taken so much time, money and effort to build, far from being instrumental in the fighting of May and June 1940, played only a peripheral part.[2] The West Wall, its sole purpose realised during the invasions of Czechoslovakia and Poland, did little more than provide Hitler's Field Headquarters during the invasion of the Low Countries and France – a fortification in the rear of the Line near Münstereifel codenamed *Felsennest*, or crag's nest. That neither of the defensive lines played a significant role in the fighting has been used by some as evidence to demonstrate that these fortifications were no more than expensive white elephants. Such an argument, however, misses the key point behind the construction of these defences. They were built as deterrents, just as nuclear weapons are today. The effectiveness of the Siegfried Line in dissuading France and Britain from attacking has already been illustrated and it is likely that the Maginot Line would have had a similar effect on the thinking of the German High Command had it been extended to the coast. But this is pure conjecture. The Belgian government abandoned its defensive alliance with France and left her cruelly exposed, a weakness that Hitler ruthlessly exploited.

The main entrance to Fort Eben Emael as it is today. (Author)

On the morning of 10 May 1940 Hitler launched *Fall Gelb* (Operation Yellow) with Bock's Army Group B advancing into neutral Holland and Belgium. British and French troops massed on the Belgian border anticipating a repeat of the Schlieffen Plan, advanced to meet the threat just as their fathers had twenty-six years previously. The reaction of the French and the British forces to the German incursion was just what Hitler and the German High Command expected. The matador had skilfully enticed the bull forward with his bright red cloak and he now delivered the *coup de grace* with an armoured spear which was delivered by von Rundstedt's Army Group A advancing through the 'impenetrable' Ardennes. At the same time, Leeb's Army Group C engaged the forces ensconced in the forts of the Maginot Line and in so doing ensured that neither they nor the thirty or so divisions stationed behind the line could be released to blunt the *sichelschnitt*, or sickle slice, as Guderian's 2nd Panzer Division, in the van of von Rundstedt's attack, raced for the coast.

The plan worked almost without a hitch. The German armoured spear reached the coast on 19 May, trapping the élite units of the French and British armies with their backs to the sea. They fought on desperately with many escaping the pocket, picked up at Dunkirk by one of the vessels in the armada that set sail from British ports. The remnants of the French Army not caught in the pocket fell back – Paris fell on 14 June and eight days later France agreed to an armistice. Symbolically, Hitler insisted it be signed in the self-same railway carriage that had been used when Germany's surrender had been accepted in 1918.[3] For Hitler the wrongs of the First World War had been righted.

But if the Siegfried Line had been innocuous in the fighting of 1940, its role now that France had been defeated was even less clear. The western border of the Third Reich was now the English Channel and if Britain could be defeated there would be no threat in the west. Plans for the invasion of Britain – *Operation Seelöwe* (Sealion) – were drawn up and ships and barges prepared to carry Hitler's invasion army. Meantime, the *Luftwaffe* began its momentous struggle with the Royal Air Force for dominance of the skies which was crucial to the success of any amphibious landing. The failure of Göring's *Luftwaffe* to defeat the RAF in the Battle of Britain led to the postponement of Operation Sealion and its ultimate cancellation. Hitler now turned his attention east. Troops who had been preparing to cross the channel were now moved to Poland and Prussia in preparation for Operation Barbarossa, the invasion of the Soviet Union. By the spring of 1941 Hitler's invasion force was ready and in June the operation began.

THE ATLANTIC WALL

Hitler's decision to turn east left the Atlantic seaboard exposed to attack, not full-scale invasion because Britain was still too weak to consider such grandiose plans, but small-scale commando raids. To counter this threat work began in December 1941 to fortify key installations.[4] At the same time the Commander in Chief West, Field Marshal von Witzleben, ordered a reconnaissance of the coast to identify key defensive sites with a view to constructing a more extensive series of fortifications. His plans, however, came

La Batterie du 'Chaos', Longue-sur-Mer, France which formed part of the Atlantic Wall. (Author)

to nought. Lacking the necessary materials and manpower to undertake the work the plans were shelved and von Witzleben was replaced in March 1942.

In that same month, Hitler entrusted the defence of the Channel and Atlantic coast to von Rundstedt and impressed on him that any Allied invasion was to be halted on the beaches. Almost immediately, and somewhat unexpectedly, the ability of the German forces in the west to repulse a large-scale landing was tested. In August 1942 the Allies launched Operation Jubilee, the abortive landing at Dieppe. Although an unmitigated disaster for the Allies, it highlighted the vulnerability of the coast to attack and in September Hitler ordered the construction of fortifications along the coast similar to the West Wall.

Initially construction work was concentrated on U-Boat pens and the defence of harbours and ports which would be vital to any Allied landing. The work was to be undertaken, as it had been latterly on the West Wall, by the Organisation Todt with technical guidance provided by military engineers.[5] Because of this the fortifications were constructed using many of the lessons learned from the building of the West Wall. Only a limited number of bunker and pillbox types were to be built and then these were to be replicated all along the coast. Indeed, a number of the standard designs from the West Wall were used because they were deemed suitable for coastal defence, specifically the 100 and 500 series. However, it was recognised that coastal defence brought with it special requirements, for example, the need for coastal batteries. As such the 600 series was introduced and by the time of the invasion models going up to number 704 had been developed. This standardisation had a number of advantages: construction was far more rapid and pre-planned structures could be fabricated by semi- or unskilled labourers,

An Atlantic Wall shelter mounting a 50mm anti-tank gun at St Aubin-sur-Mer, France. (Author)

which was crucial in the latter stages of the war as manpower was severely constrained. However, this standardisation also resulted in compromise, as the position often did not provide the perfect tactical solution.

The construction programme was due to be completed by May 1943, but Albert Speer, now in charge of the work after the death of Fritz Todt in an air crash, was not convinced that the work could be completed in time. This was due in no small part to the fact that resources tended to be funnelled to other theatres, particularly the eastern front. The build-up of British and American forces and the increased likelihood of an Anglo-American invasion forced a strategic rethink and on 3 November Hitler issued Directive 51. The main thrust of this was the strengthening of the defences along the coast. At the same time Hitler appointed Erwin Rommel to speed up the construction of the defences and to take command of the German forces who would meet any Allied invasion. Rommel recognised that the massive superiority of the Allies on land, sea and in the air meant that if they secured a foothold on the European mainland they would be all but unstoppable. Any invasion force therefore had to be immediately thrown into the sea. Such sentiments coincided with those of the Führer who was insistent that ground should never be surrendered and who placed great store in the defensive value of fortifications, the more so after the failed Dieppe landings where the ability of coastal defences to repulse an amphibious assault was, to Hitler at least, clearly demonstrated.[6]

However, Rommel's efforts to construct a line of consistently strong defences were undermined by von Rundstedt who was nominally in command. Von Rundstedt was a great believer in defence in depth and he ordered the construction of the so-called *Zweite Stellung*, or second position which was to be built some distance inland from the coast. Rommel considered this to be a distraction. It was imperative that the Allies were prevented from landing and as such every effort should be concentrated on the coastal defences. His argument eventually prevailed and in April 1944 construction work on the second position was brought to a halt. Recognising that time was short and with shortages of men and material he concentrated on extemporised defences, rather than complex bunkers. Obstacles were constructed on beaches to make the use of landing craft more difficult if not impossible. Many of these obstacles were developed from models used in the West Wall such as the steel 'hedgehogs' and the curved steel *Hemmkurvenhindernis*. Minefields were also extensively used just as they had been along the border with France – in all some six million mines were laid (although this was far short of the 50 million planned). Ultimately it was planned to construct some 15,000 bunkers, pillboxes, observation posts and radar installations along the coast of occupied Europe as part of the so-called 'Atlantic Wall'.[7] That this target was not reached by the time of the Allied invasion of June 1944 was no fault of Rommel's. Indeed, it was only as a result of his efforts that the Atlantic Wall could be described as a wall at all rather than a series of strongpoints.

Notwithstanding the fact that he never actually visited the Atlantic Wall, Hitler expressed his satisfaction with the progress that had been made. However, his confidence was not shared by Rommel or his subordinates. Considerable progress had been made in strengthening the defences but it was clear that certain sections of the wall were far stronger than others. The Pas de Calais, for example, a prime invasion target, was heavily fortified while the beaches of Normandy and Brittany, although clearly much less likely to be the preferred choice for a landing because of the distance from the British Isles and the distance from the landing beaches to the heart of Germany, were only relatively lightly defended. If the Allies were to strike at one of these weak points and secure a foothold then it would be difficult to stem their advance and certainly the 'impregnable' West Wall could no longer be relied on to deter, let alone stop, an Allied attack.

EMASCULATION OF THE WEST WALL

With attention focussed on the construction of the 'new West Wall', or Atlantic Wall, the 'old West Wall' was largely abandoned. Even before the invasion of France and the Low Countries the first tentative steps were taken to dismantle the border defences. This work was initially confined to obsolete works or works which were located in areas of little or no strategic importance. With the defeat of France guidance detailing future policy on the Siegfried Line was issued. This stipulated that no new construction could be justified and that those sites where no concrete had been poured would have their reinforcing rod framework dismantled and the hole filled in. The remainder of the defences were to be left standing to meet any future eventuality. As Westphal noted, 'Sceptics such as Rundstedt had never even in 1939 attributed great value to the West Wall, yet after the victory over France they held it not to be altogether wise to scrap it without more ado. One would never know when it might not be urgently needed.'[8] However, all provisions and ammunition were to be removed and all the weapons, interior furnishings, including

With the war in the west over, every small piece of land suitable for cultivation was utilised. Here a vegetable plot has been planted by the garrison of a West Wall bunker, August 1940. (Bundesarchiv)

Enlisted men relieve the boredom of the Phoney War by 'landscaping' their bunker, May 1940. (Bundesarchiv)

the ventilation and optics, insofar as they were not built in, were to be removed to facilities at Fortress Engineers Headquarters.[9] Outside the shelters the barbed wire was removed, as were some of the larger obstacles. The work was to be completed by the spring of 1941 and indeed much of it was, although regions varied.

Much of the demolition work had to be completed by prisoners of war (POWs) since the construction battalions had been withdrawn at the start of the campaign in the west. These men, almost 9,000 alone in the region of Nordrhein-Westfalen, were moved to secure camps where they were divided into work groups. These work groups were tasked with filling in obsolete construction sites and removing wire fencing overseen by men of the remaining construction battalions. The POWs were prohibited from collecting weapons and ammunition and from working inside bunkers. As the demolition and disarmament work neared completion the POWs were employed in the construction of anti-aircraft bunkers around Aachen while others were sent to work in weapons production.

The redeployment of the majority of the fortification engineers meant that only a skeleton crew was available to maintain the bunkers. This necessitated a drastic reorganisation of the remaining personnel. Over the whole length of the West Wall five fortifications administrations were set up with 62 supervisory groups[10] and 361 sub-groups. This meant that each sub-group was responsible for the care and maintenance of 40–50 bunkers, depending on the density of defences in that specific area.

Each supervisory group included within its ranks a fortifications technical officer, a senior guard, an office auxiliary, a line tester, two communications mechanics and two fortification workers. The sub-groups consisted of a guard and two fortification workers. The personnel for the sub-groups were largely recruited from the local population, because it was often not possible to accommodate external recruits. The guards were entrusted with the keys to the

In spite of the war and the proximity to the front a farmer cultivates his field as in peacetime, April 1940. (Bundesarchiv)

bunkers and were employed to check them weekly and to note any deterioration in their state. The workers were employed to carry out repairs and to maintain the camouflage. Unfortunately, because many of them were smallholders they were generally more interested in working their land than maintaining the defences and as such over the next four years the fortifications fell into disrepair, or worse. In one instance GIs advancing through the line reported that a farmer had used an abandoned bunker as the base for a chicken coop and had over-wintered his potatoes and turnips in the surrounding trenches![11]

Bunkers situated in isolated locations were even more difficult to maintain. These were often handed over to local communities, forestry commissions or other authorities for use as cellars, air raid shelters or forest huts under the condition that the bunkers were maintained and guarded. Invariably, they were neglected and as time passed Mother Nature reclaimed what was rightfully her own. The harsh shape and hue of the new concrete structures gradually melted into the background as they became cloaked in moss and shrouded by brambles and ferns. However, the peace of this latter day Arcadia was soon to be shattered and the defences called upon once again in the service of the Fatherland, only this time the mettle of Hitler's impregnable West Wall would be genuinely tested.

Notes

1. A Linden tree leaf had stuck on his perspiring skin, just between his shoulders. The small spot on his back remained unprotected.
2. Indeed, not only was the Maginot Line incidental to the fighting, it also generated a false sense of security and a defensive mentality while at the same time sapping French manpower with men stationed in the forts and in the rear.
3. It was subsequently destroyed to ensure that history could not repeat itself.
4. Immediately after the defeat of France there were no plans to fortify the coast of continental Europe, save for the construction of seven coastal batteries which were to support the invasion troops as part of Operation Sealion.
5. Rivalries between the Organisation Todt and the armed forces continued and were exacerbated by inter-service rivalries. Unlike the West Wall the German Army no longer bore the sole responsibility for providing plans for the defences; the navy and air force also had specialist requirements. Thus, naval commanders insisted on batteries being built with a view of the sea in order to enable them to engage naval vessels, while the Army insisted that batteries be built in the rear to enable the beaches to be covered.
6. Hitler overemphasised the importance of coastal defences when assessing the reasons for the failure of the Dieppe landings. In fact Allied failings were as much to blame for the fiasco. The landings had inadequate air and naval support, in particular, the lack of a heavy preliminary bombardment, and poor intelligence about the defences and the German order of battle.
7. For a detailed description of this the reader is encouraged to refer to *Hitler's Atlantic Wall* by A. Saunders (Sutton, 2001).
8. S. Westphal, *The German Army in the West*, p.74.
9. Ultimately much of this equipment was used to furnish the installations of the Atlantic Wall.
10. The number of sub-groups that a supervisory group was responsible for varied enormously. In heavily fortified areas like Geilenkirchen and Aachen a supervisory group might be responsible for six or seven sub-groups, whereas elsewhere it might only be three.
11. Not surprisingly, in September 1944 as the Allies approached the German border the authorities desperately tried to locate the keys but found that many had been lost or misplaced in the intervening years.

CHAPTER 4

Desperation

JUNE–SEPTEMBER 1944

Now Hagen knew exactly where Siegfried was vulnerable.

From the Rhine Saga 'Siegfried and Kriemhilde'

On 6 June 1944 the much-heralded invasion of Fortress Europe began with five separate landings along the Normandy coastline. The beaches bristled with obstacles of all descriptions and behind these were positioned pillboxes for machine and anti-tank guns, all linked by trenches, which were sited to enable the defenders to bring a withering cross-fire to bear on any invasion force brave or foolhardy enough to attempt a landing. But for all the cunning demonstrated by the engineers who decided which defences should go where, for all the effort of the labourers who built the defences, and in spite of the grim determination exhibited by the soldiers who manned the defences, Hitler's Atlantic Wall, with one murderous exception, was unable to prevent the landing of the Allied forces. By the end of the day, with the help of airborne forces parachuted into the rear, sizeable footholds had been secured on four of the five beaches.

The forward observation post at Pointe du Hoc which was captured by US Rangers on D-Day. (Author)

The exception was Omaha beach. A naturally strong defensive position, the Germans had heavily fortified the beach making a successful landing all but impossible. Its capture, however, was a necessary evil if a broad front was to be created with the link-up of the British Second Army on Gold, Sword and Juno beaches, and the US First Army landing at Utah. Thus, on the morning of D-Day when the first wave of troops hit Omaha beach they were met with a devastating hail of machine gun and small arms fire that decimated the leading elements. Those who could get forward sought sanctuary behind the seawall. The situation became critical, but with close support from naval vessels bringing direct fire to bear on troublesome enemy positions, with inspired leadership, and with tremendous bravery, the soldiers of 1st and 29th Infantry Divisions were able to make their way off the beach and secure a foothold, albeit tenuous.

Events on Omaha beach aside, the Allies had pierced the Atlantic Wall with relative ease. But this did not mean that the Siegfried Line would be breached so easily. The Atlantic Wall had been built as a thin line of defences (only relatively late on had defences been built further in land to protect against outflanking manoeuvres) designed to prevent the Allies gaining a foothold on the European continent. The Siegfried Line, by contrast, was built in depth and was designed to draw the enemy in and destroy it. Also the Siegfried Line was relatively short – 350 miles – by comparison with its larger brother the Atlantic Wall that stretched from Norway to the border with Spain.

But thoughts of breaching the Siegfried Line were far from the minds of the Allied High Command in June 1944. After the initial success of the landings, the Allies in the following days and weeks, were able to do little more than consolidate their positions around the beachheads; a task greatly aided by Hitler's reluctance to commit his reserves to Normandy for fear of a second, more powerful, landing in the Pas de Calais. Nevertheless, by the end of July the Allies were in a position to strike and on the 25th of the month Operation Cobra was launched. Following a massive aerial bombardment of the German lines, American forces broke the German defensive perimeter that had hemmed in the invaders and captured Avranches. Despite a strong counter-attack at Mortain the Americans – with General Patton now to the fore – continued the advance wheeling east. At the same time the British and Canadians advanced from their positions around Caen heading south with the two forces eventually meeting at Falaise. Thousands of German soldiers were either killed, wounded or captured in the operation and German vehicles – too numerous to count – littered the battlefield. The battered remnants of the German Army fell back in headlong retreat to the Seine. On 25 August Paris fell and the immediate collapse of resistance in the west seemed nigh. All that lay between the Allies and Berlin seemed to be the Siegfried Line and the Rhine.

GERMAN ASSESSMENT OF THE SITUATION POST D-DAY

The reaction to the Allied invasion from Hitler and the German High Command, as the Allies had hoped, was confused. Hitler did not believe that the Normandy landings constituted the main Allied thrust; he was convinced that another landing would be attempted in the Pas de Calais or on the Mediterranean coast and as such he refused to commit his reserves to the battle. The consequences of this inaction were clear, if not to Hitler, then to senior German officers. As Grand Admiral Dönitz wrote on 12 June 'If the enemy succeeds in fighting his way out of the present bridgehead and gains freedom of action for mobile warfare in France, then all of France is lost. Our next line of defence would be the Maginot Line or the old Siegfried Line.'

Von Rundstedt, the Commander-in-Chief West, and the Commander of Armoured Group West, General Freiherr Geyr von Schweppenburg, were less than happy with this strategy. Hitler's decision to keep the majority of his forces in reserve and his insistence that not an inch of territory be relinquished unless absolutely necessary meant that the commanders in the west were left with no alternative but to adopt a reactive defence, plugging gaps as they appeared and, in so doing, passing the initiative to the enemy. They suggested adopting an 'elastic defence' (essentially retreating to more defendable positions) which they believed would restore the initiative to the defenders. This proposal was forwarded to Hitler's headquarters where it received a cool reception. If von Rundstedt's proposal for elastic defence was 'considered dispassionately', it was argued, then it implied that France should be conceded to the enemy and that German forces should retire as quickly as possible to the shortest line of defence – the West Wall.

Not surprisingly, Hitler categorically rejected the idea of elastic defence, arguing that such a strategy was impractical because Allied air superiority prevented any major troop movements. Indeed, Hitler was so disgusted with the idea that von Schweppenburg was relieved of his command and von Rundstedt was sent on leave and replaced by Field Marshal von Kluge, despite the fact that the latter had only just recovered from a serious car accident.

The new commander inherited a hopeless situation. Even by the middle of July Hitler refused to commit the forces of 15th and 19th Armies – the latter of which included three armoured divisions. Thus, when the Allies launched Operation Cobra there were insufficient forces to counter, or even slow, the attack. The German defences were unhinged and Hitler's forces were thrown into headlong retreat. Only now did Hitler finally accept the enormity of the situation and that he had been deceived. On 24 August, the day before the fall of Paris, Hitler issued his orders for the construction of a new West Wall.

The Gauleiters in the west were made responsible for the construction of the new defences which included mobilising civilian labour and the provision of their accommodation and rations. However, Himmler, as Chief of Army Equipment and the Replacement Army, was made responsible for all military aspects of the construction in accordance with the directives from the High Command of the Armed Forces. This included the tactical siting of individual positions; construction priorities; and the form the construction should take based on both tactical requirements and, importantly, on the materials available. In addition, the Todt Organisation was to provide the necessary building equipment and provide the technical expertise.[1] Overseeing the whole project, and characteristically involving himself with even the minutiae, was Hitler.[2] In his directive he specifically ordered that: 'The intended organisation of the construction, and the manpower to be raised, will be reported to me as soon as possible . . .' and that

'Reports on progress and the state of construction will be submitted to me . . . on the 1st and 15th of each month.'[3]

Hitler's directives for the renovation of the West Wall were long overdue.[4] In August 1944 a survey of the defences concluded that the years of neglect and the advances in weaponry had taken their toll and in some cases had rendered defences useless. The insides were often dusty or damp or both.[5] Fields of fire were obscured and minefields and barbed wire had been removed and could not easily be replaced. Bunkers and pillboxes were too small to mount the larger, more powerful, modern guns; the anti-tank positions had been designed to accommodate the 37mm PaK, which was now disparagingly described as the 'door knocker' because it was ineffectual against the thicker sloping armour of the new tanks. Some bunkers were capable of mounting the more powerful 75mm PaK but even this had been superseded. More worryingly, it was discovered that the smaller pillboxes were unsuitable for the standard MG42 machine gun; they had been designed to mount the MG08 or MG34 which had both been gradually phased out. Indeed, the situation was so bad that General Westphal suggested dispensing with the concrete defences and developing a series of new field works better suited to defeating the threat that Germany now faced. His suggestion was not seriously considered but it was clear that a considerable amount of work would be needed if the West Wall was to slow, let alone stop the relentless Allied juggernaut.

At the end of August the Gauleiters met to formulate a plan of action. The upshot of this meeting was a decision to start work on the border defences at the beginning of September using labourers who had variously volunteered, been cajoled, or forced to report for duty. Besides members of the local population, workers from the greater Reich and forced labour from conquered territories were also employed, supplemented by youngsters from the Hitler Youth and the Labour Service. It was hoped that this *levée en masse* would yield one million workers for the construction of the new defences. However, by the middle of September it was clear that this forecast was wildly over-optimistic with only 235,000 workers employed and even with this not inconsiderable workforce it would take at least six weeks to make any significant improvement.

To ensure that the workers were given sufficient time to renovate the old defences and construct new ones a further directive was issued on 3 September. This stated that the German forces in the west were to 'dispute every inch of ground with the enemy by stubborn delaying action.'[6] This uncompromising directive was, unusually, diluted with a hint of realism. It was accepted that penetrations would occur and that rather than hold every inch of ground to the last man, troops were to avoid encirclement so as to ensure that manpower was available for the manning of the West Wall. To help stem the Allied advance and fulfil the requirements of the directive, troops currently holding positions in the West Wall were pushed to the front and their places taken by the new *Volks Grenadier* Divisions (People's Infantry).[7] It was hoped that by the end of September sufficient of these units would be available to stabilise the front and allow exhausted units, particularly the armoured divisions, to be withdrawn behind the West Wall to rest and refit.

Nor was this a pipe dream. The manpower reservoir, despite the fact that Germany had been at war for five years, was still relatively healthy. Women who saw front-line service with the Red Army and in Britain were extensively employed on farms and in factories, had, up to this point, only played a small role in the war effort – being largely confined to the home to look after the children of the 'Thousand Year Reich'. Now women born between 1919 and 1928 were ordered to report for war duties. Children above the age of twelve were also required to do their bit whether it be in the factory or helping to man the anti-aircraft batteries. The jobs that these women and children undertook freed up men for the front. Men in 'reserved occupations' that clearly did not warrant such treatment were whisked away to undertake basic training and then ordered to take up positions in the West Wall – as were members of para-military organisations who had previously been deemed too old, too young (the call-up age now ranged from 16 to 50), or unfit for service in the Wehrmacht. The armed forces were also vigorously combed for men. Officers and men serving in the various headquarters and in static installations who had thus far led a relatively sheltered existence were now ordered to the front.

But even these extreme measures were not deemed sufficient to raise an army strong enough to man the western defences; more drastic steps needed to be taken. Consequently, men who were suffering from minor ailments or certain disabilities were also conscripted. Men with stomach complaints were formed into *Magen* battalions, while men who were deaf or were hard of hearing were placed in *Ohren* battalions. Such units brought with them their own problems, not the least of which was giving orders to members of the *Ohren* battalions, or, more worryingly, inspecting their positions in the dark, which brought with it the very real possibility of being shot as an already edgy sentry opened fire and asked questions later.

This irregular force was largely untrained, inexperienced and disorganised. Leaders were few and equipment was scarce. Most of the heavy weapons had been lost in the retreat from France and even rifles were in short supply. Those vehicles that had survived the retreat had little petrol and ammunition with which to challenge the enemy armour even if the weather prevented Allied ground attack aircraft, which now dominated the skies, from seeking out their prey. But this ramshackle force was all that was available to the German High Command and it needed to be rushed to the front as soon as possible. A signal intercepted from Blumentritt, the Chief of Staff to the Commander-in-Chief West, on 3 September, explained how 'An Allied thrust towards Trier would tear open the West Wall before it was ready for defence'.[8] Fortunately for the hard-pressed German defenders the Allies saw the major opportunity for success not in the south but in the north and this permitted Hitler one last chance to shuffle the pack.

On 7 September he issued a new directive. This put von Rundstedt in charge of all *Wehrmacht* (and *Waffen SS*) personnel in the west (*Luftwaffe* and naval units had been pressed into service to stem the Allied advance) and all non-military organisations and formations. Two days later Hitler issued a further directive which stipulated that, as from 11 September, von Rundstedt was additionally to be placed in command of the western defences, relieving Himmler of the responsibility. On the same day lead American units made tentative forays into the outworks of the West Wall. Recognising the enormity of the situation von Rundstedt, on 15 September, issued a clarion call to the forces under his command. He stressed the importance of the West Wall to the defence of Germany and instructed his men to hold these positions to the last round.[9] His public declarations of faith in the strength of the West Wall, however, were in marked contrast to his personal feelings. There were insufficient troops to man all the defences and it therefore seemed to him to be madness to try and defend the West Wall simply for the sake of it. Nor were the defences structurally or tactically sound. This had been recognised in 1939 and the situation had deteriorated in the intervening years, not simply because the defences had been abandoned, but because of the increased potency of weapons now fielded by the Allies. To von Rundstedt the most sensible solution was to abandon the West Wall and retreat to positions on the east bank of the Rhine. He attempted to convince Hitler of the merits of this strategy, but the architect of the West Wall would not be swayed. Hitler had now adopted a bunker mentality both literally and metaphorically. On 14 September Jodl recorded in his diary the Führer's diktat that 'in the Siegfried Line every foot of ground, not merely the fortifications, is to be treated as a fortress.'[10]

ALLIED ASSESSMENT OF THE SITUATION AFTER D-DAY

The Allies, like the German forces they faced, were similarly exhausted by the beginning of September, but their tiredness was due to the relentless pace of the advance which had seen them cover over 300 miles in seven weeks. Not surprisingly their perception of the situation in the west during this period was the complete reverse of that of Hitler and his generals. Thoughts were dominated by optimism and hopes of an early end to hostilities.

After the initial period of consolidation the Allies, by the end of July, were ready to break the German shackles and go on the offensive. On 25 July Operation Cobra was launched with the Americans breaking out of their beachhead at St Lô. At the same time the British and Canadians made a measured advance from their foothold around Caen. In mid-August the two armies met at Falaise trapping a large part of the German forces in the so-called 'Falaise pocket'. A week later as the Allies prepared to enter Paris the mood in SHAEF was euphoric. It was widely believed that 'The August battles have . . . brought the end of the war in Europe in sight, almost within reach.'[11]

And they had good reason to believe that this was indeed the case. Allied intelligence estimated that in the Battle for Normandy the Germans had lost 400,000 men, 1,300 tanks and 3,500 guns. So severe were the losses suffered by the German Army in France that MI14 believed that Hitler could not muster sufficient forces to man the Siegfried Line. They calculated that only 15 divisions (including four Panzer Divisions which could field some 600 tanks) were available to man the defences and even by the end of September, as the last vestiges of German manpower were sent to the front, the Army would only be able to field 20 divisions and this was nowhere near enough to hold the Siegfried Line,[12] especially since these troops were believed to be low-grade, inadequately equipped and poorly trained.[13] In a note dispatched on 6 September 1944 SHAEF concluded that:

'a. The enemy is not at present able to defend either the Siegfried Line or the Rhine adequately, in spite of the apparent strength of the former, the natural obstacle of the Rhine will probably offer greater difficulties to our advance.

b. Speed is essential, as the enemy has the capability of withdrawing from other fronts or forming further forces to oppose us. We should advance on a wide front, extending and breaking through rapidly wherever he is weakest.

c. The most important areas in Germany lie in the north, and the Siegfried Line can be outflanked there. Our main effort should be in the northern sectors.'[14]

Both military and political leaders broadly accepted these conclusions.[15] Indeed the British war cabinet, for planning purposes, posited 31 December 1944 as the date for the end of the war. But in spite of this presumptuousness, in spite of all the opprobrium heaped on the Siegfried Line in Britain and elsewhere, and the arrogance of Allied generals[16] and in spite of the fact that the Siegfried Line defences had been largely abandoned for more than four years, some still harboured doubts about the ease with which the Allies would advance into Germany. The most vocal of these was the British Prime Minister, Winston Churchill. He was only too well aware from the First World War, of the resilience of the German soldier, especially with his back to the wall – literally and metaphorically on this occasion. He noted that, 'The fortifying and consolidating effect of a stand on the frontier of the native soil should not be underrated. It is as least as likely that Hitler will be fighting on January 1 as that he will collapse before then. If he does collapse before then, the reason will be political rather than purely military.'[17] Not for the first time Churchill's prescience in respect of the Siegfried Line was uncanny. But Churchill's pessimism was influenced as much by logistical difficulties as the Siegfried Line. Churchill was acutely aware that the Allies could only utilise one major port (Cherbourg) and that much of their equipment, men and munitions was still being landed over the Normandy beaches. Failure to bring another large port into use would undoubtedly slow the Allied advance and give the defenders valuable breathing space to release units from Italy and the Balkans and raise a new army to man the defences of the Siegfried Line.

This concern prompted Eisenhower, the Supreme Allied Commander, to commit a significant portion of 21st Army Group's resources to the capture of a port.[18] Meantime, the main part of his force was to continue to press east towards Germany in the hope of finishing the war by Christmas. How this was to be achieved was hotly debated and was influenced, in part, by the passionate rivalries that existed between the commanders of the two main powers – Britain and the United States.

Two broad strategies emerged – an advance on a broad front that would necessarily stretch the defenders to breaking point and so lead to ultimate victory, a strategy favoured by Eisenhower – and a narrow front strategy with all resources concentrated in one thrust aimed at smashing through the enemy frontline, overrunning the enemy's industrial heartland in the Ruhr (and so diminishing his ability to continue fighting) and then head for Berlin. Montgomery, commander of the 21st Army, favoured this strategy.

Both plans had their merits, but the worsening logistical situation meant that whichever plan was adopted would dangerously overextend the already stretched supply lines and might leave the Allies exposed to a German counterstroke.[19] This dilemma exercised the minds of the Allied commanders and in particular Montgomery who first considered the idea of a daring airborne operation in Holland. This would not only ease the logistical problems, but would also circumvent the Siegfried Line. The plan also had the added bonus of utilising the élite airborne troops enjoying a well-deserved rest in Britain after their successful exploits in Normandy in June and July.

AIRBORNE OPERATION

The initial plan developed by Montgomery and codenamed Operation 'Comet' only envisaged dropping one division – 1st British Airborne – behind enemy lines. They would capture the strategic bridges in Holland and provide an airborne carpet over which 21st Army Group would advance. Eisenhower, despite his disagreement with Montgomery over strategy, was nevertheless supportive of his idea and gave the plan the go-ahead, only for the operation to be cancelled because of fears over the ability of a single division to successfully carry out such a daring mission. As it transpired, this did not prove to be the death knell for the airborne operation in Holland, but the beginning of a much larger operation as Eisenhower now agreed that in addition to 1st British Airborne division, 82nd and 101st US Airborne divisions would be made available. Operation Market Garden was born.

The plan was to establish a series of eight bridgeheads across the various canals and rivers that criss-cross Holland and barred the Allies' way into Germany, with the final bridgehead being across the lower Rhine at Arnhem. The capture of the bridge at Arnhem would leave the Ruhr at the mercy of the Allies and the Siegfried Line impotent. This element of the operation – codenamed 'Market' – involved 101st US Airborne dropping at Eindhoven; 82nd US Airborne to the south of Nijmegen and the 1st British Airborne at Arnhem. Once the bridgeheads had been secured an armoured thrust by Horrock's 30th Corps (supported by 8th and 12th on either flank) – codenamed 'Garden' – would link up the various stepping stones so creating a continuous corridor through Holland, across the Rhine and, importantly, outflanking the Siegfried Line.

But Operation Market Garden was not the only plan for an airborne assault designed to obviate the need for a full-scale attack on the Siegfried Line. The American attempt to bounce the Siegfried Line in September 1944 had met with a severe rebuff and it was clear that a concerted effort would be needed. To aid this attack it was envisaged dropping an airborne force to the east of Aachen to attack the line from the rear. An attack in the rear by élite airborne troops against reserve and militia units manning defences that were designed to counter a frontal assault, it was hoped, would ensure 'that a break [in the Siegfried Line] can be had without undue difficulty'.[20]

Operation Naples, as it was codenamed, was certainly a daring proposition and was not without its drawbacks. Flak units would make re-supply of the airborne troops extremely difficult and as such close air support would be needed. Also there was the very real possibility of friendly fire casualties. To overcome this difficulty it was suggested that the two forces should attack on slightly different axes – the airborne force to the north, the ground force to the south and then at a prearranged time the two would swing towards one another. In spite of these difficulties, Operation Naples was concluded to be a practicable operation.

The potential units identified to undertake this operation included 6th British Airborne Division, but its involvement was discounted because they had only returned from the Continent on 10 September and would not be ready for action until 1 October. Likewise, 17th US Airborne Division, due to a shortage of equipment, could not be employed. This left only 82nd and 101st US Airborne Divisions and they could only be used with the proviso that they had not been allocated to another operation. But in the interim they had; Operation Market Garden had been given the go-ahead.

On 17 September the attack began as planned and initially enjoyed some success. The 1st British Airborne Division, despite stronger resistance than expected due to the presence of 9th and 10th SS Panzer divisions which were refitting in the area, managed to capture the north end of the road bridge at Arnhem. The 101st US Airborne captured its objectives and 30th Corps was soon across the Wilhelmina Canal and heading north to link up with 82nd US Airborne Division which had captured the bridges leading to Nijmegen at Grave. But the airborne division had insufficient strength to capture the bridges at Nijmegen. Only with the arrival of the 30th Corps was this possible and by now the operation was well behind schedule and was beginning to unravel. The 1st British Airborne Division stoically resisted strengthening German attacks, but eventually the lightly armed troops had to relinquish their hold on the bridge and those paratroopers that could were withdrawn across the Rhine. Operation Market Garden had failed. Montgomery's rapier had been shattered. The Siegfried Line would have to be smashed with hammer blows.

A New West Wall?

In 1939 or 1940 the West Wall might arguably have been capable of absorbing such blows. Four years later, however, the scenario was very different and to use an allegory that would have been familiar to the thousands of Americans now poised to assault this last bastion of the Third Reich, the cavalry was not about to ride to the rescue. If the West Wall was to successfully rebuff the forces ranged before it, it would have to do so using the mish-mash of units available and the anachronistic defences, which were being feverishly renovated and supplemented by new, often improvised, fortifications.

Some of the new 600 and 700 series of standard construction models developed for use in the Atlantic Wall were now to be used to strengthen the West Wall. These models were built to construction thicknesses B and A, but were generally much simpler affairs than those that had been constructed in the original building programme of the late 1930s. They tended to be on a single level and used much less concrete. This streamlining, however, was born of necessity rather than choice as a paucity of time and materials took its toll. This was graphically demonstrated in standard construction model 702. In this instance the special beds for bunkers were replaced with three-tier bunk beds, a wooden interior door was used instead of a gas-proof door and the steps to the external fighting position or 'ringstand' were removed.

Parallel to the development of these larger concrete structures, smaller concrete field works were developed. The 'Koch bunker'[21] was simply a concrete tube buried in the ground which was integrated into the trench system. Over 5,000 of these were completed in the West Wall and examples can still be seen to this day. A slightly more elaborate example was the 'Tobruk'. First used by the Italians in the defence of Tobruk – hence its name – this was essentially a sunken, open-topped, concrete-lined foxhole. They were ideal for strengthening the West Wall, being quick to build and requiring little in the way of materials. By October 1944 forty-seven different types had been developed that were capable of mounting a myriad weapons, principally machine guns, but also mortars, anti-tank and anti-aircraft guns. Some were even fitted with tank turrets taken from captured tanks but also from older German models such as the Panzer I and II.

An interesting development of this concept was the standard construction model 687 which mounted a Panzer V Panther tank turret. The bunker itself was constructed below ground level and consisted of three rooms: the fighting compartment which housed a motor to rotate the turret; an ammunition storage room; and a small ante-room which acted as the crew's living quarters – it had a stove but no beds. The turret was mounted directly above the fighting compartment and could be rotated 360 deg.. Being low to the ground it was not easy to spot and even more difficult to put out of action, although its immobility was undoubtedly a severe handicap.

The Organisation Todt also developed a steel shelter specifically designed to mount a Panther turret. This was much quicker, simpler and cheaper to build and was the ideal weapon for strengthening the West Wall in the straitened circumstances in which the German High Command found itself in the autumn of 1944. First used in Italy in the spring of that year, the shelter was made up of two steel boxes that were mounted on top of each other and buried in the ground so that just the turret was visible. The lower box had three rooms: the living quarters with bunks and a stove; a storeroom; and an entrance area which was linked to a communication trench and fitted with a ladder that linked the upper and lower boxes. The upper box mounted the turret and acted as both the fighting compartment and the store for the ammunition.

A Panther tank turret that was mounted on a timber framework now on display at the Westwall Museum, Niedersimten. (Author)

An improvised German anti-tank gun position near Hochwald, Germany. It was captured by the Canadians in March 1945. (Canadian National Archives)

By the closing stages of the war even this expedient was proving difficult to manufacture and install, so a timber framework was developed which could support the turret and baseplate. A number of these were completed but the design was beset by problems, not the least of which was 'sagging' of the steel baseplate which caused the turret to jam.

Optimistic plans for the construction of these shelters were envisaged. Thirty-three turrets were to be installed east of Aachen along the Roer River. However, by the beginning of December the American forces had reached the river and it proved all but impossible to install them without precipitating a heavy barrage from enemy guns. In the end it was only possible to emplace two turrets. The remainder were withdrawn to the so-called *Erftstellung* which protected Cologne and Bonn (although it is not clear how many were finally built). To the south it was planned to locate thirty turrets with concrete bases along the Upper Rhine and a further thirty-three on a section of the front running from Saarbrücken to the Rhine, but it seems that few, if any, were actually completed.

As the situation deteriorated on the western front the Germans resorted to increasingly desperate measures. Steps were taken to scour the depots and stores for any armaments that could be pressed into service. An abundance of weapons was discovered, mostly from obsolete tanks, but also some more powerful modern weapons including the main armament from the fearsome *Jagdpanther* with its 8.8cm gun. These were mounted on makeshift steel frameworks to provide improvised anti-tank weapons. With the once mighty Third Reich forced to resort to such desperate measures the end was surely nigh. Talk was of peace by Christmas – just as it had been in the summer of 1914 . . .

Notes

1. *Einsatzgruppe* 'West' which had been established to construct the Atlantic Wall retreated in some disorder from the coast, but by October its 6,000 OT and 130,000 foreign workers were assigned to *Einsatzgruppe* V refortifying the West Wall. N. Thomas, *Wehrmacht Auxiliary Forces*, p.17.

2. Already Hitler had ideas for the new line. He noted in his directive that 'The line will be built so that the first construction is a continuous tank obstacle. Preparations will be made for creating a no-man's land beyond our positions facing the enemy, and a continuous and tightly coordinated system of defences in depth will be achieved. This will be continually strengthened at strong-points by the adjacent line of permanent fortifications.' H.R. Trevor Roper (ed.), *Hitler's War Directives 1939–45*, p.184. Moreover, those parts of the Maginot Line, Hitler stated, that could sensibly be incorporated in to the line were to be rebuilt, and those that could not were to be destroyed.

3. *Ibid*, p.183.

4. On 1 September, with the Allies now at the German border, Hitler issued a further directive which reiterated much of what he had written in his directive of 24 August, the only additions being that neighbouring Gaus were now to provide labour to help in the construction of the line and the *Luftwaffe* was to provide anti-aircraft defences while the work was undertaken.

5. The occupants' discomfort was exacerbated in the actual fighting when American mortar, artillery and small arms fire was directed at the entrance of the structure. This made any attempt to leave the bunker, even to answer a call of nature, suicidal, making the already unpleasant conditions all but unbearable.

6. *Ibid*, p.189.

7. *Volks Grenadier* Divisions were approximately half the strength of a regular division – circa 8,000 men. The division was divided into three regiments (sometimes two) which in turn had only two battalions. They fell under the auspices of the SS rather than the Army.

8. F.H. Hinsley, *British Intelligence in the Second World War, Its Influence on Strategy and Operations*, Vol. 3 Pt 2, p.375.

9. Note to the last round, not the last man – again realism had prevailed over fanaticism.

10. Gen. W. Warlimont, *Inside Hitler's Headquarters 1939–45*, p.478.

11. F.H. Hinsley, *op. cit*, p.368.

12. The accepted wisdom in 1939/40 was that an infantry division for every five miles of front would man any threatened sector of the line. On this basis the Germans could defend a frontage of 75 miles – 100 miles at most – but the line stretched for 350 miles.

13. The only other units that might conceivably be freed to bolster this force were the flak defences around the Ruhr which might, in extremis, be called upon to carry out an anti-tank role.

14. PRO, WO219/2886 Operation Naples I: Forcing of the Siegfried Line: outline plans September 1944.

15. In a note to senior commanders on 4 September Eisenhower wrote 'The only way the enemy can prevent our advance into Germany will be by reinforcing his retreating forces by divisions from Germany and other fronts and manning the more important sectors of the Siegfried Line with these forces. It is doubtful whether he can do this in time and in sufficient strength . . .' A.D. Chandler Jr., (ed.), *The Papers of Dwight David Eisenhower: The War Years: IVs*, p.2115.

16. Patton insisted that given the supplies he would '. . . go through the Siegfried Line like shit through a goose'. C. Whiting, *The Battle for the German Frontier*, p.14.

17. W. Churchill, *Triumph and Tragedy, Vol.VI, The Second World War*, p.171.

18. Antwerp was captured on 3 September, but Walcheren Island and Beveland peninsula, which dominated the Scheldt estuary, were not cleared until November, making capture of the intact port facilities something of a Pyrrhic victory.

19. A German counter-attack was not seriously considered to be feasible, but could not be completely discounted.

20. PRO, WO219/2886, *op. cit.*

21. Named after its supposed designer, Gauleiter Koch.

CHAPTER 5

Defeat

SEPTEMBER 1944–MAY 1945

After the strenuous hunt, Siegfried knelt down at a spring to quench his thirst. At that moment, Hagen thrust a hunting spear between Siegfried's shoulders. With his last strength, Siegfried turned around and saw the deadly hatred in the eyes of his murderer. He bled to death . . .

From the Rhine Saga 'Siegfried and Kriemhilde'

THE GAMBLE

The bitter struggle to secure a foothold on the European mainland during June and July 1944 had by August been transformed into a wholesale rout of the German forces in the west. In a little over three months the Allied armies were at the German border, well ahead of even the most optimistic predictions. Allied planners, prior to D-Day, had anticipated reaching this position by D-Day plus 330, that is 2 May 1945. This '*blitzkrieg*' presented the Allies with the very real possibility of bringing an early end to the war, perhaps even before Christmas. But with every silver lining there is invariably a cloud and for Eisenhower and his generals it was the critical nature of the logistical situation. The speed of the advance and the sheer number of divisions that needed to be supplied (which exceeded the number planned for) meant that supplies were not reaching the front in sufficiently large quantities to allow both Montgomery and Bradley's army groups to forge ahead at their current rate.

The inability of the Allies to capture a serviceable, deepwater port meant that men and matériel were still being brought to the Continent via the landing beaches and the Mulberry Harbour. Once ashore the difficulties multiplied. The shattered rail network[1] meant that from Normandy supplies had to be transported across France by road, but there were too few lorries to meet demand and as a result it became increasingly difficult to furnish front-line units with sufficient supplies, especially of fuel. This in itself would not have been an insuperable problem had the Allied armies paused at the Seine to regroup as it was envisaged that they would. But they did not. The desperate state of the German forces, understandably, inclined the commanders in the field to gamble and to continue the advance. It was recognised, however, that without an improvement in the supply situation it would not be possible to pursue this strategy indefinitely. This left the Allied commanders with three alternatives:

(i)   Pause, and allow the logisticians time to move supplies from the beaches to the frontline;

(ii)   Capture a deepwater port intact;[2] or

(iii)   Continue the advance until the lack of fuel and ammunition forced a cessation.

The first option was dismissed because, it was argued, it would give the German forces time to regroup and strengthen the defences of the West Wall, while the second option was deemed unfeasible because Hitler had turned all the major ports into fortresses and had ordered the defenders to defend them to the last man. This left only one alternative which was reluctantly adopted. Reluctantly, because Eisenhower and his staff accepted that it was extremely risky and in a letter to the Combined Chiefs of Staff Ike noted that, '. . . At the moment and until we have developed the Channel ports and the rail lines therefrom, our supply situation is stretched to the breaking point, and from this standpoint the advance across the Siegfried line involves a gamble which I am prepared to take in order to take full advantage of the present disorganized state of the German armies in the west.'[3] The Supreme Commander's decision was vigorously supported by Omar Bradley, the commander of Twelfth US Army Group, who somewhat optimistically, thought 'that with an all-out effort we could crack through the Siegfried Line, reach the Rhine and establish beachheads on the east bank within a week.'[4]

The task of realising Bradley's aim in the first instance fell to General Hodges, the commander of First US Army. He was less convinced of the merits of 'pursuit without pause' and his initial reaction on reaching the German border on 11 September was to have a brief respite in order to allow time to get supplies of ammunition forward before launching a coordinated attack on 14 September. Hodges's proposed course of action, or more accurately inaction, was based, not unreasonably, on the assumption that the German Army, bolstered by the defences of the West Wall and now fighting for German soil, would offer much sterner resistance to that exhibited in the pursuit across France. Militating against this supposition were intelligence reports indicating that relatively few soldiers were available to man the defences and that they were so disorganised it would be difficult for the German commanders to organise a coherent strategy. If this was the case it would be pure folly, argued General Collins, VII Corps Commander,[5] to delay; the momentum should be maintained and he asked permission to make a reconnaissance in force the following day.[6] Collins' request was approved and in an apparent *volte-face* Hodges also ordered V Corps, commanded by General Gerow, to do likewise.

Gee

General Gerow's corps was to advance through the Eifel region which abutted the Belgian Ardennes and which shared many of its characteristics; it was hilly, and densely forested, streams were many and roads were few. Dominating V Corps' immediate front was the Schnee Eifel, a 2,300-foot high ridge that ran parallel to the border with Belgium. In short, the area was ideally suited for defence and, to make matters worse, a series of concrete fortifications had been constructed, although they were thinly dispersed and were in a narrow, single belt. The question was: did the Germans have sufficient men and equipment to man the defences and take advantage of the terrain?

On paper at least I SS Panzer Corps, which faced V Corps, was more than capable of defending the Eifel. However, two of the divisions were so depleted that they had been absorbed by 2nd SS Panzer Division,[7] which defended the Schnee Eifel, with 2 Panzer Division guarding the West Wall to the south. That these divisions were nominally Panzer divisions was something of a misnomer because they had but a handful of tanks and self-propelled guns between them, and only a few more artillery pieces. These divisions were 'reinforced' by the garrison troops who manned the bunkers, but there were so few of them that even in a sector of the line that could boast fewer fortifications than any other portion of the line south of Aachen, they could man no more than a fifth of the positions. It was in this parlous state that the defenders awaited the American onslaught; they did not have long to wait.

On 12 September General Gerow ordered the three divisions under his command to advance in the form of a latter day troika: the 4th Division was to head for the Schnee Eifel; 28th Division to the southwest of this feature; and 5th Armored Division further to the south. His attack was not designed as an attempt to break through the Siegfried Line, but was a precursor to the co-ordinated attack planned for 14 September and he instructed his divisional commanders accordingly.

Bloody Bucket[8]

With this in mind General Cota, the commander of 28th Division, planned to advance with just two regiments. They made good initial progress and were the first units to come into contact with the fortifications of the West Wall, capturing a number of outpost pillboxes unopposed. When this news filtered through to the staff at German Seventh Army headquarters it caused something of stir. They believed that V Corps had penetrated the West Wall before the defenders had had time to take up their positions. This was not the case and when the men of the Bloody Bucket Division resumed their attack the following day they came under rifle and automatic weapons fire from enemy pillboxes. Unable to call upon their armoured support which was undergoing vital repairs after the pursuit across France, and with few specialist 'bunker busting' weapons such as flamethrowers or satchel charges available, the infantry had to resort to the use of towed 57mm anti-tank guns. These were manhandled into position and opened fire on the troublesome pillboxes. The results were disappointing. The small-calibre guns were unable to pierce the concrete walls and did little more than 'dust off the camouflage'.[9]

The stalemate gave the tank crews and field workshops time to overhaul the battered and broken steel chargers and on 14 September the infantry advanced once more, this time supported by their armour. Almost immediately the revivified tanks were balked by 'dragon's teeth' which everywhere marked the front edge of the West Wall defences. Only by blasting the teeth with TNT[10] could the tanks get forward to support the infantry but this was made almost impossible for the engineers by the covering fire from an enemy pillbox. An impasse such as this is often unlocked by cunning, luck or sheer bravery and in this instance it was the latter.

Recognising the critical nature of the situation one engineer took it upon himself to break the deadlock. Using the teeth for cover and showing due deference to the division's motto – 'Fire and Movement' – he carefully made his way toward the troublesome pillbox loaded down with explosives. He safely reached the aperture and secreted himself in such a way that the defenders' gun could not depress nor traverse far enough to shoot at the intrepid engineer before placing his charges and seeking sanctuary on the roof of the shelter. When the charges were detonated both the pillbox and the engineer were dispatched. Thankfully, despite being catapulted into the air and landing in the midst of the dragon's teeth, he was not seriously injured. He gingerly made it to his feet and signalled to his compatriots that it was now safe to move forward. Such acts of bravery meant that by 16 September 28th Division had broken through the West Wall – but the price had been high. Although many of the pillboxes were not manned, those that were presented the infantry with a challenge for which they were not adequately armed, trained or prepared. Many of the defences were manned by little more than a lightly armed skeleton crew which in some instances had only taken up its position hours before the veterans of 28th Division attacked. Yet they inflicted on this experienced unit such heavy casualties that there were insufficient reserves to exploit the breach, nor were any of the other divisions from V Corps able to switch the axis of their attack to exploit this opportunity and Gerow was forced to suspend the operation.

Ivy

To the north of 28th Division, 4th Division advanced towards the imposing heights of the Schnee Eifel. The attack was to be delivered by two regiments – 12th Infantry to the north and 22nd Infantry to the south with 8th Infantry in reserve. Little evidence existed on the enemy's disposition to dissuade General Barton, 4th Division's commander, from putting in his attack and on the morning of 14th September the two regiments advanced towards a lateral road that followed the crest of the ridge.

The men of 12th Infantry made good progress and reached their objective without incident. The greatest impediment to the regiment's advance was the difficult terrain, rather than enemy pillboxes, which were unerringly quiet. Once the ridge had been breasted the regiment moved northeast along the road only to find that the earlier situation was now reversed. The going was now much easier but a manned pillbox which was only silenced with the help of the unit's armoured support temporarily halted progress. Their momentum lost, the doughboys dug in.

To the south 22nd Infantry fared less well. A shell from a German '88'[12] hit one of the supporting tanks. All too aware of the capacity of these weapons to inflict damage on the relatively poorly armoured Allied tanks, the remaining tanks sought less exposed positions. Their manouvers caused consternation amongst the infantry, which mistakenly believed that the tanks were withdrawing and they fell back in some disarray. Order was quickly restored and the infantry advanced apace, capturing a row of pillboxes and then pushing on to their objective, the lateral road on the Schnee Eifel. The commander of 22nd Infantry now committed his reserves and, in textbook fashion, began to roll up the line of the pillboxes. This proved easier than expected. Small arms fire, or a salvo from the supporting tanks, was enough to convince the occupants, mainly middle-aged men and callow youths, that resistance was futile. By the end of the day 22nd Infantry had smashed a hole in the defences two miles wide and over a mile deep. Impressive though these statistics undoubtedly were, the terrain militated against the large-scale use of armour. If the breach was to be exploited it would have to be by the 'poor bloody infantry'.

Well aware of the impressive gains made by his men and convinced that little if anything stood between him and a major breakthrough,[14] Barton now committed his reserve regiment. The men of 8th Infantry were to advance in a northeasterly direction towards the northern end of the Schnee Eifel and the so-called Losheim gap. If the regiment was successful the Schnee Eifel, which dominated his front, would be outflanked and the integrity of the West Wall compromised. At the same time the 12th and 22nd Infantry regiments were to continue their respective advances but they were now seen as supplementary operations.

The omens for a successful assault were not good and so it proved to be. Inclement weather denied the troops on the ground tactical air support that had been so important in expediting the advance across France.[15] In addition, the enemy had taken steps to slow the American advance by blocking roads and blowing bridges. More worryingly, when the enemy was finally encountered they provided a much sterner test than they had in the previous days and the commander of 8th Infantry was forced to halt the advance and start afresh the following morning.

The 12th and 22nd Infantry also noted a stiffening in enemy resistance. In spite of this, the regiments did make some progress, albeit very slow. With 8th Infantry's advance stalled, General Barton deemed that the best chance of success lay in changing the focal point of the regiment's attack. It was now ordered to abandon the thrust for the Losheim gap and instead strike between the other two regiments down the wooded slopes of the Schnee Eifel. The attack began on 16th September and by dusk the following day they had all but reached the eastern edge of the forest. But 8th Infantry's hold on the terrain, as was the case for all of the regiments of 4th Division, was tenuous. The forest was everywhere criss-crossed by fire breaks, paths and trails which enabled the enemy to infiltrate behind the front line and forced the Americans to expend their valuable resources mopping up these incursions and in so doing diverted effort from the main advance.

Meantime, 22nd Infantry suffered a serious reverse as it advanced to the south of the Schnee Eifel. The lead unit became separated from the main body of the force and was subject to a concerted enemy attack. Those troops that survived and avoided capture were forced to retire piecemeal after darkness had fallen. Fewer than half returned to American lines. This setback, together with the stalled advances elsewhere on 4th Division's front, prompted Gerow to call off the attack. Some minor engagements continued in the following days as the GIs secured more defendable positions before the front settled down. After promising starts two of Gerow's divisions had been forced to abandon their attempts to 'bounce' the Siegfried Line. It was now incumbent on the armoured wing of V Corps to deliver what its epithet implied that it could, 'victory'.

Victory

While the infantry divisions were seeking to break through the West Wall in the northern portion of V Corps' front, 5th Armored Division was essentially held in reserve. Its brief was to maintain contact with Third Army to the south and also be ready to exploit any breakthrough by the infantry divisions further north. Combat Command Reserve (CCR), however, was ordered to probe the West Wall in the central section of the division's front and, if the defences were found to be only weakly held, the Command was to launch an attack.

On 13 September CCR opened fire on the German lines near Wallendorf. As hoped this fusillade failed to provoke a response from the enemy reinforcing the evidence from earlier patrols which had reported that the pillboxes were not manned.[16] Indeed, closer inspection suggested that they had not been occupied in the recent past, with dust or water covering the floor. German soldiers were later seen in the locality, but in no great numbers. It was thus concluded that conditions were propitious and Gerow ordered General Oliver, the commander of 5th Armored Division, to attack.

The commander of CCR, Colonel Anderson, set off shortly after noon on 14 September. He was initially tentative, but leading elements that crossed the Sauer River experienced little or no anti-tank fire and, with his inhibitions eased, Anderson committed his main force. The *Alarmbattalion* manning this lightly fortified section of the West Wall was only equipped with small arms and although it fought tenaciously it was forced to give ground, leaving Wallendorf in flames. The tanks pressed forward and easily dealt with the few pillboxes in their path, despite the fact that the swift advance across France had prevented the unit from undertaking any specific training on how to deal with pillboxes and in spite of the fact that the concrete structures were impervious to fire from the heaviest weapon at the division's disposal – the 90mm main armament of the M10 tank destroyer. The tankers were finally halted by a large crater in the road in what seemed to be the only axis of advance.

With the armour temporarily unable to move the supporting infantry advanced alone, but they soon became disorientated in the fog and the failing light and had to laager for the night. By the morning of 15 September another route suitable for tanks had been found and the armour was able to resume its advance. Unfortunately, this new axis of advance brought the Command up against eight Panzer Mk IV tanks and their supporting infantry. The ensuing engagement saw three of the enemy tanks destroyed and the rest forced to beat a hasty retreat. Having quashed this resistance the armour moved quickly forward and by nightfall it was some six miles inside Germany with the defences of the West Wall far behind.

The ease with which 'Victory' Division penetrated the West Wall at Wallendorf may be viewed as a damning indictment of the West Wall and the futility of concrete defences. In point of fact this section of the West Wall was not heavily fortified. Engineers had decided that the terrain in the area was such that relatively few defences were needed. To make matters worse for the German High Command, the attack, quite by chance, had been directed against the weakest section of the German LXXX Corps' front. Moreover, it was also close to the boundary between, not only First and Seventh Armies, but also Army Groups B and G. As such there was bound to be a certain amount of confusion as to who was responsible for countering the incursion.

Gerow was unaware of the enemy's difficulties and was unconcerned. He was keen to take advantage of this stroke of luck and exploit the situation which he did. General Oliver was ordered to swing north and cut in behind the defenders who were holding up the attacks of 28th and 4th Divisions. Combat Command B (CCB) was allocated the task and on 16 September it crossed the Sauer into the Wallendorf bridgehead.

By now, however, the German High Command had recognised the magnitude of the situation and all available units were scraped together to counter the threat. Indeed, von Rundstedt was so concerned about the burgeoning bridgehead that on 15 September he issued a special order of the day which read, 'The fight for German soil must increase fanaticism. Every pillbox, every village must be defended until the Allies bleed to death. It is no longer a question of operations on a grand scale. The only task is to hold our positions until we are annihilated.'[17] Yet although the situation for the German High Command was grim, it was not as hopeless as it seemed. The 5th Armored Division had advanced some six miles but it actually only controlled the roads. This left the engineers tasked with constructing a bridge over the Sauer and, more worryingly, the artillery that was needed to support any new attack, dangerously exposed to ambush by German forces infiltrating US – lines and that is exactly what happened. German raiding parties harried the rear units and delayed the deployment of the artillery until late on 16 September. Since any new advance was reliant on indirect fire support it would be impossible to launch any further offensive action until the following morning. However, the stiffening German resistance and the parlous supply situation inclined Gerow to adopt a more cautious approach and he ordered Oliver to postpone any further offensive action.

On 17 September the German forces made a concerted effort to destroy the bridgehead at Wallendorf and in all likelihood they would have succeeded had the weather not improved and allowed ground attack aircraft to pummel the enemy tanks and artillery. Even so, the decision was taken to reduce the size of the bridgehead so that it could be defended more easily. Heavy shelling and further assaults, together with the realisation that the opportunity for further offensive action had all but disappeared, subsequently prompted Gerow to give the order to abandon the bridgehead altogether. The West Wall, though compromised, had held and although the battle had not been won neither had it been lost. One section of the front had been stabilised and reserves could be moved to more critical areas.

With the benefit of hindsight, it could be argued that Gerow should have gambled and pressed ahead with the advance, even if it increased the risk of running out of fuel. As Westphal notes, 'If the enemy had thrown in more forces he would not only have broken through the German line of defences which were in the process of being built up in the Eifel, but in the absence of any considerable reserves on the German side he must have effected the collapse of the whole West Front within a short time.'[18] But Gerow was unaware of the desperate state of the German defences and based his decision on the evidence available to him at the time. Regrettably, the opportunity had gone and the front settled down until December when the role of attacker and hard-pressed defender was dramatically reversed.

Lightning Joe

On Gerow's left was VII Corps under the command of General 'Lightning Joe' Collins. He faced the unpalatable prospect of attacking the West Wall to the south of the strategically and symbolically important city of Aachen where the defences were known to be far more numerous and constructed in much greater depth than those facing V Corps. Recognising that any hesitation on his part might lead to a bloody and protracted battle, he interpreted the order for a reconnaissance in force of the West Wall in its broadest possible sense. He planned to launch a *coup de main* in the hope of catching the German defenders off balance and breaking the West Wall before the Germans had had time to man the defences. This strategy was not without its risks considering the supply situation, but Collins deemed it better to break the back of the West Wall and, if necessary, halt the advance for re-supply rather than wait for fuel and ammunition and then launch a full-scale attack when the Germans had had time to overhaul and even strengthen their defences.

To maximise the chances of success Collins planned to avoid a direct assault on Aachen itself and the possibility of fierce house-to-house fighting, and instead strike south of the city with the ultimate objective of capturing the second, much thicker band of fortifications, which lay to the east of the city in a line north-south. The spearhead of the attack would be delivered by 3rd Armored Division which was to drive east towards the Roer River, while 1st Division protected its left flank around Aachen and 9th Division its right flank.

One of the bunkers that barred the way to the American forces in the autumn of 1944. This example was located at Hanbruchest, near Aachen. It was captured intact but was demolished after the war – the blast of the 800lb of explosives was so powerful that it lifted the roof of the shelter and caused superficial damage to a nearby house. (Public Record Office)

One of the bunkers that protected the town of Stolberg. This example was disguised as a garage and is shown here during demolition after the war. (Public Record Office)

Spearhead in the West

The attack by 3rd Armored Division began on 13 September with two combat commands advancing abreast along the Stolberg Corridor, which lay to the south of Aachen and skirted the northern fringe of the Huertgen Forest. Combat Command A (CCA) was to advance towards the town of Stolberg with Combat Command B (CCB) further to the south. Each combat command was in turn divided into two columns that were named after their respective commanders.

Almost immediately after setting off, the advance of Task Force Doan of Combat Command A was brought to a shuddering halt. The attacking infantrymen were pinned down by fire from enemy pillboxes and although the supporting tanks brought accurate long-range fire to bear on the enemy positions it proved to be ineffectual.[19] Attempts to clear a path through the dragon's teeth in order to more closely support the beleaguered infantrymen were less than successful; destroying the teeth one at a time with the tanks' main armament proved to be impractical and blasting the teeth with TNT was slow and highly dangerous.[20] The advance had faltered at the first hurdle which did not auger well considering these defences formed part of the narrower band of pillboxes to the west of Aachen known as the Scharnhorst Line.

The tankers' luck now turned. During the period when the West Wall had been effectively abandoned a farmer had built an earth and stone ramp in order to use a secondary road near to the main line of Task Force Doan's attack.[21] This was discovered on the afternoon of 13 September. A flail tank was ordered forward over the ramp but became stuck. The crew, under heavy fire, managed to disentangle the flail and it pressed forward followed by other tanks of the task force. However, the lucky break proved to be something of a mixed blessing. The supporting infantry was still pinned down by fire from the pillboxes and could not disengage to assist the tanks. This left them exposed to attack by enemy infantrymen armed with Panzerfaust[22] who accounted for four of the tanks while others were knocked out by German self-propelled guns. Reinforcements were ordered forward to ensure that the momentum was not lost and in spite of further losses, Task Force Doan pushed through the first band of defences.

Further to the south Task Force Lovelady of CCB enjoyed a much easier opening to its advance. As it approached a series of pillboxes near Rott, the occupants, seeing the tanks and not rating their chances, turned tail and fled.[23] The only resistance came in the form of a Panther tank that accounted for four medium tanks, before it was disabled. A demolished bridge prevented any further progress by the Task Force and it laagered for the night.

Their compatriots in Task Force King, a slightly smaller unit than Task Force Lovelady, attacked at the same time but were faced by dragon's teeth and a greater density of pillboxes. The commanding officer considered these defences too strong for his force and requested support. While awaiting the arrival of reinforcements King ordered a probing attack but it was unable to make any headway and with darkness falling the unit dug in for the night.

The following day Task Force Lovelady bridged the river that had blocked its advance and another river further on. Aside from this and some small arms fire it advanced unmolested past ghostly, silent pillboxes. By noon on 15 September it had passed the last bunker of the Schill Line; the West Wall was now behind it and ahead was only open country.

The advance of Lovelady's force through the Siegfried Line eased the path of Task Force King (now Task Force Mills after Colonel King was injured in the previous day's fighting) which now advanced through the Scharnhorst Line with relative ease. But its smooth progress was not to last. The breach in the defences formed by Task Force Lovelady precipitated a German counter-attack comprising a number of tanks and self-propelled guns. This attack was repulsed but so as to avoid further encounters with enemy armour Mills switched the axis of his advance and now followed the route taken by Task Force Lovelady. Although understandable, this action meant that the penetration of the line was only narrow and vulnerable to counter-attack.

A destroyed bunker that covered a road leading to Stolberg, near Aachen. It, and others like it, did little to stem the advance of 3rd Armored Division in September 1944. (Author)

Combat Command A resumed its attack on 14 September but its progress was hindered by the need to wait for 16th Infantry of 1st Division to advance around Aachen and protect the Command's northern flank. By nightfall on 15 September the infantry had made up the lost ground and on the following morning CCA was able to continue its advance. Just as had been the case for Lovelady and Doan on the first day of their attack, the occupants of the bunkers facing CCA beat a hasty retreat. This was clearly not a ruse to entice the force into a trap but it worked in much the same way. As the armour pressed forward it was caught in the open by seven German assault guns which knocked out six of the eight tanks.[24] Reinforcements were brought in from 16th Infantry and these together with the armour from the CCA, after some of the fiercest fighting for the Siegfried Line to date, overcame the assault guns and pillboxes. Only a few bunkers now stood between the Combat Command and the River Rhine.

Hitler's Nemesis

Desperate to exploit this breakthrough Collins ordered forward 47th Infantry (9th Division), which had been protecting 3rd Armored Division's right flank. On 14 September it advanced, meeting only light and sporadic resistance. One instance worthy of note, however, demonstrated how in wartime farce exists in almost equal measure with tragedy. A platoon leader from 3rd Battalion advancing at the head of his men on the road out of Roetgen came across two enemy soldiers who he challenged and ordered to surrender. Unbeknown to him, however, they were at the entrance to a large bunker which was so well camouflaged it was impossible to see from a distance. Believing the game was up a further 15 soldiers emerged from the gloom of the shelter and surrendered. By 15 September, helped by such instances of good fortune, the *Raiders* had penetrated the Scharnhorst Line. The official history of the division recounts that the 'Next night, in the music-halls of England, over the radios of America and on the streets of Allied cities was whistled the tune *We're Gonna Hang Our Washing on the Siegfried Line*! But the 47th was not stopping to do washing – not just yet!'[25] Enemy attempts to stop the advance of 3rd Armored Division resulted in there being insufficient forces on 47th Infantry's front to prevent them mopping up the pillboxes in their path. Soon it was advancing through the second belt of fortifications, aided by the capture of a German engineer's map which detailed all the defences in the area. Amazed at the lack of enemy activity the Raiders on 17 September emerged on the other side of the Siegfried Line. 'What had taken the German nation many years to construct had been breached by the 47th C.T. in a little more than three days!'[26]

Further to the south the two remaining regiments of 9th Division were ordered into action opposite the Monschau Corridor. The corridor offered an excellent avenue of advance through the dense forest of the region. This had been recognised by German engineers before the war and they had fortified it accordingly. More significantly, 'regular' soldiers of the German 89th Division manned the positions. Against this immensely strong position General Craig, the commander of 9th Division, ordered 39th Infantry to seize the corridor itself and to link up with 47th Infantry near Dueren, while 60th Infantry secured the right flank which involved capturing a ridge that dominated the mouth to the corridor. On 14 September, 60th Infantry commenced its assault but almost immediately the troops of the lead battalion were met by a hail of machine-gun and small arms fire. It was clear that reinforcements would be needed to seize the ridge and so a further battalion was ordered forward. The ridge was now attacked from both ends in a pincer movement, but still no significant progress was made. Not until armour was ordered forward on 16 September were the pillboxes cleared and even then it took two further days of fighting.

In the valley below, the grenadiers of 89th Division inflicted on the soldiers of 39th Infantry a similar reverse to that meted out to their compatriots on the ridge above. On 15 September tanks were ordered forward and with the infantry launched a coordinated attack. This proved to be more successful – albeit achieved in an unorthodox manner. The pillboxes proved impervious to the shells fired by the supporting armour, but the impact of the rounds distracted the occupants of the pillboxes sufficiently to allow the infantry to push grenades through the firing apertures. Although achieving the objective it was a slow and dangerous task and so the reserve battalion was ordered forward on a wide flanking manoeuvre to cut in behind the pillboxes, which they did. But even then it took a further day of fighting to finally capture the position. As the official historian of the campaign notes: in the Monschau Corridor '. . . 39th Infantry had been discovering how much backbone concrete fortifications can put into a weak defensive force.'[27]

Some of the dragon's teeth near Lammersdorf that blocked the path of 9th Division in September 1944. (Author)

The increased resolve of the enemy, the sheer exhaustion of the troops, whose numbers had been severely depleted in the previous days' fighting, and inadequate supplies, meant that Collins had to call a halt to the attacks of both 3rd Armored and 9th Infantry Divisions and consolidate. The rest of the month of September was spent fighting to secure more defendable positions in what was later to be described as the battle of the Huertgen Forest.[28] This involved attacking and destroying in the region of 125 bunkers, which taught the engineers in particular valuable lessons.[29] They soon realised that the pillboxes and blockhouses of the Siegfried Line were very different and that the traditional weapons – pole charges and flamethrowers – were not always effective. As such a six-step plan was developed that was suitable for destroying pillboxes of any size.[30]

1. Approach as close as possible with an infantry platoon and engineer section.
2. Use a tank, tank destroyer, anti-tank gun, or bazooka for supporting fire.
3. Suppress the pillbox with artillery or mortars.
4. Use direct fire weapons to suppress apertures and entrances.
5. Close in with infantry and engineers.
6. Destroy the pillbox by using demolitions on the roof or by using the point blank fire of supporting weapons.[31]

The final step depended very much on the thickness of the concrete roof. Using anything from sixteen to twenty-four beehive charges a small recess would be formed into which was packed a two hundred pound block of TNT. This would either destroy the bunker or traumatise the unfortunate occupants to the extent that in most cases they would surrender.

But impressive statistics and lessons learned could not disguise the fact that the Allies gamble had failed and with it went the chance of an early end to the war. There were many reasons for this: poor weather ensured that the Allies could not bring their aerial superiority to bear and also hampered observation for accurate artillery fire; shortages of ammunition and fuel handicapped Allied commanders who were inclined to adopt a cautious rather than an adventurous strategy; and the difficult terrain sapped the strength of the exhausted Allied units while at the same time providing ideal opportunities for stalling tactics. But a key factor was the West Wall. The defences meant that relatively few soldiers, often poorly equipped and trained and frequently of non-military age could delay, or even stop in their tracks well-equipped, experienced units that had fought their way from Normandy to the German border in a little over three months. This valuable respite gave the German High Command time to reorganise its decimated forces and to bring forward fresh troops to establish a continuous front. As such the West Wall, for all its failings, contributed to the so-called 'miracle of the west'.

An American Sherman tank eases its way through the belt of dragon's teeth near Aachen, September 1944. (Hulton Getty Images)

For the German High Command the second half of September had been an anxious time; the Allies had not only reached the German border but significantly in a number of places they had broken through the Siegfried Line and were in prime position to strike for the Rhine. However, just as the Allies appeared ready to deliver the *coup de grace* they slackened or even stopped their advance. This hesitance bemused von Rundstedt and his Chief of Staff, Westphal. They reasoned that the Allies had 'over-estimated the German defensive strength. Certainly, the permanent fortifications along the West German frontier must have contributed to this judgement, but if the enemy had known their true condition he would hardly have treated them with such respect.'[32] They were quite unaware of the logistical nightmare that the Allies were experiencing, although they had not dismissed this possibility. 'It is also possible that difficulties of supplies, particularly those for motorized formations, had cropped up, so that there had to be a pause in the operations.'[33] Whatever the reason, they were mightily relieved and used the respite to strengthen their position and await the next attack.

Cowboy Pete[34]

The XIX Corps under General Corlett was on the northern flank of First Army's advance and was tasked with piercing the West Wall north of Aachen and then wheeling south to link up with VII Corps, so encircling the city. Their progress, however, was slowed by fuel shortages which meant that the corps was immobilised for four days and was not in position to attack the line until 20 September.

Even then the assault had to be delayed as a number of factors conspired to make the attack too risky to undertake. Firstly, the advance of Montgomery's forces to the north left a yawning gap between 21st Army Group and First Army which neither force had the reserves to fill – and certainly not XIX Corps, which only had two divisions.[35] Secondly, XIX Corps was short of ammunition and Corlett was not prepared to attack without artillery support, especially as it was evident from the experiences of V and VII Corps that enemy resistance was strengthening and more especially because changeable weather meant that tactical air support could not be guaranteed. Hodges therefore permitted Corlett to postpone the advance indefinitely.

As it transpired, the assault was only postponed by a few days. D-Day was now set for 1 October and in spite of the delays the original plan was retained: 30th Division would lead the attack and would then swing south to meet up with VII Corps and encircle Aachen. The 2nd Armored Division would follow in its wake, but instead of heading south it was to drive east to seize crossings of the Roer River. Meantime, 29th Division, which had recently joined the Corps, was to make diversionary attacks on its front to the north of the main thrust.

Old Hickory

To accomplish this arduous task, General Hobbs, the commander of 30th Division, envisaged launching a three-pronged attack: the main attack was to be delivered by two regiments, 117th Infantry to the north and 119th Infantry to the south with 120th Infantry attacking a German salient outside the West Wall. They were to attack on a narrow front approximately nine miles north of Aachen so as to avoid the possibility of house-to-house fighting in the city and also the heavily fortified positions around Geilenkirchen. To ease their advance a massive preparatory bombardment was to be delivered in order to eliminate the pillboxes that had been identified by aerial and ground observation. In addition, aircraft were to bomb enemy lines on a scale not seen since the bombing of St Lô that preceded the American breakout from Normandy.[37]

Based on past experience, even a bombardment on this scale was unlikely to destroy the enemy's positions, so Hobbs took it upon himself to ensure that his men received adequate training in the art of pillbox assault. Such training had been undertaken while the unit prepared for combat in the United States and while stationed in the UK, but few, if any, of those soldiers remained in the frontline because of the heavy casualties suffered by the division. Opportunities to train were now very limited and battalions were withdrawn from the line for two days of intense training before returning to the front.[38] This training included familiarisation with specialist weapons including bazookas, flamethrowers and beehive charges; lessons in pillbox assault tactics; and dry runs. Specialist troops including engineers and tankers were also drilled in their specific tasks.

As it turned out, the tankers' first involvement in the battle was the provision of indirect fire support. On the day of the attack the weather again closed in and prevented the planned aerial bombardment and much reduced the artillery fire to the extent that the barrage, despite being bolstered by fire from the tanks and tank destroyers, did little more than remove the camouflage from a number of pillboxes that had not previously been identified.[39] These and other bunkers already pinpointed, forty-five in total, were engaged by self-propelled 155mm guns of 258th Field Artillery Battalion firing from point-blank range.[40] Yet, even this powerful weapon did not guarantee a kill, although it did at the very least widen the firing aperture, which significantly eased the engineers' demolition job. In spite of this minor success, Corlett and Hobbs were minded to postpone the attack until the following day when aerial support might again be available.

The weather on 2 October was much improved and it was possible to deliver the pre-planned air strikes but as on previous occasions they proved to be unavailing.[41] Undeterred, the soldiers of 117th Infantry crossed the Wurm River and, drawing on their recent training, stormed the enemy pillboxes. It was a textbook operation. Supporting fire from artillery, mortars and machine guns kept the defenders away from the apertures which allowed the infantry to advance over the open ground[42] and using flamethrower, pole charge or bazooka, silenced or destroyed the first band of pillboxes with only minor casualties. The bazooka was particularly effective. Private First Class Pantazapulos of A Company, 1st Battalion 117th Regiment recounted how, when he fired his bazooka, 'The shot sure caused a lot of commotion and tore a hole three feet wide in the firing slit. I put in another one and the dust was still thick when Private Sirotkin ran right up to the pillbox and shoved a pole charge into the hole. That finished most of them.'[43] The success of the infantry was all the more commendable because it was achieved with no armoured support; the tanks had become bogged down in soft ground and did not get forward until the fighting was over.

Similarly, on 119th Infantry's front the armour was unable to get forward to support the men on the ground, but here the consequences were far more serious. The infantry managed to cross the river and capture a number of pillboxes (including one disguised as a house), but pillboxes concealed in the forest proved more troublesome. Because of the trees the artillery observers were not accurately able to locate them and once the barrage lifted and the infantry attacked they were met by a hail of bullets. The commanding officer committed all of his reserves to the attack, but this failed to break the deadlock and the troops dug in for the night.

Hell on Wheels

Into the small bridgehead created by the 30th Division, the tanks of Combat Command B of 2nd Armored Division arrived ready for the second phase of the operation. This was undoubtedly a risky manoeuvre since the space was so confined, but worries about a possible German counter-attack, especially against 119th Infantry whose hold on the east bank was tenuous, overrode these concerns and on 4 October Task Force 2 of CCB attacked the enemy positions. Again it was a textbook attack. Artillery fire forced the defenders to seek shelter in their pillboxes and, once the barrage lifted, the tanks were quickly on to their respective targets, firing armour-piercing shells at the loophole or door. It was initially felt that the 155mm self-propelled guns would be needed, but it was discovered that the 75mm armoured piercing round not only penetrated the steel door but also, disconcertingly for the defenders, had a tendency of ricocheting around inside. Not surprisingly, the defenders quickly emerged and were dealt with by the supporting infantry. The following day Task Force 2 resumed its attack and using the same tactics achieved almost identical results before being stopped on 6 October by infantry supported by anti-tank guns.[45] Task Force 1, however, was less fortunate. It ran into a German counter-attack and made very little headway.

Meanwhile, 119th Infantry attempted to expand the bridgehead by trying to outflank the enemy through 117th Infantry's zone. A battalion of infantry supported by tanks adopted similar tactics to those used by Task Force 2 for 'bunker busting'; the tanks engaged the enemy pillboxes before desisting and allowing the infantry to attack. This tactic they repeated (11 times in total) until the tanks ran out of ammunition with only one pillbox still in enemy hands. The failure to capture this one pillbox was to come back and haunt the battalion because it subsequently became the focal point for a counterattack that saw four of the pillboxes recaptured. Ironically, the Germans adopted exactly the same tactics used by the doughboys of 30th Division. Fortunately, GIs in two of the captured pillboxes had learned the valuable lesson that holing up in the pillbox was fatal and, despite heavy enemy fire, they remained in their trenches and foxholes and were able to deal with the subsequent infantry assault. With the arrival of armoured support[46] the four pillboxes were recaptured.

This German counter-attack was to be the last major enemy action against XIX Corps' bridgehead. German commanders found it impossible to assemble a force of sufficient size to threaten the American hold on the east bank of the Wurm. Those forces that could be mustered were instead used piecemeal against American attempts to expand the bridgehead and, more significantly, to prevent the link-up between XIX and VII Corps around Aachen.

By 7 October the bridgehead was some six miles wide and almost five miles deep. Not surprisingly, then, when Hobbs reported to Corlett he was able to declare that, 'We have a hole in this thing [the West Wall] big enough to drive two divisions through.' He then confidently asserted that, 'I entertain no doubts that this line is cracked wide open.'[47] Hobbs' conviction was undoubtedly correct, but, as with the attacks of First Army's two other corps, success had come at a terrible price. Between them 30th Division and 2nd Armored Division had suffered 1,800 casualties including 200 killed.

The Big Red One

By early October Hodges's objective was clear: First Army was to encircle Aachen and then to strike east into the heart of Germany. Less than six miles separated the forward elements of XIX Corps to the north of the city and VII Corps in the south and in light of previous experience the link-up between the two was only thought to be a few days away. Having crossed the Wurm, 30th Division was to continue its sweep south while 1st Division struck north with the common objective of Wuerselen. If they were successful, the circle around Aachen would be closed and the defenders of the city doomed.

The troops of the 'Big Red One' had first set eyes on Aachen and the Siegfried Line almost a month before on 13 September. The defences had initially been viewed with unease, but on reflection it was concluded that they 'could not be so much after all and certainly not enough to worry a Division which had battered its way across France and Belgium and now even a corner of Holland. The talk of the 'dragon's teeth' did not terrify the boys at all; this fairytale nomenclature, in fact, probably served to lessen the First's awe of the German creation.'[48] Moreover, because the enemy had not had a chance to man the defences properly there was a misguided belief that the division had conquered the West Wall before the defences had been genuinely tested. 'We found otherwise very soon, and kept on finding out more for weeks to come, all of it extremely disagreeable.'[49]

The unit tasked with writing the next disagreeable chapter of the Siegfried Line story was 18th Infantry Regiment, which was already familiar with the defences of the West Wall, having fought its way through the first band of pillboxes. It was now tasked with fighting through the much thicker Schill Line to the east of Aachen and seizing a series of objectives each defended by a maze of pillboxes. Realising this, the commander of 18th Infantry established pillbox assault teams, which received specialist training in pillbox reduction and were armed with flamethrowers, Bangalore torpedoes, beehives and pole and satchel demolition charges. In addition, 745th Tank Battalion was to provide direct fire support, while an air–ground liaison officer was attached to each battalion should air attacks be needed to neutralise particularly awkward enemy positions.

Launching the attack before first light on the morning of 8 October the infantry advanced to its first objective. The defenders were taken completely by surprise and their positions were captured almost without a shot being fired. That afternoon the second objective was also captured but this time the special weapons and tactics that had been developed for attacking pillboxes were fully utilised, together with a great deal of courage.[50] Finally, on the night of 9 October, 'two companies slipped through the darkness past the yawning apertures of enemy pillboxes to gain the crest of Ravels Hill [the final objective] without firing a shot. Even mop-up of eight pillboxes at dawn the next morning was accomplished without shooting.'[51]

In just two days 18th Infantry had captured all its objectives, but it was now subjected to intense counter-attacks and the pillboxes that prior to the attack had posed so many problems now came to the doughboys' salvation, providing shelter against the enemy barrage. The enemy's attempts to dislodge the men of 18th Infantry lasted almost a week but were resisted by the infantry that was supported by both heavy artillery concentrations and air attacks.

In parallel with 1st Division's attack, the Old Hickory Division advanced south to complete the encirclement. Much of the hard work had seemingly already been done in the previous days' fighting and Hobbs certainly believed that the job was finished. Indeed, there seemed to be reasonable grounds for optimism since it was initially envisaged that the defences of the West Wall could be avoided. But the plan of attack did not allow for a spirited rearguard action by the hard-pressed defenders. The German High Command was well aware of the threat to Aachen and did everything in its power to prevent the link up, even ordering a number of raids by the *Luftwaffe*. So effective were these counter-measures that Hobbs was forced to change his plan of attack. Two battalions of 119th Infantry were now ordered to cross the River Wurm to the west bank and then advance south, while the third battalion was to advance along the east bank. The 116th Infantry Regiment was to resume the direct assault towards Wuerselen with 117th and 120th staging diversionary assaults on the division's eastern flank.

The change of plan once again brought 119th Infantry into contact with pillboxes of the West Wall and again they stalled the infantry's advance. Drawing on its experience from the earlier fighting, 2nd Battalion employed tactics that had proved so successful previously; seven pillboxes were captured, together with 50 prisoners. Pressing home the advantage and helped by the diversionary attacks of 117th and 120th Infantry and also by the main assault on Wuerselen by 116th Infantry, 119th Infantry finally made contact with 1st Division on the evening of 16 October – the encirclement of Aachen was complete and, five days later, Aachen fell.

Hitler's Nemesis – battle rejoined

In early October General Hodges identified certain key objectives that would need to be captured in order to ease the passage for a renewed general offensive across the River Roer towards the Rhine. One of these objectives was the village of Schmidt which, if captured, would outflank the pillboxes defending the Monschau Corridor that had stopped the advance of 9th Division in September.

The task of seizing the village, which lay in the heart of the Huertgen Forest, fell to General Craig's 9th Infantry Division. For many of the men of the division this meant another encounter with their own nemesis – the defences of the West Wall. Indeed, the Raiders of 47th Infantry had already attempted to advance on this front in September but, having broken through the defences, did not have the strength to exploit the breach. Now, however, with the arrival of the Ninth US Army,[52] the First Army was able to readjust its front and this meant that two regiments were now available to resume the attack: 39th Infantry and 60th Infantry, the same regiments that had had such a bloody baptism in the Monschau Corridor the month before.

The attack was to be launched on 5 October with both regiments advancing abreast, the *Falcons* of 39th Infantry on the left and the *Go-devils* of 60th Infantry on the right. However, poor weather meant that, once again, the ground attack aircraft were unable to identify their targets and the attack was postponed until the following day. Clear skies ensured that the preliminary bombardment was delivered as planned, but despite being guided to their targets by flares the bombing was ineffectual and enemy resistance was sufficiently strong to rebuff the *Go-devils'* first foray. The *Falcons* made some progress against the enemy pillboxes, but with supporting armour unable to move forward because all the tracks and firebreaks were either blocked or mined, they paid a high price in casualties. The defenders in their bunkers, by contrast, untroubled by artillery or bombs, and with no direct fire from US tanks, were able to direct accurate mortar and artillery fire, which exploded in the boughs and branches of trees and rained shrapnel down on the forest floor killing and injuring countless GIs in their exposed positions.

Late on 8 October tanks and tank destroyers to support the two regiments were finally able to get forward. Their presence tipped the balance in the favour of the hard-pressed infantrymen and some progress was made. However, with losses mounting, the advance slowed and was stopped altogether on 39th Infantry's front when, on 12 October, the Germans launched a powerful counter-attack. A less powerful counter-attack on 60th Infantry's front, though unsuccessful, also held up the advance.

By 16 October it was clear that Craig's offensive had stalled and with no prospect of the depleted force resuming an attack the two regiments were withdrawn to rest and recuperate. The division had suffered losses in the order of 4,500 men.[53] As the official historian notes, a casualty for every yard advanced.

This artillery fort at Kleinau was, unusually, constructed above ground level. The structure was demolished in November 1948. (Public Record Office)

Bloody Bucket – the pail overflows

The job of capturing Schmidt now fell to 28th Division of V Corps.[54] With the ranks of the division now replenished after the losses of September, General Cota planned to use all three regiments at his disposal in the attack, although only one, the 112th Infantry, was to actually assault Schmidt. To prevent a repeat of the counter-attack that had thwarted 9th Division's attempt on the village, 109th Infantry was to secure the northern flank while 110th Infantry wheeled to the southwest in order to attack the defences of the Monschau Corridor from the rear. At the same time a combat command of 5th Armored Division would make a frontal assault on the defences of the corridor in the hope that the pincer would succeed where the earlier frontal attack had failed.

On 2 November, slightly earlier than initially planned, the men of 109th Infantry began their advance. They made some progress but were distracted by enemy infiltrations and the need to seek shelter against the devastating 'tree bursts' which added to the grunts' misery in the Stygian darkness of the forest.

To the regiment's right, the 112th Infantry, enjoying slightly more success, also made steady progress and by nightfall was in position to strike at Schmidt itself the following day. By the afternoon of 3 November Schmidt had been captured. However, its stay was to be a short one. A determined enemy counter-attack forced both 112th and 109th Infantry to retreat as the Germans fought to secure the strategically important village which it was hoped would be one of the jumping off points for the Ardennes Offensive.

While the bulk of 28th Division was locked in a sanguinary struggle to capture Schmidt, 110th Infantry attempted to outflank the defences that covered the rear of the Monschau Corridor. This proved to be far from straightforward as its route was barred around Raffelsbrand by a series of pillboxes.[56] The two battalions tasked with capturing these positions were pinned down by machine gun and mortar fire and, with no direct fire support,[57] were forced to resort to desperate measures; a number of attempts were made to get forward with satchel charges but the infantrymen were killed when the explosives they were carrying were detonated by enemy fire. Demoralised, the infantry fell back to reorganise themselves and prepare for a new attack the following day, but this was also unsuccessful.

On 8 November 110th Infantry resumed its attack and 'for five more terrible days . . . two mutilated battalions tried to reduce the pillboxes' but its efforts were in vain; 'The lines at the end remained almost the same.' That could not be said of the regiment's fighting strength. 'One battalion, for example, though strengthened at one point by ninety-five replacements had but 57 men left, little more than a platoon. In the rifle companies not one of the original officers remained and only two of the non-commissioned officers.'[58]

The second attack on Schmidt had developed into one of the most costly divisional actions that the American army undertook in the whole of the Second World War. In total the division suffered 6,184 casualties. Gerow's V Corps had failed to capture Schmidt and this portion of the front now reverted to VII Corps so that it could deliver the main attack to capture the River Roer.

Following a path blasted by US Army Engineers an American jeep and trailer passes through dragon's teeth of the Siegfried Line. (Hulton Getty Images)

LAST CHANCE

The battles of September and October to breach the West Wall demonstrated that the fighting on the western front had entered a new phase. The pursuit was over and the Allies could now expect a bloody battle of attrition. In a note to his senior officers on 28 October Eisenhower reappraised the situation thus: 'Since my last directive . . . of 4 September the enemy has continued to reinforce his forces in the west. Present indications are that he intends to make the strongest possible stand on the West Wall in the hope of preventing the war spreading to German soil . . . Limitations of maintenance and transportation prevented our overrunning of the Siegfried Line before the enemy's resistance stiffened. We now have to deploy superior forces in the forward area and furnish them adequate resources for intensive fighting.'[59] To do this, the port of Antwerp had to be made fully operational and all efforts were to be concentrated on this goal.[60] Nevertheless, Eisenhower was determined to maintain the pressure on the German forces in the west. The reasoning for this was clear. Firstly, the enemy was suffering heavy losses in simply trying to stem the Allied advance; losses which Eisenhower hoped would grind the Germans into submission.[61] Secondly, a pause in the Allied offensive would give the enemy time to build new defences to seal off the Allied incursions into the West Wall and to train new soldiers. Thirdly, to halt the advance now would give

German industry, in spite of the Allied bombing, time to produce new tanks and guns but also significant numbers of the new jet aircraft that might threaten Allied air superiority. Thus, in spite of the difficulties with supplies, the poor weather and the heavy casualties, the 'broad front' strategy would continue with attacks launched in the first half of November involving First, Third and Ninth Armies – 22 divisions with their supporting formations, 500,000 men in total. This would be the last chance to smash the Siegfried Line before the worsening winter weather brought large-scale manoeuvres to an end.

But Hitler was equally determined to resist and issued an uncompromising diktat through Jodl in November. 'If as a result of negligence or lack of energy on the part of commanders or troops, the enemy succeeds in breaking in to the fortified zone (of the Siegfried Line) that constitutes a crime of incalculable consequence. The Führer is determined in such cases to bring those responsible to justice immediately.'[62] The scene was set for a bloody showdown and into this cauldron was thrown the newly formed Ninth US Army and its green divisions.

In the November offensive Ninth Army was tasked with advancing to the Roer River at Linnich and Juelich. Its ability to do so, however, was severely constrained by the town of Geilenkirchen; a heavily fortified part of the West Wall that was still in German hands. To make matters worse the town lay on the boundary between two armies and, not only that, they were commanded by different nations. The solution that was proposed was to entrust the capture of the town to the British Second Army, supported by 84th Division from the US XIII Corps.[63] Meantime, XIX Corps of Ninth Army, with its northern boundary moved slightly to the south to incorporate XIII Corps, was to attack towards the Roer, in the knowledge that its left flank was secure.

The principal British contingent allotted to the operation was 43rd 'Wessex' Division which was to attack northwest of Geilenkirchen with 84th Infantry putting in the main thrust from the south. The Railsplitters were to be supported by armour of the British Sherwood Rangers Yeomanry which included in its complement a number of 'funnies' designed specifically for this type of attack.[64] The operation was to commence on 18 November, two days after the main attack towards the Roer was launched, in the hope that this action would siphon off some of the forces defending the town. However, von Rundstedt was convinced that the main body of Montgomery's 21st Army Group was not going to attack so he ordered units from this front to the area of the American attack and as such the positions around Geilenkirchen were not weakened.

Railsplitters

The attack by 84th Division went ahead as planned. At 0700 on 18 November two battalions of 334th Infantry, their path cleared of mines by British flail tanks, advanced towards the high ground to the east of Geilenkirchen near Prummern. The 2nd Battalion experienced little resistance but 1st Battalion to their right was held up by a concentration of ten pillboxes. With the supporting armour bogged down in the clinging mud the infantry had to capture these unaided. Bringing concentrated fire to bear on the enemy positions, the defenders retreated from their foxholes into the pillboxes and then each one was assaulted in turn. Concerns over a possible counter-attack did not materialise and the regiment pressed ahead capturing its objectives: Prummern and Hill 101. The expeditious advance of 334th Infantry prompted General Bolling, the divisional commander, to press ahead with the advance. The 1st Battalion was now tasked with capturing a position overlooking Sueggerath and the Wurm valley, which would aid the advance of 333rd Infantry planned for the next day, while 2nd Battalion was to capture Mahogany Hill to the northeast of Prummern. Securing this feature would not only improve the defence of Prummern but would also facilitate the regiment's advance on Beeck.

As the events of the following day unravelled it became clear that the fortunes of the two units had reversed: the 1st Battalion succeeded in securing its objective, but the 2nd Battalion was held up, this time by German armour that prevented any attack against Mahogany Hill. Only with the commitment of the reserve battalion could the attack be resumed and even then pillboxes on the top of the hill supported by further pillboxes on the north-eastern fringe of Prummern blunted the attack. Eventually, British Crocodile flame-thrower tanks were able to get forward and dealt with the pillboxes around the village[65] which, in turn allowed the infantry to finally capture Mahogany Hill, albeit after two days further fighting.

On 19 November, 333rd Infantry opened its assault up the Wurm valley towards Geilenkirchen. The capture of the town itself proved to be less onerous than originally anticipated; surrounded on three sides, the defenders had withdrawn and only one battalion was required to mop up. The other battalion continued along the valley towards Sueggerath. The village was soon overrun and the regiment continued to advance towards its final objective, Wurm. Its progress was considerably aided by the Crocodiles which were particularly effective against pillboxes that were encountered *en route*. As Capt. Mitchell noted, 'A few squirts from the flame-throwers and the Germans poured out . . . The bastards are afraid of those flame-throwers and won't be caught inside a pillbox.'[66] However, on 21 November torrential rain, mines and demolitions prevented the tanks from getting forward and the exposed infantry suffered terribly at the hands of the defenders ensconced in their pillboxes. The battalion commander called for help exclaiming, '. . . these men are fighting and dying up here. No one is lying down. But we gotta have power to do this thing.' Finally on 22 November the armoured support was able to get forward and 'As flame-throwers on the Crocodiles went into action the Germans emerged from the nest of pillboxes that had barred the way, hands high'.[67]

The success of the Crocodiles was something of a relief for the 'poor bloody infantry' but their solace was fleeting. The heavy rain had made the ground very soft and the trailers that contained fuel for the flame-throwers became bogged down and the tanks could go no further. Indeed, the fate of the Crocodiles ultimately mirrored the attack as a whole towards Wurm and Beeck. Nevertheless, the Geilenkirchen salient had been all but cleared and a further 119 pillboxes could be added to the tally of defences destroyed.

Pinching out the heavily fortified Geilenkirchen salient of the West Wall was inevitably going to be a costly business and so it proved to be: the 84th Division suffered 2,000 casualties including 169 dead and 752 missing. However, the high rate of attrition, even for a raw, inexperienced unit, was exceptional and could not solely be attributed to the advantage afforded the defenders by their concrete casemates. After all, the United States Army had been fighting its way through similar defences for the past two months. Indeed, some units, like the 9th and 28th Infantry Divisions, had had to assault the West Wall on two separate occasions. Yet, in spite of this wealth of experience and the seemingly limitless resources at its disposal the US Army signally failed to effectively disseminate the lessons learned from previous engagements to units coming into the line.

The attack on Geilenkirchen was the Railsplitters' introduction to combat and as such the heavily fortified town was likely to be a tough baptism, all the more so because the defences were manned by 15th Panzer Grenadier Division, veterans of North Africa, Sicily and the fighting around Monte Cassino in Italy. Yet the soldiers of 84th Division had undergone no specialist training, nor had they benefited from the experiences of their compatriots in the first battles of the Siegfried Line. Yes, details of lessons learned were circulated in two official publications,[68] but there was no attempt to physically transfer knowledge between frontline units and certainly not to 'green' units like the 84th Division. As a result soldiers initially attacked pillboxes without the support of engineers

Major-General Simpson shows Field Marshal Montgomery dragon's teeth of the Siegfried Line near Aachen. (Imperial War Museum)

but also without direct fire support from tanks and tank destroyers and self-propelled guns, which had proved invaluable in the earlier fighting. This might explain why the Railsplitters' suffered casualties in the region of 60 per cent. Ultimately, it was fortuitous that the division specifically asked to be supported by the Sherwood Rangers whose Crocodiles had a devastating psychological and physical impact on the defenders sheltering in their pillboxes.

Old Blood and Guts – the goose demurs[69]

Farther to the south Patton's Third Army faced arguably the sternest challenge of the Siegfried Line Campaign. The divisions under his command faced the prospect of breaching the defences of the Saar region. Constructed to block the most direct route from France into Germany and the strategic Saar Basin, the defences were built in large numbers and in considerable depth. In 1939 they proved to be an insurmountable barrier to the French, albeit psychological rather than physical.[70]

In addition to the defences on the east bank of the Saar, a series of fortifications had been constructed running due west from Orscholz to the River Moselle and was named the Siegfried or Orscholz Switch Line. It was designed to ensure that the French could not easily outflank the Saar position[71] with an advance along the right bank of the Moselle towards Trier. The defences of the switch line were not dissimilar to those of the West Wall proper: dragon's teeth covered by a two-mile deep belt of pillboxes and bunkers which had been reinforced with fieldworks. To man the line, which stretched some 12 kilometres, was a cosmopolitan force, the bulk of which was made up of two rifle battalions of 416th Division[72] – the remainder had fallen back to take up positions in the West Wall proper.[73]

Tiger

By the middle of November, Colonel Polk's 3rd Cavalry Group, in the vanguard of the XX Corps advance, had reached the line but was ordered to halt by General Walker, the corps commander, and await the heavy armour of General Morris's 10th Armored Division, which was charged with breaching the switch line.

Combat Command A of the Tiger Division was to relieve Polk's Cavalry and when this relief was complete Morris planned to deliver a two-pronged attack on the morning of 21 November: Taskforce Standish on the left directed against Tettingen and Taskforce Chamberlain against Borg. With scant intelligence on the enemy's positions and strength both commanders, after whom the respective forces were named, were forced to feel their way forward. As enemy positions were identified their coordinates were passed to the artillery which then targeted the potential threat. It was slow going and, in spite of the fire support, Taskforce Chamberlain was unable to breach the anti-tank defences even though the defenders had not had time to block the main road to Kirf and had had to resort to explosives to blow a large crater in a desperate, and ultimately successful, attempt to halt the armour. The supporting infantry had been able to make a small incursion, but without armoured support its advance had been stymied. The anti-tank defences that faced Taskforce Standish were even more elaborate, with an anti-tank ditch as well as dragon's teeth all covered by pillboxes. Not surprisingly, Taskforce Standish was similarly balked and CCA's attack was suspended.

On the morning of 22 November the attack was renewed and enjoyed a little more success. Taskforce Standish, with dismounted infantry and engineers creating a path through the anti-tank defences and pillboxes, captured the village of Nennig in the heart of the Orscholz line. To their dismay, however, they found that the defences continued behind the village in a north-south line protecting the German right flank and so prevented the armour from hooking around the defences. Taskforce Chamberlain, meantime, abandoning the main Borg – Kirf road, attacked along the ridge to the west of the road. It pierced the dragon's teeth and seized a small salient some 800 yards in depth. Recognising the threat that this incursion posed to the integrity of the defences, the enemy soon acted to eliminate the bulge and in the afternoon the Americans were forced to withdraw behind a curtain of shellfire from the supporting artillery.

Weakened by the two attacks – Taskforce Chamberlain on 21 November alone had suffered 55 casualties and the loss of 5 (possibly 6) tanks – it was clear that CCA would need to be bolstered if it was to achieve a decisive breakthrough. General Walker had already placed 358th Infantry (of 90th Division) under General Morris's control, but he had been so confident in his division's ability to smash the Orscholz Line that he had deemed it unnecessary to throw them into the initial attacks. He now recognised the error of his ways and the regiment was ordered forward.

Tough 'Ombres[74]

One battalion of 358th Infantry – the 3rd under Captain Spivey – was to attack towards Tettingen with the ultimate objective of Sinz while another – the 2nd under Lt Colonel Schultz – was to advance from Borg towards Muenzingen, some two miles behind the main Orscholz positions; quite a task for a unit that had been reduced to two-thirds of its full complement by the fighting for Metz, and stripped of aerial support by the inclement weather.

The advance of 2nd Battalion got off to an inauspicious start with friendly fire from tanks of Taskforce Chamberlain hitting the unit soon after it had jumped off. Confusion followed and by the early afternoon 2nd Battalion had succeeded in only pushing a small contingent of men through the dragon's teeth. For the men of 3rd Battalion the opening of their attack was more propitious. Spivey had decided that a direct assault along the main road to Tettingen would be folly and instead wheeled to the right. Covered by fog his men succeeded in capturing a number of pillboxes and 84 prisoners. The weakness of Spivey's force, however, meant that these positions could not be guarded and in the fog a number were reoccupied by German infantry who inflicted heavy casualties on the unsuspecting GIs.

The following morning, 24 November, K and I companies of 3rd Battalion were to renew the attack, with the former entrusted to take the village of Butzdorf and the latter

Tettingen. The operation was delayed by a fierce enemy counter-attack as the Germans attempted to reverse the gains of the previous day. The attack was repulsed, but it delayed Spivey's advance until the afternoon. When it finally got under way progress was pedestrian, slowed by the concrete defences. On I Company's front 'Sixteen pillboxes were taken, but the slow work of buttoning-up each separate pillbox, worming close in through the mud, and knocking it out with demolition charges had consumed the daylight hours.'[75] In light of the delays, Spivey postponed the operation until the following morning. Unaware of this and less troubled by pillboxes, K Company pressed ahead and secured a foothold in Butzdorf. Its position, however, was precarious and in a fierce counter-attack all the officers of the company, including the company commander, were either killed or injured. In spite of this tremendous handicap the foothold was retained.

On the morning of 25 November I Company resumed its assault and captured Tettingen but the cost was high and only with the aid of the regimental reserve, L Company, was it possible to relieve the remnants of K Company in Butzdorf. Despite the arrival of L Company, however, the position in Butzdorf was still perilous and it was decided that the gains would have to be relinquished in order to secure the front from possible counter-attack.

For the 2nd Battalion on the right progress was no easier. A large bunker on the outskirts of Oberleuken halted the infantry's advance and it took more than five hours to finally silence it. Once achieved, the battalion was free to proceed to its ultimate objective, while 1st Battalion was tasked with mopping up the enemy in Oberleuken itself. But although 2nd Battalion succeeded in capturing Hill 388 to the west of Oberleuken it suffered heavy casualties and did not have the wherewithal to capture its ultimate objective, Muenzingen. The badly mauled regiment was withdrawn from the fray, to be relieved by 10th Armored Division.

Another concerted attack would arguably have seen the Americans break through the line, but the threat to this outwork of the West Wall was recognised by the German High Command, which considered it to have 'special importance', and so 404th Volks Artillery Corps and 21st Panzer Division (elements of which had already played a part in the fighting of the previous days) were ordered forward on 25 November. As a result Nennig, Oberleuken and Tettingen were recaptured on 27 November.

Although 358th Infantry had been withdrawn from the front this was not to be the last action of the 'Tough 'Ombres' in this campaign, their tenacity was to be tested in a crossing of the Saar River and an attack on the main defences of the West Wall.

By 29 November General Twaddle's 95th Infantry Division had already reached the Saar Heights which shielded Saarlautern and on 1 December the division entered the city. To everyone's amazement a bridge across the Saar was found to be still intact and although protected by two bunkers – part of the West Wall proper – it was captured. Twaddle's men crossed the bridge and pressed on into the heart of the West Wall[76] and, despite combat fatigue, by 18 December they had captured 146 pillboxes.

On Twaddle's left 90th Division reached the Saar near Dillingen and before dawn on 6 December 1st and 2nd Battalions of 357th Infantry crossed the fast-flowing river in assault boats. The crossing was uneventful and the battalions moved into the heart of the defences without incident. As dawn broke the enemy suddenly stirred. A number of manned pillboxes had been bypassed in the darkness and these now brought machine gun fire to bear on the crossing points as well as ordering up artillery and mortar fire. The two battalions found themselves cut off, battling both the elements and the enemy safe and dry in their concrete shelters. 'The entire area was literally studded with enemy pillboxes and advances were measured not in feet or yards but in the number of pillboxes taken.'[77] The men of the regiment fought on with dwindling numbers and supplies.

Their compatriots in 358th and 359th Infantry also crossed the Saar and encountered similar difficulties. Linking up the bridgeheads between the two regiments was hindered by a series of five pillboxes and with conventional means failing to bear fruit a willing German civilian spoke to the incumbents and managed to persuade them to surrender. Elsewhere, the reduction of pillboxes was less straightforward. John Cochrane Jr. of 3rd Battalion, 359th Infantry and an engineer from 315th Engineers were tasked with destroying a troublesome pillbox. They stealthily approached the pillbox and laid their charges at the door before retiring in some haste to a ditch. The expected explosion failed to materialise and the engineer ran back to the pillbox, at great personal danger, and repeated the operation. This time the charges blew in the steel door and the occupants who were not killed were sufficiently concussed to offer little resistance; the intrepid engineer was subsequently awarded the Distinguished Service Cross.

In spite of such heroics, on 19th December the division was ordered to withdraw back across the Saar. Events in the Ardennes meant that offensive operations had to be suspended for the foreseeable future.

Gee up!

For First Army the November offensive meant that V and VII Corps would resume their attempts to drive through the Stolberg corridor and push the enemy out of the Huertgen Forest. The main thrust was to be made on 16 November by VII Corps along the Stolberg corridor. It soon became clear, however, that to aid VII Corps' advance, V Corps would have to resume its attack in the forest which Gerow's men did on 21 November.[78] After two weeks of bitter fighting First Army was through the forest. In all 23,000 men were either killed, wounded, missing or captured by the enemy. A further 8,000 succumbed to the elements or combat exhaustion in what was undoubtedly some of the bitterest fighting of the Second World War. Not without good reason was the Huertgen Forest named the bloody forest. But for Gerow's V Corps one last challenge remained before winter curtailed further operations; the capture of the Roer River dams.

By the end of the first week in December both the First and Ninth Armies had reached the Roer River. The Roer River dams, however, were still in German hands. This was the result of tenacious defence, most notably in the fighting around Schmidt, but was also due to the concerns at SHAEF about the possible danger to US troops should the Germans decide to blow the dams. Attempts to destroy the dams by the RAF had been unsuccessful and so it was decided a ground assault would have to be launched. Gerow's V Corps stood opposite the target and logically was best placed to seize the objective.

Gerow's plan was to attack on 13 December employing a double envelopment using two divisions. The 78th Division was to attack from the west along the Monschau corridor towards Schmidt. Meantime, to the south, 2nd Division was to attack through the Monschau Forest in a northwesterly thrust towards the dams with a regiment of 99th Division protecting its right flank. For Gerow's Corps this would again entail breaching the Scharnhorst and Schill lines; defences which had held 9th Division in the previous September.

Lightning

For 78th Division only two regiments were available for the attack through the Monschau corridor, 309th and 310th Infantry. The two were to advance abreast through the Scharnhorst line with 310th Infantry on the left striking east to capture Lammersdorf, while 309th Infantry was given the ultimate objective of Kesternich. With these objectives taken 309th Infantry was to wheel south while 310th Infantry was to head northeast through the defences of the Schill line to Schmidt.

To guarantee surprise it was decided that the attack would not be preceded by an artillery barrage; such preparations invariably had no discernible effect on the concrete defences and only served to alert the enemy to the possibility of an assault. Concealed by fog and with radio silence the infantry of 310th Infantry advanced on 13 December.

Some of the dragon's teeth near Lammersdorf that blocked the path of 78th Division in December 1944. (Author)

Calamitously, the silence was soon broken by an unfortunate GI who stood on a mine. This brought an immediate response from a pillbox, but after a brief firefight the occupants surrendered, claiming that they had run out of ammunition. The 309th Infantry also made steady progress and one company reached the outskirts of Kesternich. Pillboxes on the flanks, however, held up the rest of the battalion and forced the lead battalion to suspend its advance rather than become involved in house to-house fighting.

Nevertheless Gerow and General Parker, the commander of 78th Division, were heartened by the not inconsiderable gains of the Lightning Division. They would have been less so if they had been aware that the 'lightning' advance was in part due to the fact that the 272nd Volks Grenadier Division, which was holding this sector, was in the process of being relieved so it would be fresh for the forthcoming Ardennes offensive. On the following day 309th Infantry, supported by a battalion of 310th Infantry, captured Kesternich, but their hold was only tenuous and German infantry infiltrated back into the village. More worrying still, prisoners captured in the battle were from another division, 326th Volks Grenadier Division – an orphan unit pressed into defence out of sheer desperation, or the start of something more sinister? Only time would tell.

Second to None

The southern wing of the envelopment was to be delivered by 2nd Division through the Monschau Forest. The thickly wooded terrain meant that the routes of advance open to General Robertson, the divisional commander, were limited. The most simple and direct route was the road to Wahlerscheid, so he ordered 9th Infantry to take this route, capture the village and then swing northwest. Through the breach would follow 38th Infantry, which would then strike northeast towards the Roer River dams. The attack was to be launched on the morning of 13 December – an inauspicious omen as it turned out.

The enemy's dispositions around Wahlerscheid were unknown and so it was decided not to use a preliminary bombardment, but to rely on the infantry to radio-in co-ordinates of any strongpoints as the battle developed. However, the element of surprise could not compensate for the sheer strength of the enemy positions; the village had been transformed into a veritable fortress. Barbed wire entanglements, in places ten deep, and mines protected pillboxes and bunkers with undergrowth cleared to ensure clear fields of fire. The defenders were caught off-balance by the initial attack but soon regained their composure and inflicted terrible casualties on the men in the lead companies, especially the sappers charged with cutting the wire. Night came as little relief; the ever-present threat of death or disability was aggravated by the weather as GIs, wet through, found their clothes froze during the night.

The following day an artillery barrage was ordered to soften up the defences,[79] but without accurate information it was less than effective and in at least one instance the shells fell on American troops. The inability of the artillery to neutralise the enemy positions resulted in a repeat of the carnage of the previous day when the infantry attacked again. Finally, the demoralised infantrymen were withdrawn to give the artillery full rein. A battery of 155mm self-propelled guns was also called up to engage the pillboxes over open sights. Firing 287 rounds at the fortifications, the crews were convinced that at least three pillboxes had been penetrated, but subsequent examination proved that this was not the case.

The sledgehammer had then failed to dislodge the enemy from their positions; it was now the turn of the rapier. During the fighting on 14 December one squad had managed to crawl forward and cut the enemy wire. However, in the confusion of the initial engagements the news of this success had been delayed and it was not until late on 15 December that this valuable information was passed back to company headquarters. With no alternative, the commander of 9th Infantry pushed a patrol through the gap in the wire under the cover of darkness. Once through it radioed back to headquarters and two companies were ordered forward. They also silently slipped through the gap and now attacked the pillboxes, blowing the doors off with beehive charges and killing or capturing the occupants. Soon after daylight on 16 December Wahlerscheid was in American hands and troops of 38th Infantry were advancing towards the Roer Dams.

A lone US piper plays amid the snow-covered dragon's teeth of the Siegfried Line, 25 January 1945. (Hulton Getty Images)

General Robertson was mightily relieved at the breakthrough, but was blissfully unaware that, as with 78th Division, its passage had been eased by the fact that the soldiers manning the positions at Wahlerscheid were in the process of being relieved as part of the preparation for the winter offensive and were caught in limbo by the American attack.

All along the front the West Wall had been broken but still the depleted and demoralised forces held out. Churchill's gloomy predictions about the resilience of the German army and the possibility of its resistance continuing into the New Year were now looking increasingly likely, much to the dismay of Eisenhower and his senior commanders. 'The near-miraculous revitalisation of the German army in October had come as a shock, dissipating some of the optimism. The failure of our November offensive to crack the Siegfried Line and push through to the Rhine had been a further jolt, leading Ike and SHAEF planners to conclude that we would probably be stalemated through the winter, unable to mount a decisive offensive until after the spring thaw in late April or May 1945.'[80] Hitler's Ardennes offensive would throw even this pessimistic assessment into doubt.

INTERREGNUM

As the weather worsened and the Allied soldiers prepared for what they hoped would be a quiet Christmas and New Year, Hitler launched his last offensive of the war, which later became known as the 'Battle of the Bulge'. Taking advantage of the overcast conditions which would necessarily limit the effect of Allied air power, Hitler launched Dietrich's Sixth SS Panzer Army, supported by Manteuffel's Fifth Panzer Army and Brandenberger's Seventh Army against the weakly held Ardennes section of the front. By fair means or foul they were ordered to advance to the port of Antwerp, vital to the Allies for supplies, and in so doing split the Anglo-American force in two. The intelligence staff at SHAEF had been aware for some time that Hitler planned (or rather hoped) to launch a counter-attack and on 19 October they had concluded that, 'Hitler wants a November offensive. Possibility not excluded of Sixth Panzer with I and II SS Corps plus the Para divisions (also refitting) putting in spoiling attack in north before we start large-scale offensive action.'[81] However, the massing of German forces in the weeks prior to the attack was somewhat conceitedly attributed to von Rundstedt's careful management of his forces as he prepared to meet the next Allied offensive, rather than preparation for a counter-stroke.[82]

Indeed, such was the secrecy of the operation that even von Rundstedt had been kept in the dark. When he was finally informed of the plan he was less than enamoured and urged the Fürher to change his mind. But Hitler would not back down. On 16 December, thirty divisions supported by the remnants of the once mighty *Luftwaffe* attacked. The American units caught in the maelstrom, mostly 'green' or resting units posted to this supposedly quiet section of the front, were thrown back in disarray and leading elements of Manteuffel's Fifth Panzer Army almost reached Dinant on the River Meuse (some 60 miles from their start line).[83] It soon became clear, however, that the offensive was not going according to plan and von Rundstedt implored Hitler to allow him to pull his forces back before they became ensnared in a trap, with Patton's Third Army pressing on the neck of the pocket from the south and Hodges's VII Corps ready to strike from the north. Hitler refused to authorise this course of action and almost paid a heavy price for his obstinacy.[84] On 22 December there was a break in the weather and Allied aircraft attacked the exposed German forces. This put further pressure on German supplies, which were already in a parlous state; and, with losses mounting and the vital road junction at Bastogne[58] still held by the 'battered bastards', the attack literally and metaphorically ran out of gas.

Fortunately for Hitler deteriorating weather prevented the Allies closing their pincer, but the Germans still lost 100,000 men and almost all their armour. Losses for the Allies were also high, but they could be readily replaced and with the threat now extinguished and the *Wehrmacht* further weakened, the Allies could again look to the offensive and another attempt to breach the Siegfried Line.

WINNER TAKES ALL

In his appraisal of the 'Battle of the Bulge', Eisenhower was quick to realise the critical role played by the defences of the Siegfried Line. 'The strong artificial defences of the Siegfried Line assisted the enemy to achieve strength in the attack. The obstacles, pillboxes, and fixed guns of that line so greatly multiplied the defensive power of the garrison that the German could afford to weaken long stretches of his front in order to gather forces for the counter blow.'[86] But with the failure of Hitler's Ardennes offensive would the defences be able to stem the inevitable Allied assault?

Von Rundstedt, who had never been an advocate of the defences, thought not. He was keen to retreat behind the Rhine, which he saw as the last viable line of defence. Hitler disagreed, arguing that aerial interdiction meant that it was imperative that both banks of the Rhine remain in German hands so that this vital artery remained open; and, as such, the West Wall had to be held at all costs. His orders to von Rundstedt reflected this desire, 'no soldier, no vehicle and no weapon was to cross the Rhine eastwards without the authority of an Army Headquarters . . . troops were bidden to remain in the forts of the Siegfried Line, though they might be encircled by the enemy and though their numbers were inadequate to occupy the line fully.'[87] Von Rundstedt attempted to balance his own views with those of the Führer, but Hitler's insistence on holding the West Wall clearly rankled with him. In a report to the Supreme Commander at the end of February von Rundstedt described the West Wall as a 'mousetrap'.[88] Not surprisingly, given the emotional and physical investment he had made in the West Wall, Hitler was greatly displeased and described the report as a 'shameful fabrication', ending his rant by exclaiming that, 'the enemy was trembling before this miracle of German technics'.[89] But, as with so much else, he was deluded. Almost everywhere along the front the Allies were breaching the defences.

To the north the West Wall defences were less elaborate, often little more than trenches and barbed wire, more reminiscent of the First World War than the Second. These defences were located near the Hochwald Forest and were captured by Montgomery's forces in the first months of 1945. (Canadian National Archives)

To the north, in early February 1945, 21st Army Group broke through the Siegfried Line with little difficulty, slowed only by tenacious defence and the cloying mud. The defences on Montgomery's front were far less numerous than those further south, often little more than fieldworks, although every now and again British forces stumbled across, sometimes literally, more substantial defences as Captain Sheldon, a platoon commander in the Coldstream Guards, recollected in a letter. Leading an attack on a section of the Siegfried Line, he came across two harmless-looking haystacks which turned out to be very well camouflaged pillboxes. Encounters with elaborate concrete defences were thankfully very rare. These tended to be concentrated around strategically important towns like Cleve and Goch,[90] around which the Germans constructed their defensive plans. In the advance towards the former, Sergeant-major John Walls MC of 15th Scottish Division 'ceremonially hung up his token line of washing'.[91, 92] Other

Infantry of the 2nd Gordons, 227th Brigade outside a German bunker at Kleve after its capture with 90 prisoners. (Imperial War Museum)

British soldiers outside a Siegfried Line bunker near Hochwald Forest, Germany, 4 March 1945. (Canadian National Archives)

British units did not have the chance for such celebrations. Lt Mason of the Royal Signal Squadron, 13th Medium Royal Artillery noted in his war diary that, as of 3 February, 'We were supposed to be in the Siegfried Line. I looked around for the pillboxes, dragon's teeth and gun emplacements. There were none of these things. The only defences that I saw were an anti-tank ditch and some barbed wire . . . Mud was our greatest enemy',[93] he concluded.

Lightning – strikes twice

The American forces immediately to the south were less fortunate. Here, Hodges's First Army resuscitated plans that had had to be shelved by the German counter-attack. One of the first targets was the Roer Dams and the town of Schmidt. Four attacks had been launched in this general direction from September through to December – the last being aborted when the Germans struck in the Ardennes. One of the divisions involved in this last attack, the 78th Division, had made an incursion into the West Wall in the Monschau corridor and, as this was a natural avenue of attack in otherwise difficult terrain, it was selected as the route for the new offensive. Familiar with the terrain and already *in situ* General Parker's 78th Division was logically given the task of leading, but in recognition of the difficulties experienced in earlier attacks by the determined defenders ensconced in concrete shelters the infantry was to be supported by Combat Command A of 5th Armored Division and a platoon of British Crocodile flame-thrower tanks. Facing this composite force was Lightning Division's old adversary, the 272nd Volks Grenadier Division.

From the outset the omens for the attack were good. A short, sharp bombardment prior to the assault on 31 January – the result of ammunition conservation rather than a deliberate tactic – saw the defenders remain in their pillboxes fully expecting a further half-hour barrage. It did not materialise and before they had time to respond 310th Infantry had overrun the enemy positions, including 32 pillboxes. Indeed, so swift was the advance that the supporting Crocodile tanks were all but redundant in the attack. Meantime, the supporting tanks of CCA captured Eicherscheid and 311th Infantry captured Kesternich. The division was now in a position to capture Schmidt and the Schwammenauel Dam.

Attacking on the morning of 5 February on the left wing of 78th Division's attack, 309th Infantry slipped unopposed through the Siegfried Line positions. Whether caught by surprise, or keen to survive the war, the defenders manning the pillboxes did not fire at the infantrymen as they passed the firing apertures. With its objective achieved, the regiment spent the rest of the day mopping up the 35 pillboxes that had been bypassed, so as to ensure that 310th Infantry, which was to pass through their positions and continue the attack on Schmidt, was not delayed by pockets of resistance.

The men of 311th Infantry were less fortunate. They also encountered a number of pillboxes, but the occupants of these proved less willing to surrender; each one had to be attacked and silenced. With this task successfully achieved, the infantry advanced on Schmidt and entered the town. General Parker now ordered 309th Infantry to capture the dam, which it duly did. The two targets had been captured and in the process the West Wall had been breached. More importantly, Ninth Army could now resume its advance unthreatened by the possibility of a German-engineered deluge.

Elsewhere on First Army's front, veteran units like 1st and 9th Infantry Divisions completed the job that had been started the previous year. After helping to stem the German winter counterattack, 1st Division went on the offensive at the beginning of February, 'Leaving Von Rundstedt's troops no time to do more than sweep snow from their re-occupied pillboxes on the Siegfried Line . . .'[94] On 2 February the infantry began their assault on Scheitert and Ramscheid. Once through the dragon's teeth, which had been strengthened with anti-personnel and anti-tank mines, and reinforced with tanks and tank destroyers, the 'Big Red One' captured its objectives. On 4th February the important communications centre at Hollerath was captured and the following day the Division consolidated its position, clearing enemy pillboxes before 99th Infantry Division relieved it. In the 21 days of its attack it captured 50 pillboxes and bunkers.

The 9th Infantry Division resumed its advance at much the same time. On 30 January, 60th Infantry recommenced the interminable and highly dangerous task of bunker-busting as it headed east from Monschau, while 39th Infantry advanced on Wahlerscheid, the scene of such bitter fighting in the previous December. The immensely strong pillboxes and log-bunkers in the area were soon overcome, however, as the demoralised defenders succumbed to the veterans of the *Falcon* regiment.[95]

Old Blood and Guts – the goose relents

By early February 1945 the 'Bulge' had been erased from the military maps and Patton's Third Army stood on the River Sauer opposite Echternach and Wallendorf just as Hodges's First Army had in September the previous year. Little had seemingly changed in the interim: the river still represented a formidable barrier swollen by the winter snow and rain and the far shore still bristled with pillboxes. But looks could be deceptive; much had changed on both sides. The German army had been fatally weakened by the ill-conceived Ardennes offensive and all along the front the Siegfried Line had been punctured. By contrast, although the Allies had suffered losses they had been able to replace them with fresh recruits and they had resolved the logistical difficulties that had hamstrung them the previous autumn. What had not changed, however, were the constraints placed on Patton and his reluctance to abide by them.

Patton was still confident of his army's ability to defeat the Siegfried Line and at a press conference in Luxembourg City on 1 January in responses to a question about the Siegfried Line, he answered that, 'Never in the history of the world has there been a line that could be successfully defended . . . The only way you can win a war is to attack and keep attacking . . .'[96] And that is exactly what he planned to do.[97] An order from Eisenhower of 1 February effectively put an end to Twelfth Army Group's attack, but Patton's Third Army was permitted to 'continue the probing attacks now in progress'. Patton, as ever, interpreted this order in its broadest sense-seeing this as not only an opportunity to breach the West Wall but, if successful, as a means of persuading his superiors that an offensive in the south should not be discounted. Patton thus told Middleton, the commander of VIII Corps, to go beyond the Schnee Eifel and capture the important road centre at Pruem.

Troy 'Gimpy Knee'[98]

To realise this aim Middleton ordered 4th and 90th Divisions, both veterans of the earlier fighting, to make the main attack with 87th Division securing the northern flank with First Army. The 4th Division was to strike north of Brandscheid and then turn south to capture the town before being relieved by 90th Division. The 'Tough 'Ombres' were then to advance on Pronsfeld, another road centre some five miles south of the ultimate objective, Pruem, which was to be taken by 4th Division.

Intelligence reports suggested that this portion of the West Wall was only weakly held and patrols seemed to confirm this, with a number of bunkers found to be unmanned.[99]

Moreover, because of the difficult terrain, the defences of the West Wall in this area were less numerous and had been weakened further by demolitions completed by US engineers after the fighting in September. However, the VIII commanders were not complacent; in September the scenario had not been all that different and on that occasion the German resistance stiffened markedly and Middleton expected nothing less now.

Ivy – envelops the wall

For Ivy Division, the new offensive was in many respects a case of déjà vu. It had attacked the Schnee Eifel in September and was now called upon to advance over the same ground and fight against at least one of the enemy units that it had faced in the autumn. On that occasion the division had enjoyed early success before being held as the Germans rushed reserves forward. Would the story be the same in February?

Certainly the initial advance met with success; reconnaissance by 8th Infantry Regiment early on 4 February found the first belt of pillboxes unoccupied and so General Blakeley, the commander of 4th Division, ordered the lead battalions of 8th and 22nd Infantry to attack. Their objective was a string of pillboxes on the crest of the Schnee Eifel. Having successfully stormed the ridge, follow-up battalions turned left and right to assault the remaining bunkers.

The following day, 8th Infantry continued to advance northeast, rolling up the pillboxes as it went, while 22nd Infantry advanced towards Brandscheid. The town, as the commanders of the Division were well aware from their experiences in September, was heavily fortified and the lead battalion spent the morning of 5 February assaulting eleven pillboxes that defended a crossroads above the town. Having overrun these positions, 22nd Infantry, supported by ten medium tanks and seven tank destroyers, now attacked Brandscheid itself. The armoured support targeted the numerous pillboxes that protected the town and in a manner of hours Brandscheid had fallen with the loss of only three men.

'Tough 'Ombres' – hasta la vista!

With Brandscheid secured, the attack of 90th Division could begin. On the morning of 6 February, 359th Infantry advanced in the darkness, picking its way through the dragon's teeth and silent pillboxes and capturing Habscheid without a shot being fired. Indeed, such was the success of the surprise attack that the regiment had inadvertently bypassed a number of manned pillboxes covering a gate through the dragon's teeth on the road to Habscheid. Unaware of this oversight engineers blew the barrier and promptly came under heavy fire from these pillboxes. Pinned down, the engineers were unable to sweep for mines to allow the armour to get forward to support 359th Infantry. The situation soon became critical. Without armoured support the regiment could make no further progress and was cut off and vulnerable to counter-attack. However, lacking any reserves the defenders were unable to exploit the situation and before they could act a 155mm self-propelled gun had moved forward and engaged the troublesome pillboxes. The defenders made a strategic withdrawal and the engineers were able to get to work clearing the road. The 358th Infantry was now able to pass through and relieve 22nd Infantry in Brandscheid. The timing was less than opportune because the Germans counter-attacked as the relief was in progress, but the enemy assault was repulsed.

Meanwhile, 11th Armored Division, which had been in reserve, advanced southwest of Habscheid towards the heavily fortified Losenseifen Hill. Fortunately, few of the positions were manned and those that were, taken by surprise as men of the Thunderbolt division attacked without artillery preparation. Middleton's VIII Corps had now broken through the West Wall on a front eleven miles wide and in accordance with Patton's wish Middleton urged his divisional commanders to press home their advantage.

This was easier said than done. The German High Command, who had initially paid little heed to the attack, now realised the full magnitude of the situation, having identified the presence of not only 4th Division, but also the 90th, 87th Infantry Divisions and 11th Armored Division. Generalfeldmarschall Model, commander of Army Group B, now moved the army boundaries so that Seventh Army was responsible for stemming the attack, and gave General Brandenberger, the commander of Seventh Army, permission to use 2nd Panzer Division, which had been held in reserve. These changes took some time to take effect and in the interim the 87th Infantry and 11th Armored Divisions spent 7 February consolidating their position by clearing pillboxes, while 4th Division[100] and 90th Division in the centre pressed home their attacks towards Pruem and Pronsfeld respectively.

For 90th Division this involved a two-pronged attack with 357th and 358th Infantry. The former was ordered to attack two hills, both of which were heavily fortified. The lead battalion was to attack Hill 511 and was to be followed by a second battalion tasked with capturing Hill 510. The results were mixed. Fire from enemy pillboxes halted the attack on the first objective but the supporting battalion, after a day-long struggle, was able to capture Hill 510. It was not to remain in American hands for long, however, and was to become the focal point of a seesaw battle which, by darkness on 8 February, had been settled in the favour of the Tough 'Ombres.[101]

Meantime, 358th Infantry from its base in Brandscheid launched a regimental-scale attack: the 3rd Battalion successfully captured Hill 521, but both the 1st and 2nd Battalions found their paths blocked by pillboxes. The 1st Battalion, supported by tanks, methodically reduced the pillboxes that barred its way – ten in total – and on the following day captured a further 55 before establishing contact with 359th Infantry. The 2nd Battalion fared less well. The battalion encountered a number of well-camouflaged pillboxes that had not previously been identified, which were manned by determined individuals, well drilled in the art of pillbox defence. A number of pillboxes were captured, but the defenders were resolute and it was only on 9 February, with their position undermined by advances elsewhere, that they were forced to withdraw.

With the defences of the West Wall behind them, VIII Corps' advance quickened and it soon reached the Pruem River. Unfortunately, the road network was not designed to take the traffic that is needed to support a modern army and began to disintegrate, preventing any supplies moving forward and forcing Middleton's units to dig in. This enforced hiatus only resulted in a brief delay as engineers worked tirelessly to repair the roads. On 18 February, 90th Division was ordered to advance southeast from Habscheid with a view to securing the Pruem River from Pronsfeld to Mauel where it was to join up with XII Corps. The unenviable task of leading 90th Division's attack fell to 359th Infantry, but was made less onerous by the fact that 11th Armored Division had captured Losenseifen Hill, the dominant feature in this sector of the front. Nevertheless, 359th Infantry still had to overcome a thick belt of pillboxes if it was to make any significant progress. Setting off before first light the regiment caught the defenders by surprise and the village of Kesfeld was captured, together with 48 pillboxes and over 400 prisoners, including two regimental commanders of 167th Volks Grenadier Division.

Thunderbolt

On 11th Armored Division's front, the West Wall was still largely intact and meant that the Combat Command Reserve had to overcome not only the pillboxes but also the dragon's teeth. A plan of attack was developed which envisaged CCR advancing through the Siegfried Line towards Reiff, to be followed by CCB, which would then attack the defences from the north hitting them in the flank and rear where they were most vulnerable. The preparations for the attack were helped in no small part by the capture of a German map detailing the locations of all the pillboxes and which also gave '. . . a complete description . . . of each and every box including its category, fields of fire, calibre of weapons, heating system, emergency exits, entrances, thickness of walls, location of switchboards, communications, OPs and CPs, and supplementary information concerning recent entrenchments, protective mine belts etc . . .'[102] This welter of information, together with the desperate state of the defenders, practically guaranteed success – and so it proved.

On the morning of 18 February 63rd Armored Infantry Battalion opened the assault. Engineers blasted a path through the dragon's teeth and the minefield. Through this opening the infantry poured, capturing a number of enemy positions. The enemy defenders were caught in disarray; they were in the middle of troop redeployments and were also taken by surprise as the men of Thunderbolt division, somewhat out of keeping with their nickname, attacked with no artillery preparation. Simultaneously, 55th Armored Infantry Battalion, supported by engineers and tanks, broke through the enemy defences and by dark it had captured its first objective, Leidenborn. Although most of the pillboxes encountered by the CCR were manned they offered little resistance, the occupants usually choosing to surrender when they came under sustained, accurate enemy fire.

The following day, elements of 276th Volks Grenadier Division launched a counter-attack but it was repulsed by 55th Armored Infantry Battalion, which went on to capture a further 23 pillboxes in and around Herzfeld on the back edge of the Siegfried Line. The 63rd Armoured Infantry Battalion spent the day consolidating its position before renewing its advance on 20 February, when it captured the town of Sengerich and a further ten pillboxes. The battalion spent the following day preparing for the final assault planned for 22 February, while 55th Armored Infantry Battalion seized Roscheid and its accompanying pillboxes. Combat Command R was now through the Siegfried Line and it now only remained for CCB to move through CCR's zone and roll up the enemy defences. With Eschfeld and a further ten bunkers captured by 55th Armored Infantry during the morning of 22 February the stage was set for CCB to mop up the remaining pillboxes and bunkers between 11th Armored Division and its fellow tankers in 6th Armored Division to the south. This they did soon after lunch that day. In just four days, 11th Armored Division had punched a two-mile-wide hole in the Siegfried Line and in so doing captured no less than 197 pillboxes and bunkers.

Super Sixth

On 20 February men of the 6th Armored Division crossed the Our River led by Combat Command B. Their advance was preceded by a twenty-minute bombardment of the enemy's pillboxes followed by a ten-minute pause and then a further intense one-minute barrage directed against the initial objective. Previous experience had shown that the enemy had a tendency to vacate its bunkers after the initial bombardment had finished and take up positions in trenches and foxholes ready to meet the anticipated infantry attack. It was hoped that this secondary bombardment would frustrate this tactic and catch the enemy in the open.

This attention to detail extended to the tactics developed to assault the enemy pillboxes. At its base in California the division had constructed mock defences which were used to hone the men's skills, and the lessons learned were now put to good use, initially by C Company of 44th Armored Infantry Battalion. Prior to the assault supporting tanks and tank destroyers engaged those pillboxes within range, concentrating, where possible, on the known weaknesses, principally the firing apertures. After a 30-minute cannonade the tanks desisted and two platoons, designated as assault teams, moved forward covered by the remainder of the company. When the respective assault team was in position a red smoke grenade was thrown, a signal to cease all supporting fire. With suppressing fire provided by the support team, engineers cut the barbed wire in front of the pillbox before one of the sappers advanced through the gap in the wire to dispatch the pillbox. With the position captured the assault team sought sanctuary within its confines before signalling to its supporting units and then heading for the next target. These tactics were so successful that 44th Armored Infantry suffered only one fatality in its attack and, together with 9th Armored Infantry, by midday had captured 17 pillboxes and secured their first objective.

These tactics, however, did not always guarantee success as troops of A Company 9th Armored Infantry found during this same operation. A set-piece attack was launched against one specific pillbox, but despite using five beehive charges the company could not dislodge the occupants. Indeed, far from surrendering, the defenders instructed their own artillery to shell the pillbox. Unperturbed, engineers supporting the infantry on the following day used 200lbs of TNT in an effort to destroy the position or at least persuade the zealots to surrender; but this failed, as a did a tank destroyer firing from point-blank range at the door. Finally, the engineers packed 450lbs of TNT into the recess formed by the previous explosion and detonated the charge. This had the desired effect. Dazed and confused and in some cases heavily concussed, the ten martyrs surrendered or were evacuated from the shelter with their pride if not their eardrums intact.

Combat Command B was now on a roll and the following day the tanks rumbled south, capturing Dahnen and then Dasburg, where the pillboxes covering the Our River in front of CCA were overrun, so enabling its compatriots to cross the river unmolested. In the five-day period from 20 February, when the division launched its assault on the Siegfried Line, the Super Sixth captured a staggering 253 pillboxes.

'Steady' Eddy

While VIII Corps advanced south, XII Corps under General Eddy on the night of 6/7 February pressed north to close the trap and pinch out the so-called Vianden Bulge. The attack was to be launched in the area between Wallendorf and Echternach by 5th and 80th Infantry Divisions, together with a regimental combat team of 76th Division – 417th Infantry. The first and most difficult obstacle proved not to be the West Wall defences, but the swollen Sauer River. Just 16 men of 5th Division managed to make their way across the treacherous strait. Their plight was aggravated by defenders manning pillboxes on the far bank, who were now alerted to the threat and brought heavy fire to bear on reinforcements as they prepared to cross the river. Despite ordering tanks and tank destroyers to the river's edge to engage the pillboxes and the 'We Will' spirit of the men in the Red Diamond Division, the enemy fire and the swiftly flowing river prevented any further troops getting across.

Blue Ridge

To the north and south of 5th Division, the 80th Division and 417th Infantry Regiment respectively enjoyed better fortunes. After successfully traversing the river, the 80th Division captured Wallendorf while 417th Infantry set about reducing the pillboxes that might hinder further crossings of the river. The raging torrent however prevented further reinforcements getting forward and it was not until 11 February that the river was finally bridged and a firmer foothold secured. Even then a thick belt of pillboxes separated the bridgehead of 80th Division from that of 5th Division and 417th Infantry. By mid-day on 12 February the defenders had been winkled out of these pillboxes and the bridgehead consolidated. The two divisions, together with 76th Division, now crossing the river and, reintegrating 417th Infantry into its ranks, set about securing a more defendable bridgehead, work that was completed by 17 February.[103] The 80th Division was now ordered to advance north to Mauel with a view to meeting up with VIII Corps and closing the circle.

By this time, Patton's intentions were evident to the local German commanders, who requested to withdraw to the east of the Pruem River. Model, already unhappy that Seventh Army had failed to stem the American advance and determined to follow Hitler's order that no German territory should be relinquished, declined Brandenberger's request. Brandenberger was subsequently relieved of his duties and replaced by General Felber,[104] who was in the unusual position of having to decline a request for withdrawal which he had instigated. However, aware of the consequences of not retreating from the bulge, he engineered a strategic withdrawal under the pretence of overwhelming American strength and his men lived to fight another day.

Into this vacuum on 18 February advanced 80th Division. The 318th Regiment was tasked with advancing from Wallendorf to Hill 408 just outside Meetendorf which it did in three days. Meantime, its compatriots in 319th Infantry headed for Niedersgegen and in so doing cut off the German forces still ensconced in their bunkers on the Our River. The task of mopping up these pillboxes fell to 53rd Armored Infantry of 4th Armored Division. By nightfall on 21 February it had completed this assignment and in the process captured 337 prisoners. Enemy resistance in the sector had effectively collapsed and by 23 February the Vianden Bulge had been cleared. Thus, 'two corps of the Third Army in just over three weeks had penetrated the West Wall in some of the most forbidding terrain to be found along the Western Front . . . the enemy's prepared defenses lay behind, and only a miracle could enable the Germans to man another solid front in the Eifel.'[105]

Pilgrim

By this time Third Army had also cleared the Saar-Moselle triangle, but it had proved to be a far tougher challenge than anticipated. The blunting of Hitler's ill-starred offensive meant that resources, albeit limited, could be spared to eliminate this salient. This involved the capture of the Orscholz or Siegfried Switch Line which protected the base of the triangle and which had shown its defensive strength during the abortive attack of November.

As it transpired, the only resource that could be spared for the operation was the inexperienced 94th Infantry Division.[107] After cutting its teeth in the fighting to contain the garrisons of Lorient and St Nazaire, the division had moved across France to the German frontier. *En route* the men of the division had passed through Verdun, the scene of such bitter fighting in the First World War, little realising that they were to write a similarly bloody chapter in the history of the Second. Such a morbid prospect, however, was far from the minds of the troops as they headed towards Germany, their bodies and minds numbed by the freezing temperatures. On 7 January the division relieved elements of 90th Division that had been holding the line and the men began familiarising themselves with their new surroundings. Soon thereafter the division's commander, Major General Malony, received his brief. His orders were to seize this outwork of the West Wall and in so doing compel the German High Command to expend men and matériel in its defence that might otherwise be used in the Ardennes. D-Day was set for 14 January.

The assault was launched by 376th Infantry on the morning of D-Day and soon the villages of Tettingen and Butzdorf had been captured with little resistance from troops manning the defences. A strong enemy counter-attack led by elements of 11th Panzer Division forced the infantry to retire from Butzdorf, but, bogged down in the snow and harassed by artillery fire, the German counter-attack foundered and the 11th Panzer Division could do little more than help the overstretched 416th Infantry Division hold the line.

His strike against the centre of the line halted, General Malony decided to launch his next attack against Orscholz itself, which was the eastern anchor of the position on the

River Saar. The 1st Battalion of 301st Infantry was to be in the van. On the night of 19 January Companies A and B set off for their forward assembly area just in front of the enemy's dragon's teeth. Loaded down with equipment and in driving snow it was tough going. Nevertheless, the exhausted troops arrived at their jump off points at the pre-ordained time. Company B safely slipped through the dragon's teeth and seized a number of enemy positions, but Company A became mired in a minefield hidden by the deep snow. The explosions alerted the enemy in pillboxes and fieldworks who brought a withering fire to bear on the unfortunate infantrymen. The 2nd Battalion was ordered forward in an effort to rescue the situation but only succeeded in adding to the casualty figures. The supporting armour was unable to get forward because the ground, although frozen, was not sufficiently hard to take the tanks' considerable weight. The attack was called off and the isolated troops of B Company were forced to surrender to the enemy.

Switching the focus of the attack back to the centre, General Malony ordered 302nd Infantry, on the left, to capture Butzdorf. This opening was to be exploited by Combat Command A of 8th Armored Division which was to roll up the defences in front of 376th Infantry attacking on the right, enabling the regiment to capture Sinz. The attack was launched on 26 January, but as is so often the case with such elaborate manoeuvres, the operation, although partially successful, did not go according to plan. The men of 302nd Infantry were held up, preventing the armour from getting forward. This delay was critical, because CCA had only been attached to 94th Division for 48 hours,[108] so General Malony committed 301st Infantry in a desperate attempt to clear a path for the tanks before they were withdrawn from the attack. All was not lost, however. In spite of the fact that the defences on its front had not been cleared, 376th Infantry pressed forward towards Sinz and secured a foothold in the village.

Building on this platform, 302nd Infantry, on 2 February, was directed against Kampholz Woods situated to the southeast of Tettingen. This was a particularly tough nut to crack because the approaches were covered by a series of pillboxes. Indeed, so effective were the pillboxes that the regiment took almost a week (until 8 February) to capture the last of them. In the interim, 301st Infantry captured Sinz, but despite repeated attempts could not capture the nearby Bannholz Woods, defended by 11th Panzer Division. By this point, however, the commander of 11th Panzer Division was becoming increasingly concerned at the way his élite division, which had fought with distinction on the eastern front and had taken part in Operation Barbarossa, was being utilised. Eventually the division was relieved and replaced by the weakened 256th Volks Grenadier Division. Intelligence concerning the withdrawal of 11th Panzer Division eventually filtered through to General Walker, XX Corps commander, and on 15 February he ordered a full-scale attack.

The 301st Infantry Regiment was to attack from Sinz towards Munzingen, with 376th Infantry protecting its left flank. At the same time 302nd Infantry was to advance from Kampholz Woods and roll up the pillboxes to the east. On 19 February the assault began with 301st Infantry experiencing only sporadic resistance. 'An occasional group of Germans would fight tenaciously, particularly when protected by pillboxes or bunkers, but in the main the opposition bore no comparison to that put up earlier by the panzer

One of the bunkers that formed part of the Orscholz Switch Line captured by men of 94th Infantry Division. (Author)

division.'[109] Similarly, 302nd Infantry, in its attack from Kampholz Woods, suffered at the hands of soldiers of 416th Infantry Division holed up in their pillboxes and it was only with the arrival of the armoured support on the morning of 19 February that it was able to progress. However, it was clear that the Orscholz Switch Line had been broken and 10th Armored Division, which had been held in reserve, was released to press home the advantage. By 21 February the Saar-Moselle triangle was clear. It now only remained to pierce the West Wall proper.[110]

PATTON'S GAMBLE

The West Wall in this sector was built covering the Saar River and was up to three miles in depth where the terrain, which was dominated by steep wooded slopes, offered an opportunity for a breakthrough. The first obstacle to be negotiated, however, was the river. Patton hoped to cross during the night of 21–22 February, but the assault boats were delayed and did not arrive until dawn on 22 February. Desperate to prevent the enemy manning the defences on the east bank Patton took a gamble and ordered 94th Infantry to immediately cross the river. Concealed by early morning mist men of 302nd Infantry crossed the Saar near Taben and captured the first defences of the West Wall with little or no fighting. To the north opposite Serrig, 301st Infantry enjoyed a less auspicious start. Covered by the same heavy fog the men of 3rd Battalion set out in their boats across the river, but the defenders, despite their inability to identify clear targets, brought enough fire to bear to disperse the attackers. Moreover, many of the boats were lost in the swift current and prevented the battalion getting across until later in the day when new boats had arrived. Nevertheless, by the close of the day, 301st Infantry had secured a bridgehead and had made contact with 302nd Infantry.

But if the crossing had gone badly for 301st Infantry, it was even worse for 376th Infantry supporting 10th Armored Division in its crossing near Ockfen. The boats to cross the river did not arrive until midday when the fog had cleared, and attempts to generate an artificial smokescreen proved unsuccessful, as heavy enemy fire from the pillboxes on the far bank made it impossible to get the smoke generators into place. General Morris was forced to defer the attack, and it was not until darkness had fallen that the 3rd Battalion was able to attempt a crossing. Somewhat surprisingly, in light of the earlier enemy reaction, the assault teams made it safely across the river without a shot being fired from the east bank. Having landed they made short work of the enemy pillboxes and in so doing opened the way for the remainder of the battalion to cross.

For 1st Battalion the crossing was less straightforward. Company C made the far bank but then came under heavy fire. Fortunately in the darkness the enemy was unable to discern any clear targets and was thus only able to fire blind. The tracer fire, however, gave the attackers a clear idea of the enemy dispositions and drawing on their experience of assaulting concrete defences in the Orscholz Switch Line the pillboxes were systematically silenced. The tenaciousness of C Company paved the way for another company to cross the river, while the final company, due to lack of boats, crossed downstream using 3rd Battalion's boats – as did 2nd Battalion.

Through the bridgeheads secured by 94th Division, the tanks of 10th Armored Division poured. SHAEF had stipulated that this division was to be held in reserve to meet any unforeseen eventualities[111] and as such it was only available to Patton until 25 February.[112] The division therefore had to be employed at the earliest opportunity and it was imperative that it made quick gains, which it did. Combat Command A smashed its way to the confluence of the Saar and the Moselle to ensure that any defenders remaining in the West Wall positions along the Saar could not fall back and defend Trier, while another task force and CCB headed for Trier itself. In front of them lay dense concentrations of pillboxes protecting the ancient city. But 2nd Mountain Division, which had been rushed forward to meet the threat, arrived too late to man the defences and 10th Armored Division entered the city on 1 March.

'The Orscholz Switch, the Saar-Moselle triangle, Trier, and the heavily fortified section of the West Wall around Trier – all were taken. With the success of the operation the Third Army had torn a gaping hole in the West Wall from Pruem to a point below Saarburg.'[113] But, despite his success, Patton was denied the opportunity to cross the Rhine. Instead, Third Army was ordered to eliminate the last major German concentration to the west of the Rhine – the so-called Saar-Palatinate triangle.[14] The area was heavily fortified along the German border with thick belts of pillboxes and bunkers running from Trier through Saarbrücken to the Rhine. These defences had deterred the French five years previous and now stood in the path of General Patch's Seventh Army.

In clearing the Saar-Moselle Triangle, General Walker's XX Corps had already pierced the West Wall around Trier, which offered Patton an excellent opportunity to outflank these defences. Of course, Third Army also had a foothold in the West Wall around Saarlautern from advances in December.[115] Utilising these incursions, Third Army was to drive east so as to outflank this part of the West Wall, while the three corps of Seventh Army applied pressure all along the front from Saarbrücken to Hagenau, but with the main thrust delivered along the Kaiserlautern Corridor.

General Patch was a much more cautious and measured commander than Patton and he believed that to break the West Wall fortifications on his front, which it should be remembered were still largely intact and manned by units of the First Army, which were in reasonable shape, he would need to launch a setpiece attack. This would require not only reserves of men and matériel but would also necessitate slight changes to unit boundaries, all of which would take time. Thus, Patch had no plans to attack before 15 March.

Patton, by contrast, was determined to keep the German forces opposite him off-balance and in so doing hopefully increase his chances of success. He therefore planned to launch his attack on 12 March with the aim of advancing to the River Nahe which it was agreed would be the boundary between the Third and Seventh Armies.[116]

Patton's attack was swift and in strength and by 16 March, before the bulk of Seventh Army had reached the West Wall, lead elements of Third Army had reached the River Nahe. Patton now not only threatened to annihilate the German Seventh Army but also to cut off General Foertsch's First Army in the West Wall. This possibility had not escaped the note of Eisenhower and the Allied High Command and on 17 March Ike gave permission to Patton to exploit the situation; he was to strike for the Rhine and cut off the German troops holding the West Wall in front of Patch's Seventh Army. Given his head, Patton pressed ahead with his eastward advance and with German resistance melting like snow before the sun, the first of his units – 90th Division – reached Mainz on the Rhine by 20 March.

The situation for the German First Army was now critical. Forbidden to withdraw across the Rhine by order of the Führer unless forced to do so, General Foertsch's troops faced being enveloped. However, the intransigence of the German High Command in respect of withdrawal had softened a little by this stage and units were able to pull back if they were threatened with encirclement and annihilation. Thus, units of First Army manning the defences in the western portion of the West Wall were withdrawn. This enabled troops of the Seventh Army to finally pierce the West Wall and plans were put in place to exploit this gap and outflank the defences to the east. But General Foertsch was wise to this and withdrew XIII SS Corps which for two days had held the advance of XV Corps. This left only XC Corps holding the eastern stretch of the line; two understrength Volks Grenadier divisions and an infantry training division against the five divisions of VI Corps. Yet, just as had been the case on the rest of First Army's front, 'it was less the hard fighting of the VI Corps that would determine when the West Wall would be pierced than it was the rampaging thrusts of the Third Army . . . in the German rear.'[117]

And so it proved to be. When VI Corps attacked on 21 March it found that most positions had been abandoned. By the following day defence of the Saar-Palatinate was all but over. Some fanatical troops continued to fight on in the pillboxes of the West Wall, but those who could had retired, fighting a rearguard action until, on 23 March, they were finally given permission to withdraw across the Rhine to fight in the ultimate *Götterdämmerungschlacht*.

RELIEF

By the first week in March the Siegfried Line was little more than an uncomfortable memory; and, on 7 March, it became an irrelevance when Hodges's First Army captured the Ludendorff Bridge at Remagen. Troops were soon pouring across the Rhine, the last major obstacle between the Allies and victory.

Winston Churchill flanked by, left to right, Field Marshals Montgomery and Brooke, with Maj Gen Simpson, examine dragon's teeth of the Siegfried Line near Aachen. (Imperial War Museum)

After the war the site of this pillbox was chosen as a German war cemetery and the structure used to mount three imposing crosses. (Author)

In that same week Churchill and Field Marshal Sir Alan Brooke visited the front to congratulate Montgomery, Crerar[118] and Simpson and to discuss the final operations of the campaign with Eisenhower. While he was visiting, Churchill took the opportunity to tour the battlefields and, as the procession passed through a section of the West Wall, Churchill ordered his car to stop, so that he could take a closer look at the dragon's teeth. Addressing the entourage he implored, 'Gentlemen, I'd like to ask you to join me. Let us all urinate on the great West Wall of Germany.' To the assembled pressmen who now jostled for the best shot he suggested that perhaps, 'This is one of those operations connected with this First World War which must not be reproduced graphically.' They obliged. Churchill unzipped his fly and with the other dignitaries duly urinated on the concrete defences. Field Marshal Sir Alan Brooke later recalled the event, commenting wryly that, 'I shall never forget the childish grin of inner satisfaction that spread all over his face as he looked down at this critical moment.' Churchill was clearly relieved in all the senses of the word![119]

Notes

1. The Allied bombing and demolitions by the retreating German forces meant that the rail network was all but unusable.
2. By the end of August it was calculated that over 90 per cent of all the supplies on the Continent could be found in depots near to the Normandy beachhead, although this was partly as a result of the fact that the build up of supplies in Normandy had exceeded expectations.
3. A.D. Chandler Jr. (ed.), *The Papers of Dwight David Eisenhower: The War Years: IV*, p.2124.
4. O.N. Bradley and C. Blair, *A General's Life*, p.321.
5. The V, VII and XIX Corps made up First Army.
6. A reaction that was much in keeping with his moniker 'Lightning Joe'.
7. To make matters worse 2nd SS Panzer Division had no ammunition for its anti-tank guns and artillery pieces.
8. The nickname given to the division by the Germans because of the blood-red keystone insignia and the vicious fighting tactics of the unit during the Normandy campaign.
9. C. B. MacDonald, *United States Army in World War II. The European Theater of Operations: The Siegfried Line Campaign*, p.45.
10. Or in one instance simply shooting at the teeth point blank with the main armament of the tank.
11. The division's nickname comes from the Roman numerals IV – Ivy.
12. The name given to the German 8.8cm Flak which could be used against both air and ground targets.
13. One interested onlooker, reporting for *Collier's*, was Ernest Hemingway. In an article he dispatched in October 1944 he described one instance of how troops of 4th Division cleared one of the pillboxes they encountered. 'The Krauts wouldn't come out when we talked to them. So we pulled the TD [tank destroyer] right up to the back of the steel door we had located by now and that old Wump gun fired about six rounds and blasted the door in and you ought to have heard them wanting to come out. You ought to have heard them yell and moan and scream and yell, 'Kamerad!'. . . They started to come out and you never saw such a mess. Every one of them was wounded in five or six places from pieces of concrete and steel. About eighteen men came out and they got down in the road. They expected to get shot. But we were obliged to disappoint them . . . There were legs and arms scattered all over the place.' C. Whiting, *The Battle for the German Frontier*, p.29.
14. A view shared by General Gerow, the corps commander.
15. It was already becoming clear, however, that air support was unlikely to have as significant an impact in the battle for the West Wall. Troops of 22nd Infantry that witnessed a sortie by P47 fighter-bombers noted, 'The bombs hit smack on top of the seven-foot-thick concrete-and-steel pillboxes. From our angle we could see no damage at all. No roofs were caved, no huge cracks appeared. Probably the Jerries had hellish headaches from concussion, but nothing was visible. All the great show did was raise dust.' G. Astor, *The Bloody Forest. Battle for the Huertgen: September 1944–January 1945*, p.51.
16. Elements of 85th Reconnaissance Squadron had crossed the Our River in the vicinity of Gemünd on 11 September. Unbeknown to them they had crossed the river in full view of an enemy pillbox which fortunately was unmanned. As it transpired none of the eighty or so pillboxes that they inspected were occupied.
17. C. Messenger, *The Last Prussian: A Biography of Field Marshal Gerd von Rundstedt 1875–1953*, p.206.
18. S. Westphal, *The German Army in the West*, p.174.
19. One pillbox was hit by approximately fifty rounds from a tank destroyer and appeared to have been silenced, but its crew resumed firing when the infantry started forward again. When eventually called on to surrender one of the defenders replied, 'Go to hell – we'll fight it out!' The twelve-man crew later surrendered somewhat dazed and confused as a result of the concussion of the shells hitting the shelter.
20. It was subsequently found that the easiest and quickest solution to the problem of dragon's teeth was to dismantle the gates or remove the I beams that were used where the dragon's teeth intersected with roads. In one instance even this proved unnecessary because the steel gate had not been locked!

21. An after-action report (probably reflecting the experiences of 3rd Armored Division, although this is not explicit – WO219/5129) written at the time implies that engineers constructed the ramp, but the author has adopted the description of events quoted in the Official US History and the Divisional History.
22. A hollow charge anti-tank weapon.
23. This reaction was not surprising. Many of the defenders were often boys or old men. The occupant of one shelter later confessed that he was told he was required simply to clean out the shelters prior to their occupation by regular troops only to find himself embroiled in the fighting. There were even reports of women being found in the blockhouses but whether these women actually took part in the fighting or were simply sheltering there is unclear.
24. The bunkers of the West Wall were generally able to mount nothing larger than the 3.7cm Pak. Thus, anti-tank guns (and self-propelled guns) tended to be deployed in well-camouflaged field positions which were extremely difficult to spot. However, once they opened fire and revealed their position they were easily dealt with by artillery and infantry assault.
25. Capt. J. B. Mittelman, *Eight Stars to Victory: A History of the Veteran Ninth US Infantry Division*, p.242.
26. *Ibid*, p.247.
27. C.B. MacDonald, *op. cit*, p.94.
28. In fact much of the fighting was for the Roetgen and Wenau forests, but to the GI on the ground one evergreen forest looked much like another.
29. The 15th Engineer Combat Battalion received a Distinguished Unit Citation for the dangerous work that they undertook in the period to 23 October.
30. Although on at least one occasion they had to resort to an alternative solution. When 39th Infantry was attacking Lammersdorf on 16 September they came across a pillbox that seemed impregnable. A prisoner was brought forward to plead with the occupants to surrender but they would not and were entombed by a dozer.
31. P.R. Mansoor, *The GI Offensive in Europe: The Triumph of American Infantry Divisions, 1941–1945*, p.187.
32. S. Westphal, *op. cit*, p.176.
33. G. Blumentritt, *Von Rundstedt: The Soldier and the Man*, p.254.
34. The nickname given to General Corlett at West Point because he was raised in Colorado.
35. 2nd Armored Division on the left wing and 30th Division on the right.
36. The division was named in honour of President Andrew Jackson whose nickname this was.
37. This unnerved the veterans of 30th Division who well remembered the casualties incurred as a result of 'friendly fire' in this operation.
38. The 3rd Battalion of 120th Infantry Regiment in Division reserve, however, was able to spend most of its time honing its assault skills.
39. According to the history of the 30th Infantry Division French and British intelligence from before the war provided the location of 90 per cent of the pillboxes on the division's front.
40. This expedient was not without its dangers, however, because it meant that the crew, normally used to the relative safety of a position some miles behind the front, was now up at the sharp end and very vulnerable to enemy fire in an open fighting compartment.
41. Indeed, the bombing was so ineffectual – even the use of napalm – that prisoners captured later and interrogated about the effect of the aerial bombing, asked, 'What bombing?'
42. A captured German officer later admitted that machine gun crews in the pillboxes were often reluctant to open the loophole to fire because of the possibility of being shot.
43. R.L. Hewitt, *Work Horse of the Western Front: The Story of the 30th Infantry Division*, p.115.
44. The engagement was also famous for the report from one of the regiments that they had 'Fired at haystack with machine gun. Shots bounced off.' *Ibid*, p.112.
45. During the attack by Task Force 2 Sgt. Ezra Cook, after capturing a pillbox, found the telephone still in working order and called the occupants in the next pillbox and convinced them to surrender.
46. The tanks had had to retire to re-arm and undergo emergency maintenance.
47. C.B. MacDonald, *op. cit*, p.279.

48. H.R. Knickerbocker *et al*, *Danger Forward: The Story of the First Divisions in World War II*, p.278.
49. *Ibid*, p.279.
50. Captain Brown, a company commander, despite being wounded three times, personally led the attack on Crucifix Hill and knocked out three pillboxes himself and was later awarded the Medal of Honor.
51. C.B. MacDonald, *op. cit*, p.287.
52. General Simpson's Ninth Army was initially squeezed into the front line on the right of the First Army but at the end of October 1944 was redeployed to the left flank and to the south of the Second British Army.
53. The Germans had also suffered heavily – 1,300 prisoners and 1,500–2,000 casualties.
54. Responsibility for the capture now fell to V Corps because VII Corps was to launch the main drive to the River Roer and an attack on Schmidt would have drained its strength. This necessitated a temporary adjustment to the boundary between the two corps.
55. Despite the fact that they had been reinforced by 12th Infantry from 4th Division.
56. And where no pillboxes existed emplacements had been fashioned out of logs that proved to be almost equally difficult to capture.
57. The dense forest, the lack of suitable roads and mines prevented any armour getting forward.
58. C.B. MacDonald, *op. cit*, p.372.
59. A.D. Chandler Jr (ed.), *op. cit*, p.2257.
60. The port had been captured on 4 September, but the first shipment was not docked until 28 November.
61. Eisenhower was unaware of the enormous efforts to which Hitler was going to raise a new army in the west so that by December he would be ready to launch the Ardennes offensive.
62. Gen. W. Warlimont, *Inside Hitler's Headquarters 1939–45*, p.479.
63. It was deemed prudent to attack the town in a pincer movement but under the direction of one army, even if this meant that an American division was temporarily attached to the British Second Army.
64. The 'funnies' included Crocodiles – flame-throwing tanks; Flails – Shermans with a spindle extension in front with heavy chains that rotated and beat the ground discharging any mines they came into contact with; and AVREs (Armoured Vehicle Royal Engineers) carrying Petards – powerful explosive charges that were fired like a mortar and specifically designed for the demolition of concrete defences.
65. Rain had turned the roads and tracks into a quagmire and together with the danger of mines made progress all but impossible. Major John Semken, commander of A Squadron Sherwood Rangers Yeomanry, had three tanks destroyed by mines under him. Neither his crew nor he suffered any physical injuries, but after the third mine detonation he was reported as missing. The unit padre later found him in a captured pillbox very 'bomb happy'. He later recovered and helped the Sherwood Rangers Yeomanry become the first British unit through the Siegfried Line.
66. C.B. MacDonald, *op. cit*, p.554.
67. *Ibid*, p.555.
68. The Combat Lessons Branch produced 'Battle Experiences' and 'Immediate Reports'. The former was designed to provide units with up-to-date information on, among other things, assaulting pillboxes.
69. See Chapter 5, Desperation, Footnote 16.
70. Indeed, the defences of the West Wall around Saarbrücken were considered to be so strong that to aid Third Army's advance the Allied High Command again considered the possibility of an airborne operation somewhere in the area behind the line between Merzig and Pirmasens. A paper written on 3 November 1944 which discussed the operation, codenamed Operation 'Choker 1', considered various drop and landing zones, but concluded that they were too scattered and too near to built-up industrial areas, so the idea was dropped. PRO, WO219/2891 Operation 'Choker I': to assist in attack on the Siegfried Line from rear of Saarbrücken, November 1944.
71. The position had been constructed on the assumption that Luxembourg would remain neutral, which was no longer the case.
72. The other elements being two service companies which had been converted to infantry, a fortress machine-gun battalion and a battalion of engineers.

73. It should be noted, however, that during 22 November, 416th Division was reinforced with armoured infantry from 21st Panzer Division.

74. The 90th Division was also known as the Alamo Division.

75. H. M. Cole, *United States Army in World War II. The European Theater of Operations: The Lorraine Campaign* (Center of Military History, United States Army, Washington, 1950), p.496.

76. The defences at this point were the thickest along the entire border.

77. J. Colby, *War From the Ground Up: The 90th Division in World War II*, p.326.

78. By this time 28th Division had been relieved and its place taken by 8th Division which was at full-strength.

79. Poor visibility prevented any air attacks.

80. O.N. Bradley and C. Blair, *op. cit*, p.342.

81. F.H. Hinsley, *British Intelligence in the Second World War, Its Influence on Strategy and Operations,* 4 Vols, p.407.

82. A presumption no doubt helped by Hitler's careful choice of codename – 'Wacht am Rhein' (Watch on the Rhine) – with its defensive connotations.

83. Dietrich's attack to the north had been blunted and Manteuffel's success was recognised too late to reinforce it.

84. Hitler drew parallels between the reticence of some to back the continuation of the offensive and the less than wholehearted support he received in 1939 and 1940 for his offensive strategy. '. . . I was told verbally and in writing that the thing could not be done, that it was impossible . . . we've built the Siegfried Line so why don't we let the enemy bang his head against it and then possibly attack him afterwards? . . . It's exactly the same today. Our relative strength is no less than it was in 1939 or 1940. On the contrary if in these two attacks we succeed in destroying both these American groupings then the balance will swing clearly and finally in our favour . . . ' Gen. W. Warlimont, *op. cit*, p.492.

85. Men of the 101st Airborne Division who were rushed to the front at the start of the German offensive and who were subsequently cut off.

86. D. Eisenhower, *Crusade in Europe*, p.378.

87. Gen. W. Warlimont, *op. cit*, p.506.

88. In a report on 6 March Westphal, von Rundstedt's Chief of Staff, gave an equally blunt assessment of the value of the West Wall which further infuriated the Führer.

89. S. Westphal, *op. cit*, p.194.

90. The fortification of Goch continued until the town was attacked. It was defended by two anti-tank ditches, mines, barbed wire and a series of concrete pillboxes with steel embrasures.

91. W.D and S. Whitaker, *Rhineland The Battle to End the War*, p.64.

92. Which was more than the 1st Rifle Brigade did, much to the disappointment of Brigadier Wingfield, commander of 22nd Armoured Brigade.

93. Imperial War Museum, 89/13/1, Mason, Lieutenant W.E.

94. H. R. Knickerbocker et al, *op. cit*, p.349.

95. Capt. J. B. Mittelman, *op. cit*, p.300.

96. M. Blumenson, *The Patton Papers 1940–1945*, p.613.

97. In private, however, he was little more reticent. In a letter to Beatrice (his wife) on 28 January he informed her of the start of a new attack, but concluded the paragraph 'Unfortunately we have to storm the Siegfried Line as a starter', *Ibid*, p.630.

98. Middleton had relinquished command of 45th Division because of arthritis in his knee, but Eisenhower had requested his return, telling General George Marshall, Army Chief of Staff, that, 'I don't give a damn about his knees, I want his head and his heart. And I'll take him into battle on a litter if we have to.'

99. This section of the front was held by under-strength Volks Grenadier divisions, with the regular units withdrawn to refit or to meet the expected attack further north. To make matters worse the line of the VIII Corps' advance was along an inter-army boundary between LXVI Corps of Fifth Panzer Army and XIII Corps of Seventh Army in the south.

100. The 4th Division by this time was already through the main defences of the West Wall. The

division's reward for breaching the line was to be withdrawn and sent to another sector of the front to repeat the feat. This they did with the help of 'Iron Mike' – the name given to the awesome 155mm gun on the self-propelled gun carriage.

101. During the engagement men of the 357th Infantry Regiment were the victims of a new and unsavoury German tactic. German defenders would withdraw from their pillboxes and allow the GIs to advance. Almost immediately these positions would come under heavy and accurate artillery and *nebelwerfer* fire which forced the infantry to seek shelter in the only safe haven available – the recently vacated pillboxes. Once inside they found that the enemy covered their only escape route; they were trapped. Whole platoons were decimated before the men learned that it was safer outside the bunker than in.

102 H.D. Steward, *Thunderbolt: The History of the Eleventh Armored Division*, After Action Report.

103. After crossing the Sauer and fighting its way through one of the most densely fortified sections of the Siegfried Line, the Onaway Division was faced with the daunting task of storming the 'Katzenkopf' position that barred its way to the Rhine. The Katzenkopf was one of the biggest bunkers constructed by the German army and although not bristling with weaponry – one of Hitler's criticisms of such positions – it certainly posed a significant challenge to anyone who was foolhardy enough to attack it, boasting in its arsenal machine guns, a mortar and retractable flamethrower. In the end the defenders of the fortress slipped away into the darkness and the men of 76th Division captured one of the most powerful works of the Siegfried Line without a fight.

104. As commander of XIII Corps, and a subordinate of Brandenberger, he had asked to withdraw in the face of Middleton's attack.

105. H. M. Cole, *op. cit*, p.115.

106. The division was originally nicknamed the Pilgrim Division when formed in the First World War, but when the division was reactivated it had lost its New England identity and received a new sleeve insignia, but no new nickname.

107. The division included within its ranks high school graduates fresh out of class, rear echelon troops integrated into units as makeshift infantrymen, or men out of the stockades.

108. 8th Armored Division was a green unit and had only been attached to Third Army for combat training.

109. *Ibid*, p.127.

110. A veteran of the battle (R. Kingsbury of E Company 376th Infantry) candidly conceded that in his opinion if all the pillboxes had been manned the attack would, in all likelihood, have been unsuccessful. However, sufficient empty pillboxes existed to allow the regiment to advance avoiding direct attacks on manned positions which tended to result in heavy casualties.

111. The Allies had almost been embarrassed by the Ardennes counter-attack and Eisenhower was determined to avoid a repeat by maintaining a strategic reserve.

112. Patton subsequently secured a further extension of 48 hours and thereafter Bradley avoided the telephone so that SHAEF could not contact him to withdraw 10th Armored Division.

113. *Ibid*, p.134.

114. The Moselle formed the left-hand edge and the Rhine the right with the French/German border the base.

115. Patton had not been able to exploit the foothold because of the need to stem the German advance in the Ardennes.

116. Although Patton made it clear to his corps commanders that should the opportunity arise they were to strike for the Rhine.

117 *Ibid*, p.262.

118. The Commander in Chief of 1st Canadian Army.

119. On March 2 Patton had visited Bitburg and had seen the West Wall for the first time. In his diary he wrote, '...I have seen the dragon's teeth, a useless form of amusement.' M. Blumenson, *op. cit*, p.651. No doubt relieved that his confident predictions of September had finally been realised.

Conclusion

Gunter and Hagen placed the dead body in front of Kriemhilde's door in the castle. She found him cold and rigid on her threshold, when she was about to go to church in the morning. With a loud cry she sank to the floor.

From the Rhine Saga 'Siegfried and Kriemhilde'

In the period immediately after the First World War, Germany was a shadow of the imperial power that had threatened the status quo in Europe in 1914. Emasculated by the victorious powers at Versailles and weakened from four years of war, she posed no threat to those states that shared a common border. As the years passed the fledgling democracy restored the country's industrial, economic and (surreptitiously) military strength and worked to ease the restrictions imposed on her under the terms of the Paris peace settlement. As the fortunes of the sleeping giant were revived, neighbouring states took steps to guarantee their security. Alliances were signed and, almost without exception, concrete fortifications were erected along their respective frontiers. France established the mighty Maginot Line and provided advice and expertise to Czechoslovakia so that she

Block 2 of Fort Eben Emael as viewed today. It originally mounted two 60mm cannons. (Author)

could construct her own, albeit much smaller, border defences.[1] The Netherlands and Belgium also invested heavily in concrete and steel, perhaps most notably Fort Eben Emael that protected the strategically important Albert Canal. Even Poland, which had always seen the Soviet Union as the major threat, latterly built a series of fortifications on her western border to deter any possible German aggression.

In the final analysis, the time, money and effort invested in these defences realised a meagre return. At best their contribution to the defence of these countries was inconsequential and at worst it was deleterious. The majority of the Czech defences were constructed in the Sudetenland, which was ceded to Germany as part of the Munich agreement in September 1938. In the following March the rest of the country was occupied without any of the defences being tested in combat.[2] The Polish defences enjoyed some success but they were far from complete and did not seriously slow, let alone stop, the German advance. The Dutch defences were subdued by a mixture of deception and airborne assault, while the more elaborate Belgian fortifications, although providing a sterner test, similarly failed to stem the irresistible German attack. Even the immensely strong defences of Fort Eben Emael, the jewel in Belgium's defensive crown, were quickly overwhelmed by a daring and highly publicised paratrooper attack. In the end '. . . most of Belgium's defensive positions proved of no significant value.'[3]

The failure of the Belgian and Dutch defences to stem the German *blitzkrieg* left France's northern border dangerously exposed to attack. This had not been fortified for fear of upsetting her neighbour, with whom she had a strategic alliance, and little progress had been made in extending the Maginot Line to cover this vulnerable portion

A munitions train transports victorious German soldiers on a tour around the Hackenberg fort of the Maginot Line, August 1940. (Bundesarchiv)

of the front when Belgium effectively adopted a neutral status. The German army now sliced through this lightly fortified section, leaving the garrisons ensconced in the major forts of the Maginot Line as little more than interested onlookers. Some small-scale attacks were launched against the defences but they were not crucial to the outcome of the battle for France. When the end came many of the forts were still intact, their troops determined to fight on until ordered to surrender by their superiors.

To many commentators, both at the time and in later appraisals, the inconsiderable part played by fortifications in the initial engagements of the war proved that they were little more than expensive white elephants. Undoubtedly, this argument has some merit in respect of the defences constructed by France and her allies. It is more difficult, however, to apply this logic to the West Wall as one historian has endeavoured to do, postulating that, 'when war came the Maginot Line fulfilled its limited purpose admirably, while the Germans never reaped any substantial military benefit from the West Wall.'[4] Certainly, the fortifications of the West Wall were not tested at the outset, but to assert that the West Wall did not benefit Germany is to miss the point. The West Wall was constructed as a deterrent against possible attack in the west while Hitler realised his aims in the east. In this regard it was most successful and the same author later concedes as much noting that, 'whatever its shortcomings in 1938 the West Wall served Hitler's purpose for the Anglo-French allies were mightily impressed.'[5] Indeed, the western powers were so concerned at the potential for casualties should they launch a frontal attack against the Siegfried Line that they demurred. As such the West Wall was instrumental in solving the perennial problem of war on two fronts and enabled Hitler to conquer much of Continental Europe.

In the dark days that followed the end of the First World War such a coup seemed impossible. In the Hall of Mirrors at Versailles the victors had decided that as well as drastically reducing the size of Germany's armed forces, her western border was to be demilitarised, there was to be an army of occupation and, to ensure that Germany complied with the terms of the peace settlement, a series of control commissions were to be created, including one specifically tasked with administering issues associated with fortifications.

As time passed the raw, open wounds left by the war healed and the Draconian restrictions imposed on Germany were eased. The army of occupation was withdrawn as were the control commissions. However, limitations relating to Germany's armed forces were retained and she was still prohibited from building fortifications in the Rhineland, despite the fact that since 1929 France had been busily building a massive bulwark which was clearly aimed at, and visible from, Germany. The building of the Maginot Line and the failure of the western powers to disarm as they had promised rankled with the Germans, especially the nationalists. It was no surprise therefore that when one of the most extreme nationalist parties, the National Socialists, came to power it was bent on remedying these injustices. Conscription was reintroduced, the armed forces were modernised and expanded and, most controversially, the Rhineland was remilitarised. Soon thereafter work on rudimentary border defences began with the introduction of the *Pioneerprogramm*. Generally, the fortifications were small in scale but were built in considerable depth, drawing heavily on the lessons learned in the First World War. They were constructed under the aegis of the army with the building work contracted out to private companies. Progress was unremarkable in what was considered a long-term plan to fortify the western frontier. Initially, Hitler was unperturbed, but it soon became clear that if he were to realise his aims in the east there would need to be a significant increase in both the speed and scale of the project. This led to the inauguration of the *Limesprogramm* in May 1938 and later that year the *Aachen-Saar programm*. Believing that such an undertaking in the timescale required was beyond the capability of the army Hitler passed responsibility for the West Wall to Fritz Todt, the architect of the new German motorway network. The army retained responsibility for all the tactical input, but this only served to generate friction between the two which was exacerbated by Hitler's constant interference. The disharmony and challenging targets meant that the shelters were often poorly designed and constructed or were sited so that they were unable to provide all-round defence.

These shortcomings were well known in France and Britain despite the best efforts of the German security forces and the image portrayed by Goebbels's Propaganda Ministry of an impregnable concrete barrier. Yet the western democracies were reluctant to call Hitler's bluff. The reasons behind this reticence stem, in the main, from the First World War and the overriding desire in France and Britain to avoid another European conflict. Thus the respective governments in Paris and London went to tremendous lengths to appease Germany which culminated in the Munich agreement. When this failed to satiate Hitler they were left with no alternative but to declare war.

The fateful decision taken, the French army boldly advanced towards the Siegfried Line in accordance with its agreement with Poland. However, the Saar Offensive, as it was grandly called, was small in scale and although perhaps launched with the best of intentions was little more than a sop to Poland rather than a genuine attempt to smash the West Wall. The advance was halted and soon thereafter the troops were withdrawn from their exposed positions to the relative safety of the Maginot Line. The possibility of further offensive action was not completely discounted, however, despite the accepted wisdom that a successful defensive campaign, as it had done in the last war, would sap the enemy morale and lead to victory. Papers were drafted, views were passed backwards and forwards between the defence ministries and committees were formed to consider the various issues that arose. Political expediency and geography dictated where the blow would have to fall, but the strategy to be adopted and when an attack might be launched required further consideration.

In the end two potential strategies were developed – 'destruction' and 'surprise'. The former entailed using a massive artillery bombardment in the hope of destroying the enemy defences and creating the conditions suitable for the infantry and tanks to exploit. The latter entailed the development of weapons specifically designed to overcome the defences, as had been the case in the last war when the Hindenburg Line had been undone by the introduction of the tank.

Seemingly neither strategy could be implemented immediately: to deliver a barrage of sufficient magnitude to destroy the Siegfried Line would require the production of even greater numbers of weapons, while a surprise attack necessitated the development and mass production of new weapons. Both alternatives would take time, but that was a commodity that was in short supply. By the time the briefing papers had been written and discussed, by the time the committees had been formed and the terms of reference agreed it was too late. Poland was defeated and the might of the *Wehrmacht* had been transferred to the west where it was readied to launch lightning war on the ill-prepared and uncoordinated forces of the western powers.

In point of fact the British and French had weapons in 1939 that, on paper at least, were capable of shattering the German fortifications. A number of guns were powerful enough to destroy the German bunkers, they had flamethrowers and explosives, and mine countermeasures had also been developed. Indeed, they were equipped with almost everything that the Americans had when they attacked the Siegfried Line in 1944. They lacked the ground attack aircraft but these played a limited role in the later fighting because of the difficulty of hitting such small targets and the poor weather. With the benefit of hindsight it is easy to conclude that a genuine attempt should have been made to breach the German border defences in 1939. However, the French and British High Commands lacked confidence in their own ability and that of their men, nor was there a political will to attack. As such they resorted to type and a defensive psychosis gripped the political and military leadership. In so doing they forgot Napoleon's maxim that the side that stays within its fortifications is beaten, and so it proved to be. France was defeated and Britain stood almost alone. Another four years would pass before the Tommies, now supported by millions of GIs from the United States, would return to the European mainland and this time the West Wall might actually be tested and a genuine attempt made to 'hang out the washing'.

In the interim the fortifications on Germany's western frontier were stripped of their weapons and fittings and then largely abandoned. The Führer now turned his attention to an even more impressive line of defences along the coast of occupied Europe, but the power of the Allied invasion force proved irresistible. Still Hitler refrained from renovating the border defences for fear of generating panic, but with the fall of Paris he succumbed to the inevitable. The original defences were readied for action and new, often improvised, fortifications were constructed. This work continued, in spite of the difficulty and danger, throughout the battle for the Siegfried Line. To man the defences men were conscripted from all sections of the community, irrespective of age or ability. Realistically, it was never going to be possible in a few weeks to construct a series of defences capable of defeating a modern, mechanised army with unrivalled air superiority and certainly not when the positions were manned by a 'people's army', with little in the way of heavy equipment and short of supplies of ammunition and fuel. Certainly the Allied High Command thought so, with Patton a particularly strong critic. He described the Siegfried Line as, among other things, '. . . a monument to human stupidity. When natural obstacles – oceans and mountains – can be so readily overcome, anything that man makes, man can overcome.' In spite of such declarations, the soldier on the ground often harboured misgivings and the thoughts of one GI quoted in *Yank Magazine* echoed the sentiments of many. 'I don't care if the guy behind that gun is a syphilitic prick who's a hundred years old – he's still sitting behind eight feet of concrete and he's still got enough fingers to press triggers and shoot bullets.'

As it transpired, the pessimism of the infantryman on the ground proved more prescient than the optimism displayed by the general in the rear. The first attempt to 'bounce' the line was made in September and was to set a worrying precedent for the later battles. With little in the way of reserves either in terms of supplies or men Hodges's First Army took a gamble in the knowledge that the defences were only lightly held. The gamble failed and Eisenhower turned his attention to Operation Market Garden, the daring airborne operation to outflank the Siegfried Line. Initially reports emanating from the Netherlands were positive, but gradually it became clear that the plan had also failed and a concerted effort would be needed to smash Hitler's West Wall. Thus in late autumn a series of attacks were launched to breach the defences, but each was rebuffed with heavy casualties. 'Time and again they attacked the wall on four different national frontiers many miles apart. Repeatedly they were repulsed, suffering substantial losses. Platoons surrendered, companies were wiped out, whole battalions fled in disorder. Divisions were decimated in a matter of days, losing thousands of men for a few paltry square yards of useless terrain.'[6]

Of course it would be an oversimplification to heap all the praise for the so-called 'Miracle in the West', on the West Wall. A number of other key factors played a crucial role. Firstly, the Americans were not prepared to assault the defences of the Siegfried Line. Most units had received rudimentary training for attacking fortified positions when based at their respective camps in the United States, but losses during the invasion of Normandy and the subsequent pursuit meant that few veterans remained in the front line. The speed of the advance meant that this deficiency could not be easily rectified. Thus, the men of 4th, 9th and 28th Infantry Divisions and 3rd and 5th Armored Divisions had to learn the hard way, which inevitably resulted in higher casualty figures. The performance of American units did improve, but a failure to properly disseminate the lessons learned from the earlier fighting meant that the likes of 84th Infantry Division in its attack on Geilenkirchen in November 1944 and 94th Infantry Division in its attack on the Siegfried Switch Line in February 1945 made many of the same mistakes that their compatriots had in September.

This problem was exacerbated by a lack of intelligence. Many of the bunkers of the West Wall had been carefully disguised as houses or other structures and those that had not had now blended seamlessly into the landscape after four years of neglect. This rendered aerial reconnaissance useless and meant the Allies had to rely on British and French intelligence gathered before the war, which, not surprisingly, was less than perfect.[7] The infantry on the ground had to hope that the preliminary bombardment, if it did not destroy the enemy positions, would at least remove any camouflage and expedite any assault. If not, a burst of tracer fire from a machine-gun might pinpoint a target as the shells ricocheted off the concrete. If all else failed the grunts would have to advance blind and hope that the enemy was asleep or the positions were empty. Fortunately, this was often the case.

This bunker at Hechelsheid was camouflaged by means of a house that was built on top. The house was inhabited by civilians and was still used after the war. (Public Record Office)

The lack of troops to man the positions was a major headache for the German High Command, but von Rundstedt, never a fan of the defences, seemed to thrive on the challenge and his generalship was another factor in the ponderous advance of the Allies. In September 1944 he was again given command of the German forces in the west after his enforced sabbatical. He soon moulded the shattered remnants of the German army that had escaped from the debacle in France and the newly conscripted raw recruits into a cohesive fighting force. The wily *Feldmarschall* then deployed the limited resources at his disposal to check Allied incursions and frustrate their attempts to breakthrough the Siegfried Line.

However, it is still extremely unlikely that the Germans would have held the West Wall positions as long as they did, even with von Rundstedt's inspired leadership, if it had not been for the Allies' logistical difficulties. As the first American units reached the outworks of the West Wall, which were predominantly unmanned, reserves of fuel and ammunition were almost exhausted. Supplies still had to be brought across the landing beaches or through Cherbourg, the only major port captured up to that point. Hitler had recognised the importance of deep-water ports to the success of the Allies' advance and had ordered local commanders to defend them to the last man and, when capture seemed inevitable, to put them out of commission, which they did with a remarkable degree of success. Soon whole armies had to pause as shortages began to bite. By December the supply situation was much improved, but with the weather deteriorating and the troops exhausted after six months of hard fighting, large-scale operations were suspended as Eisenhower and his generals reconsidered their strategy. But just as they contemplated their next move, the Germans struck in the Ardennes.

Having carefully nursed his dwindling resources of men, tanks, fuel and ammunition, Hitler launched his last-gasp effort to wrest the initiative from the Allies in the west. The Battle of the Bulge, as it became known, gave Hitler a series of Pyrrhic victories as the inexperienced American troops stationed in the Ardennes were overwhelmed by élite SS and Panzer units and retreated in some disarray. However, Hitler's army could not maintain the momentum. With little fuel and a break in the weather allowing Allied aircrews to wreak havoc, Hitler's storm-troops were held up well short of their ultimate goal. Few were able to escape the carnage and none of the heavy equipment made it back

German prisoners of war are marched to the rear through dragon's teeth of the Siegfried Line. (Imperial War Museum)

to German lines. With the last reserves of men and matériel expended the West Wall could not be effectively manned and, as Machiavelli noted more than four hundred years before, '. . . fortresses without good armies are incompetent for defence'.[8] And so it transpired. In the first months of 1945 the Allies cut through the defences with relative ease and once they were across the Rhine the sections of the West Wall still in German hands had to be abandoned.

The West Wall, like the Atlantic Wall and the defensive lines in Italy and the East had been conquered. Never designed to repel an enemy attack indefinitely and with no prospect of relief, the forces manning the hopelessly outdated defences could do no more than delay the inevitable. This they did with a remarkable degree of success. Indeed, not only did this multifarious force manning the West Wall stop the Allied advance – in the three months after entering Germany the Allies' deepest penetration was 22 miles – it also inflicted terrible casualties on the Allies.[9] Moreover, it enabled Hitler to establish a powerful strike-force which was used in the Ardennes counter-offensive. Had Hitler decided against launching his ill-starred offensive and instead fully manned the defences the battle for the Siegfried Line would have been far more costly. Fortunately he did not, and many veterans of the campaign have lived long and fulfilling lives as a consequence.

Notes

1. Known as the 'Benes Line'.
2. A number were subsequently destroyed by the Germans as they tested the effects of artillery and anti-tank guns on this type of fortification, which they hoped would provide useful lessons if it proved necessary to assault the Maginot Line.
3. J.E. Kaufmann and R.M. Jurga, *Fortress Europe – European Fortifications in World War II*, p.118.
4. T. Taylor, *Munich: The Price of Peace*, p.109.
5. *Ibid*, p.689.
6. C. Whiting, *West Wall: The Battle for Hitler's Siegfried Line*, p.xiv.
7. However, in at least one instance pre-war intelligence proved invaluable, identifying 90 per cent of the pillboxes on 30th Division's front.
8. Niccolo Machiavelli, *Discorsi XXIV,* 1531.
9. In the Siegfried Line Campaign (up until the Ardennes offensive) First Army alone suffered 7,024 killed, 35,155 wounded and 4,860 missing and captured. It is estimated that total American battle casualties in this period were in the region of 68,000 with a similar number of non-battle casualties (frost-bite, fatigue etc).

Postscript

Some of the castles again became ruins, and their remnants look nowadays as witnesses of a varied history upon the hurried visitor. Other castles are still in very good condition, and they can still be visited.

Father Rhine Tells His Sagas

During the battle for the Siegfried Line countless bunkers, pillboxes and dragon's teeth were destroyed. The fate of many was sealed during the fighting itself, but many more were demolished in the lull that followed in order to ensure that the defences could not be reused by the enemy should they launch a successful counter-attack. The importance of this pre-emptive measure was learned very early on. In the first engagements of the battle in September 1944 engineers of 3rd Armored Division, after piercing the Siegfried Line around Roetgen, destroyed a number of pillboxes and obstacles to prevent their re-occupation and also to identify the best method of reducing such structures.

In the following six months many more of the defences were destined to meet the same end and after the war the destruction continued. Some shelters were blown up out of sheer malice (like the French efforts to destroy the *Katzenkopf*), while others were razed to the ground as the British and Americans conducted experiments on the various structures in order to better understand their strengths and weaknesses. The findings were soon gainfully employed as the Americans demolished countless structures including all the fortifications around Aachen.[1] The postwar scrap metal drive also saw many of the steel turrets and plates removed.

Despite the ravages of war, the best efforts of the occupation forces and postwar development, many of the fortifications survived until relatively recently. However, now the German government has taken it upon itself to destroy the remainder of the West Wall on the pretext that the crumbling fortifications represent a threat to public safety. This has caused a great deal of concern in Germany among local residents, fortification and heritage groups and, somewhat surprisingly, environmental groups.[2] Even more surprisingly, the proposed action of the German government has generated some column inches in the British tabloid press. Not normally one to share the views of Fleet Street's finest, the leader writer in the *Daily Express*, quite correctly, described the plan to fill in bunkers and grind down the dragon's teeth as an act of vandalism that was not only a terrible waste of money but would besmirch the memory of many brave men who lost their lives in the battle for the Siegfried Line.

Undoubtedly, some of the structures may be dangerous but they could be made safe without the need to destroy or bury them. Ironically, at a time when the government in Berlin is embarking on a plan to expunge one of the most visible reminders of the last

One of the bunkers at the Vogeslang prior to demolition (top left), following the detonation of 700lb of explosives in September 1948 (right) and views of the bunker after the dust had settled (bottom left) and today. (Public Record Office)

NEW MOVE TO DEFEND NAZI LINE THAT OUR TROOPS WANTED TO HANG WASHING ON

We'll go to the wall to save the Siegfried

An excerpt from the Daily Express *published in April 2000 detailing the demise of the Siegfried Line.* *(Imperial War Museum)*

war, volunteers in countries that were occupied by Hitler's forces are making efforts to preserve the German fortifications for future generations. Volunteers in Germany have also made efforts to protect sections of the West Wall and have opened a number of small, but very interesting museums, yet they have had to proceed with little or no state help. It is important that this attitude changes and that those few fortifications that remain are preserved and protected not only for their architectural and historical importance, but most importantly as a silent reminder of the brave soldiers on both sides who perished fighting for what they thought was right.

Nazism was not a happy chapter in German history, but it cannot be ignored nor should it be and it is right that there are lasting reminders of the horrors that it brought. With this in mind it is perhaps worth remembering the aphorism that seems to have a greater resonance in this instance, 'Those who do not remember the past are doomed to relive it.'[3] Let us hope not.

Notes

1. However, it was recognised that further reconnaissance would be needed because a number of structures had been discovered by sheer chance. A report written at the time noted that, 'Two such pillboxes were so well camouflaged as cottages that they were not detected at 50ft distance. In addition, one other pillbox provided the foundation for a house and this would not have been detected had not another member of the party entered by a side door.' WO195/8366.
2. Many of the structures have now been colonised by plants, insects, animals and birds.
3. Centre of the History of the Resistance and Deportations, Lyon.

Timeline

	General		West Wall
1919			
January	Victorious powers meet at Versailles		
March	Conditions for German disarmament finalised		
1923			
January	Ruhr occupied by French and Belgian troops		
1925			
September	Treaty of Locarno		
1927			
January	Allied Control Commissions withdrawn		
1929			
	Work on the Maginot Line begins		
1930			
	Allied army of occupation removed		
1933			
30 January	Hitler becomes Chancellor		
October	Germany leaves Disarmament Conference and League of Nations		
1934			
19 August	Hitler becomes head of state on death of Hindenburg		Start of the Neckar-Enz line
1935			
1 March	The Saar is returned to Germany		Start of the building work on the Wetterau-Main-Tauber line
11 March	Existence of Luftwaffe made public		
16 March	Hitler introduces conscription		
1936			
		22 February	Order for the secret reconnaissance of the demilitarised zone of the Rhineland
7 March	Germany remilitarises the Rhineland		
1937			
			Difficulties with raw materials and delivery schedules lead to a lengthening of the forecast building time to 1948 and finally 1952
1938			
11 March	Germany annexes Austria	March	West Wall extended and strengthened
		1 April	General Wilhelm Adam takes over command of the 2nd Army Group

		28 May	Hitler orders the accelerated construction of the West Wall with 11,800 supplementary bunkers to be built by October 1938 – *Limesprogramm*
		June	Göring visits West Wall and issues damning report. Hitler charges Dr Fritz Todt with the completion of the construction work in the west
		1–2 July	Hitler dictates his memorandum on fortification design
		16 July	Hitler decides on the suspension of all large-scale party and state building in favour of the *Limesprogramm*
		26–29 August	Hitler visits West Wall
29 September	Munich agreement signed		
5 October	Germany occupies Czech Sudetenland	9–14 October	Hitler makes second visit to West Wall. In speech at Saarbrücken announces *Aachen-Saar Programm*
		Autumn	West Wall extended along the Dutch border
1939			
		February	Decision made to strengthen bunkers
14 March	Germany occupies Bohemia and Moravia		
31 March	Chamberlain announces France and Great Britain to guarantee Poland		
		May	Hitler makes third visit to West Wall
		24 July	Hitler makes final visit to West Wall
23 August	Nazi Soviet Pact signed		
31 August	Hitler issues War Directive 1		
1 September	Germany invades Poland		
3 September	France and Great Britain declare war on Germany		
7 September	France launches 'Saar offensive'		
17 September	USSR invades Poland		
5 October	Organised Polish resistance ends		
1940			
9 April	Germany invades Norway and Denmark		
10 May	Germany launches offensive in west. Churchill succeeds Chamberlain		
15 May	British strategic air offensive against Germany starts. Dutch Army surrenders		
26 May	Dunkirk evacuation starts		

28 May	Belgian Army surrenders		
2 June	Allies withdraw from Norway		
4 June	Dunkirk evacuation completes		
14 June	Germans enter Paris		
22 June	France signs armistice with Germany		
18 December	Hitler issues Directive 21 for the invasion of the USSR		
1941			
22 June	Germany invades USSR		
11 December	Germany declares war on USA	December	Work on 'Atlantic Wall' begins
1942			
		February	Fritz Todt killed in an air crash
19 August	Dieppe raid		
		September	Further construction work on coast defences ordered – U-boat pens, ports and harbours
1943			
		3 November	Hitler issues Directive 51 ordering the strengthening of coastal defences
1944			
4 January	Red Army crosses pre-war Polish border		
6 June	Operation Overlord starts: Allies land in Normandy		
20 July	Attempt to assassinate Hitler fails		
		20 August	Hitler's decree for levy of 'people's' labour for West Wall
		24 August	Hitler orders building of a new West Wall
25 August	Germans surrender in Paris		
4 September	Allies capture Antwerp		
11 September	First US Army reaches German border	11 September	Von Rundstedt placed in command of western defences
17 September	Operation Market Garden launched to establish bridgehead at Arnhem		
21 October	First German city captured when Aachen falls to US troops		
16 December	Germans launch Ardennes offensive		
1945			
7 March	US First Army crosses Rhine at Remagen		
25 April	Soviet and US troops meet at Torgau		
30 April	Hitler commits suicide		
2 May	Red Army captures Berlin		
7 May	Unconditional surrender signed by Jodl		
8 May	VE Day		

Typology

Construction strength B1

NO.	DESCRIPTION	CREW	CONCRETE VOLUME	MAXIMUM PRICE RM
1	MG Pillbox	5	95	26,500
1a	MG Pillbox (entrance at rear)	5	100	26,500
2	MG Pillbox with infantry section (flank)	18	195	45,000
2a	MG Pillbox with infantry section (frontal)	18	193	45,000
3	MG Pillbox with small cloche	7	144	41,000
4I	MG Pillbox with small cloche and infantry section	20	201	46,000
4II	MG Pillbox with small cloche and infantry section (flank)	20	201	46,000
5	Double MG Pillbox	10	158	43,000
5a	Double MG Pillbox (with self-contained section)	10	157	43,000
6	Double MG Pillbox with infantry section	23	229	55,000
7	Double MG Pillbox with small cloche	12	172	46,000
7a	Double MG Pillbox with small cloche and self contained fire sector	12	–	–
8	Double MG Pillbox with small cloche and infantry section	25	238	57,000
9	MG Pillbox with cover plate	5	102	35,000
10	MG Pillbox with cover plate and with infantry section (flank)	18	193	49,000
10a	MG Pillbox with cover plate and with infantry section	18	193	49,000
11	MG Pillbox with cover plate and small cloche	7	141	45,000
12	MG Pillbox with cover plate, small cloche and infantry section (flank)	20	195	52,000
12a	MG Pillbox with cover plate, small cloche and infantry section	20	197	52,000
13	Double MG Pillbox with cover plate	10	153	51,000
14	Double MG Pillbox with cover plate and infantry section	23	226	63,000
15	Double MG Pillbox with cover plate and small cloche	12	218	63,000
16	Double MG Pillbox with cover plate, small cloche and infantry section	25	235	66,000
17	MG Pillbox with extra loophole and infantry section	20	220	53,000

18	Pak Pillbox (fire sector 60°)	5	192	45,000
18a	Pak Pillbox (fire sector 30°)	5	190	44,000
19	Pak and MG Pillbox (Pak 60°)	10	230	57,000
19a	Pak and MG Pillbox (Pak 30°)	10	228	56,000
20	Pak dugout with MG loophole installation	10	192	45,000
21	Pak dugout with small cloche and MG loophole installation	12	214	53,000
22	Company commander gun position with MG loophole installation	12	203	45,000
23	Gun position with 3 loophole armoured turret	5	131	51,000
24	Gun position with 3 loophole armoured turret and infantry section	18	215	70,000
25	Gun position with 6 loophole armoured turret	10	153	90,000
26	Gun position with 6 loophole armoured turret and infantry section	23	225	105,000
27	Battalion battle HQ with MG loophole installation	18	263	59,000
28	Artillery observation post	8	180	68,000
28a	Artillery observation post with MG loophole installation	13	245	85,000

Total number constructed (B1)   **710**

Construction strength C

1	MG Pillbox	5	41	14,000
2	MG Pillbox with infantry section	18	98	27,000
3	Gun position with 3 loophole armoured turret	5	55	24,000
4	Gun position with 6 loophole armoured turret	5	54	24,000
5	Pak Pillbox (fire sector 60°)	6	112	31,000
5a	Pak Pillbox (fire sector 30°)	6	109	30,000
6	Pak and MG Pillbox (Pak 60°)	10	144	39,000
6a	Pak and MG Pillbox (Pak 30°)	10	141	38,000
7	Double MG Pillbox	10	95	28,500
7a	Double MG Pillbox with self contained fire sector	10	95	28,500
8	Pak dugout with MG loophole installation	10	*c.* 94	31,500
–	Pak Pillbox (fire sector 30°)	6	*c.* 60	–

Construction strength D

1	MG Pillbox	5	14.8	7,000
2	MG Pillbox	5	14	7,000
3	MG Pillbox	5	11.2	7,000
4	MG Pillbox	5	8.4	6,000
5	MG Pillbox with corrugated sheet metal revetment	5	14.5	6,000
–	Pak bunker	–	*c.* 11.3	–

Total number constructed (C and D)   **716**

REGULAR STRUCTURES OF THE *LIMESPROGRAMM*

NO.	DESCRIPTION	CREW	CONCRETE VOLUME	QUANTITY
1	MG Pillbox with armoured loophole	5	169	522
1a	MG Pillbox with armoured loophole (for Upper Rhine)	5	206	–
2	MG Pillbox with infantry section	18	335	57
3	Double MG Pillbox	10	257	236
10	Infantry section dugout	15	252 }	
	Infantry section dugout with added combat room	15	287 }	3,471
10a	Infantry section dugout	14	297	
	Infantry section dugout with added combat room	14	358	1,536
10b1	Infantry section dugout (forward slope) with two entrances	14	404	7
10b2	Infantry section dugout (forward slope) with one entrance	14	404	11
11	Double infantry section dugout	27	343 }	
	Double infantry section dugout with added combat room	27	380 }	1,338
18	Gun emplacement for field gun (FK16 n.A)	6	376	116
19	Stand for artillery observer (open)	6	258	230
19a	Stand for artillery observer with armoured turret 21P7	8	435	41
19b	Stand for artillery observer with armoured turret 44P8	8	400	–
19c	Stand for artillery observer and flash ranging station	6	231	3
19d	Stand for advanced artillery observer	3	189	37
19e	Stand for artillery observer and flash ranging station	6	362	–
19f	Stand for advanced artillery observer	3	308	–
20	Gun emplacement for 3.7cm Pak	6	325	591
20a	Gun emplacement for 3.7cm Pak (Upper Rhine)	–	234	–
20b	Gun emplacement for 3.7cm Pak with loophole plate	6	340	–
20c	Gun emplacement for 3.7cm Pak with loophole plate	6	340	–
22	Gun emplacement for 8.8cm Flak	9	350	56
22a	Gun emplacement for 7.5cm Flak	6	362	–
22b	Gun emplacement for 8.8cm Flak (open)	–	25	–
22c	Gun emplacement for 7.5cm Flak (open)	–	24	–
23	MG Pillbox	5	228	458

24	Double MG Pillbox without armoured loophole (Upper Rhine)	10	446	294
25	Double MG Pillbox with armoured loophole (Upper Rhine)	10	400	111
26	Double MG Pillbox without armoured loophole	10	276	156
27	Signals position	–	12	–
28	Stand for artillery observer with small cloche (Upper Rhine)	6	330	86
29	Six loophole turret with infantry section (B Small work)	23	479	24
30	Gun emplacement for 17cm naval gun	9	2,000	15
30a	Gun emplacement for 17cm naval gun (inclined body)	9	2,130	–
31	Regimental command post	32	514	146
32	Medical dugout	24	512	81
33	Ammunition dugout for 7.5cm or 8.8cm Flak	–	150	33
34	Gun emplacement for 24cm naval gun	33	4,700	2
35	Gun emplacement for 30.5cm naval gun	12	1,851	2
36	Gun emplacement for 10.5cm naval Flak	–	1,250	1
37	Ammunition dugout for 1FH, sFH and Flak	–	410	39

Total number constructed **9,700**

REGULAR STRUCTURES OF THE *AACHEN-SAAR PROGRAMM*

NO.	OLD NO.	DESCRIPTION	CREW	CONCRETE VOLUME	QUANTITY
51	–	Dugout for trench position	6	*c.* 124	–
51a	–	Dugout for trench position	6	*c.* 120	–
96	–	Gun position with six loophole turret (D) in B	9	440	17
101a/b†	15a	Infantry section dugout	15	590	
101c/d†	15a	Infantry section dugout	15	526	603
101v††	–	Infantry section dugout	15	376	27
102a/b†	16a	Double infantry section dugout	27	792	
102c/d†	16a	Double infantry section dugout	27	732	
102v††	–	Double infantry section dugout	30	588	606
103a/b†	1	MG Pillbox	6	570	
103c/d†	1	MG Pillbox	6	480	61
104a/b†	1	MG Pillbox with infantry section	18	782	
104c/d	1	MG Pillbox with infantry section	18	690	24
105a/b†	1	MG Casemate	6	564	
105c/d†	1	MG Casemate	6	470	513
106a/b†	1	MG Casemate with infantry section	18	768	
106c/d†	1	MG Casemate with infantry section	18	677	144
107a/b†	2	Double MG Casemate	12	762	
107c/d†	2	Double MG Casemate	12	707	139

108a/b†	2	MG Pillbox with MG Casemate	12	760 }	
108c/d†	2	MG Pillbox with MG Casemate	12	705	226
109a	3	Pak Casemate with periscope and flanking installation	6	741	
109b	3	Pak Casemate with small cloche and flanking installation	6	801	
109c	3	Pak Casemate with periscope but without flanking installation	6	689 }	
109d	3	Pak Casemate with small cloche but without flanking installation	6	749	20
110a	4	Gun position with three loophole turret (B) in B with flanking installation	6	610 }	
110b	4	Gun position with three loophole turret (B) in B without flanking installation	6	530	23
111a	4	Gun position with three loophole turret (B) and infantry section in B with flanking installation	18	817 }	
111b	4	Gun position with three loophole turret (B) and infantry section in B without flanking installation	18	734	44
112a	5a	Gun position with six loophole turret (B) in B with flanking installation	12	660 }	
112b	5a	Gun position with six loophole turret (B) in B without flanking installation	12	572	10
113a	5a	Gun position with six loophole turret (B) and infantry section in B with flanking installation	24	864	
113b	5a	Gun position with six loophole turret (B) and infantry section in B without flanking installation	24	778 }	
113d	–	Gun position with six loophole turret (B) and infantry section in B – two floors without flanking installation	26	977	12
114a	5b	Gun position with six loophole turret (B) in A with flanking installation	12	1,865 }	
114b	5b	Gun position with six loophole turret (B) in A without flanking installation	12	1,571	42
115a	5b	Gun position with six loophole turret (B) and infantry section in A with flanking installation	24	2,281 }	
115b	5b	Without flanking installation	24	2,032	161

115d	–	Gun position with six loophole turret (B) and infantry section in A – two floors without flanking installation	c. 26	2,172	73
115/133	–	Gun position with three loophole turret in A	24	2,281	–
116a	6	Pak and MG Casemate with small cloche and flanking installation	12	813	67
116b	6	Pak and MG Casemate with periscope and flanking installation	12	813	67
116c	6	Pak and MG Casemate with small cloche without flanking installation	12	765	67
116d	6	Pak and MG Casemate with periscope without flanking installation	12	765	67
117a†	7	Battalion or Regimental command post	20	1,092 ⎫	
117b†	7	Battalion or Regimental command post	20	1,025 ⎭	72
118	8	Medical dugout	22(33)	856 ⎫	
118b	–	Medical dugout	36	1,210 ⎭	39
119a†	(9)	Dugout for battery command post	12	999 ⎫	
119b†	(9)		12	930 ⎭	29
120a	10a	Artillery observation post (in B) with flanking installation	c. 9	629 ⎫	
120b	10a	Artillery observation post (in B) without flanking installation	c. 9	535 ⎭	96
120d	–	Artillery observation post (in B) two floors without flanking installation	c. 9	600	3
121a	10b	Artillery observation post (in A) with flanking installation	9	1,692 ⎫	
121b	10b	Artillery observation post (in A) without flanking installation	9	1,424 ⎭	23
122	11a	Munitions dugout	–	955	–
123	11b	Munitions dugout	–	530	–
124	12	Artillery shelter (in A)	8	2,312	–
125	13	Double gun casemate (in A)	40	7,000	–
126	14	Open fire position with ammunition dugout	–	1,217	–
127	15b	Infantry section dugout on a steep slope	15	406	6
128	16b	Double infantry section dugout on a steep slope	27	655	3

129a	17	Pak Pillbox with small cloche and flanking installation	6	705	
129b	17	Pak Pillbox with periscope but without flanking installation	6	635	
129c	–	Pak Pillbox with small cloche but without flanking installation	6	635	
129d	–	Pak Pillbox with periscope and flanking installation	6	705	5
130a	17	Pak shelter with small cloche and flanking installation	6	640	
130b	17	Pak shelter with periscope but without flanking installation	6	575	
130c	–	Pak shelter with small cloche but without flanking installation	6	575	
130d	–	Pak shelter with periscope and flanking installation	6	640	99
131a	–	Dugout with six loophole turret (A1) with two infantry sections on two floors in A with flanking installation	39	2,884	
131b	–	Dugout with six loophole turret (A1) with two infantry sections on two floors in A without flanking installation	39	c. 2,510	1
132a	–	Dugout with three loophole turret (B) in A with flanking installation	12	1,915	
132b	–	Dugout with three loophole turret (B) in A without flanking installation	12	1,621	–
133a	–	Dugout with three loophole turret (B) with infantry section in A with flanking installation	24	2,331	
133b	–	Dugout with three loophole turret (B) with infantry section in A without flanking installation	24	2,082	
133d	–	Dugout with three loophole turret loophole turret (B) with infantry section on two floors in A without flanking installation	24	c. 2,222	3
135a	–	Dugout for M19 with small cloche	17	975	
135b	–	(in B) on two floors	–	–	
136a	–	Dugout for M19 with small cloche	17	2,543	
136b	–	(in a) on two floors	–	–	–
137a	–	Dugout with three loophole turret (A1) in A with flanking installation	12	1,915	
137b	–	Dugout with three loophole turret (A1) in A (as 132b) with flanking installation	12	1,621	–

138a	–	Dugout with three loophole turret (A1) with infantry section in A (as 133a) with flanking installation	24	2,331	⎫
138b	–	Dugout with three loophole turret (A1) with infantry section in A (as 133b) without flanking installation	24	2,082	⎬ –
139a	–	Casemate for 4.7cm Czech fortress A/T gun and double barrelled machine gun with periscope and flanking installation	18	1,079	⎫
139b	–	Casemate for 4.7cm Czech fortress A/T gun and double barrelled machine gun with small cloche and flanking installation	18	1,079	⎬ 24
139c	–	Casemate for 4.7cm Czech fortress A/T gun and double barrelled machine gun with periscope but without flanking installation	18	1,007	⎫
139d	–	Casemate for 4.7cm Czech fortress A/T gun and double barrelled machine gun with small cloche but without flanking installation	18	1,007	⎬ 24
395	–	Dugout with observer post in tamped concrete	6–12	210	–
396	–	Dugout in tamped concrete	12–20	250	–
501	–	Infantry section dugout	c. 14	356	29
502	–	Double infantry section dugout	c. 26	629	6
503	–	MG Casemate with infantry section	18	594	60
504	–	Pak shelter with infantry section	12	537	16
505	–	Pak Casemate	6	539	12
506a	–	Pak Casemate for 4.7cm fortress A/T gun 36(t) (right)	14	778	⎫
506b	–	Pak Casemate for 4.7cm fortress A/T gun 36(t) (left)	14	778	⎬ 20
507a	–	Artillery bunker for sFH18, 10cm K (without revolving platform) with side munitions room	–	1,147	⎫
507b	–	Artillery bunker for sFH18, 10cm K with side munitions room	–	998	⎬
507c	–	Artillery bunker (507b) + (512)	–	–	28
508a	–	Artillery bunker for sFH18, 10cm K with side munitions room being under that	–	935	⎫
508b	–	Artillery bunker (508a) with the superstructure of 513	–	–	⎬ –

509	–	Auxiliary artillery observation post	6	265	–
509a	–	Auxiliary artillery observation post on steep slope	6	287	87
509b	–	Auxiliary artillery observation post	6	287	117
509c	–	Auxiliary artillery observation post flank turned towards opponent	12	497	93
509c SK	–	Auxiliary artillery observation post flank turned towards opponent (on steep slope)	12	c. 450	–
510a	–	Artillery bunker for 1FH with side munitions room	–	c. 988	27
510b	–	Artillery bunker (510a) + (512)	–	–	–
511a	–	Artillery bunker for 1FH with munitions room	–	c. 925	24
511b	–	Artillery bunker (511a) with the superstructure of 513	–	–	–
512	–	Munitions dugout for artillery bunker lateral arrangement (f.sFH 18)	–	–	–
513	–	Munitions dugout with artillery bunker lying over it (f.1FH 18)	–	–	–
514	–	MG Casemate	6	383	29
515	–	MG Casemate on steep slope	6	c. 389	28
516a	–	United artillery bunker with side munitions room	15	1,518	24
516b	–	United artillery bunker with side munitions room and added crew room	15	1,242	–
517	–	Open artillery gun position for 8.35cm Flak(t) with crew and munitions room	6	830	–
518a/b	–	Double artillery gun position	30	2,836	–
SK6a	–	Gun position with six loophole turret and flanking installation	9	483	11

Total number constructed   **3,828**

†   'a' with small cloche and flanking installation
    'b' with periscope and flanking installation
    'c' with small cloche but without flanking installation
    'd' with periscope but without flanking installation
††   Simplified version using fewer materials, for example 64 per cent of the concrete used in structure 101a/b

REGULAR STRUCTURES OF THE LVZ WEST

NO.	DESCRIPTION	CREW	CONCRETE VOLUME	QUANTITY
B	MG Pillbox	6	182	251
F	Infantry section dugout (Führer shelter)	18	289	470
K	Battle Headquarters	24	454	43
M	Munitions room	–	153	172
Pz	Pak shelter with small cloche	15	361	141
U	Double infantry section dugout	27	343	438
V	Infantry section dugout on forward slope	12	270	29

Total number constructed   **1,544**

CONSTRUCTION DESIGNS OF 1944/45

NO.	DESCRIPTION	CREW	CONCRETE VOLUME	QUANTITY
612	Artillery bunker (cannon up to 10.5cm)	–	385	It is unclear
621	Infantry section dugout as battle HQ	10	485	how many of
669	Artillery bunker (guns up to 15cm)	–	495	these
677	Pillbox for 8.8cm Pak	–	380	shelters
687	Panther turret on concrete shelter	3	175	were
701	Pak shelter (max 1 sFH)	–	380	finished
702	Infantry section dugout	Up to 12	385	
703	Pillbox for 8.8cm Pak on pivot mounting IIa	–	370	

Pak – *Panzerabwehrkanone* – anti-tank gun
Flak – *Flugabwehrkanone* – anti-aircraft gun

Bibliography

Anonymous, *Spearhead in the West: The Third Armored Division 1941–45* (Battery Press, Nashville, 1980).

G. Astor, *The Bloody Forest. Battle for the Huertgen: September 1944–January 1945* (Presidio Press, Novato, USA, 2000).

N. Bethell, *The War Hitler Won: September 1939* (Allen Lane, Penguin Press, London, 1972).

M. Blumenson, *The Patton Papers 1940–1945* (Houghton Mifflin, Boston, 1974).

G. Blumentritt, *Von Rundstedt: The Soldier and the Man* (Odhams Press, London, 1952).

O.N. Bradley and C. Blair, *A General's Life* (Sidgwick & Jackson, London, 1983).

A. Bryant, *Triumph in the West 1943–1946* (Fontana, 1965).

L.G. Byrnes *History of the 94th Infantry Division in World War II* (Battery Press, Nashville, 1982).

A.D. Chandler Jr (ed.), *The Papers of Dwight David Eisenhower. The War Years: IV* (Johns Hopkins University Press, Baltimore, 1970).

W. Churchill, *The Gathering Storm, The Hinge of Fate, Closing the Ring and Triumph and Tragedy, Vols. I, IV, V and VI, The Second World War* (Cassell, London, 1951, 1952).

J.J. Clarke and R. Ross Smith, *United States Army in World War II. The European Theater of Operations: Riviera to the Rhine* (Center of Military History, United States Army, Washington, 1993).

J. Colby, *War From the Ground Up: The 90th Division in World War II* (Nortex Press, Austin, Texas, 1991).

H.M. Cole, *United States Army in World War II. The European Theater of Operations: The Lorraine Campaign* (Center of Military History, United States Army, Washington, 1950).

P. Delaforce, *Monty's Marauders: Black Rat and Red Fox* (Tom Donovan Publishing, Brighton, 1997).

T. Draper, *The 84th Infantry Division in the Battle of Germany, November 1944 – May 1945* (Viking Press, New York, 1946).

Lt Col. G. Dyer, *XII Corps: Spearhead of Patton's Third Army* (XII Corps History Association, 1947).

J. Eastwood, *Topics of the Moment. The Maginot and Siegfried Lines* (Pallas, London, 1939).

J. Ehrman, *Grand Strategy, Vol. V, The History of the Second World War* (HMSO, London, 1956).

D. Eisenhower, *Crusade in Europe* (William Heinemann, London, 1948).

H. Essame, *The Battle for Germany* (B.T. Batsford, London, 1969).

J.H. Ewing, *29 Let's Go! A History of the 29th Infantry Division in World War II* (Infantry Journal Press, Washington, 1948).

K. Ford, *Assault on Germany: The Battle for Geilenkirchen* (David & Charles, Newton Abbot, 1989).

W. Gorlitz (ed.), *The Memoirs of Field Marshal Keitel* (William Kimber, London, 1965).

R.J. Greenwald, *Order of Battle of the United States Army: World War II ETO Divisions* (Office of the Theater Historian, Paris, 1945).

M. Gross, *Der Westwall zwischen Niederrhein und Schnee-Eifel* (Rheinland-Verlag, Köln, 1989).

R.L. Hewitt, *Work Horse of the Western Front: The Story of the 30th Infantry Division* (Battery Press, Nashville, 1980).

F.H. Hinsley, *British Intelligence in the Second World War, Its Influence on Strategy and Operations,* 4 Vols (HMSO, London 1979–1990).

G. Hofmann, *The Super Sixth: History of the 6th Armored Division in World War II* (Sixth Armored Division Association, Kentucky, 1975).

A. Horne, *To Lose a Battle: France 1940* (Macmillan, London, 1969).

D.E. Houston, *Hell on Wheels: The 2nd Armored Division* (Presidio Press, San Rafael, California, 1977).

D. Irving, *The War Path: Hitler's Germany 1933–9* (Michael Joseph, London, 1978).

J.E. Kaufmann and R.M. Jurga, *Fortress Europe – European Fortifications in World War II* (Combined Publishing, Pennsylvania, 1999).

A. Kesselring, *The Memoirs of Field Marshal Kesselring* (William Kimber, 1964).

H.R. Knickerbocker *et al., Danger Forward: The Story of the First Divisions in World War II* (Albert Love Enterprises, Atlanta, Georgia, 1947).

Marshal de Lattre de Tassigny, *The History of the French First Army* (George Allen & Unwin, London, 1952).

C.B. MacDonald, *United States Army in World War II. The European Theater of Operations: Arnaville, Altuzzo and Schmidt* (Center of Military History, United States Army, Washington, 1952).

C.B. MacDonald, *United States Army in World War II. The European Theater of Operations: The Last Offensive* (Center of Military History, United States Army, Washington, 1973).

C.B. MacDonald, *United States Army in World War II. The European Theater of Operations: The Siegfried Line Campaign* (Center of Military History, United States Army, Washington, 1984).

P.R. Mansoor, *The GI Offensive in Europe: The Triumph of American Infantry Divisions, 1941–1945* (University Press of Kansas, 1999).

C. Messenger, *The Last Prussian: A Biography of Field Marshal Gerd von Rundstedt 1875–1953* (Brassey's, London, 1991).

Capt. J.B. Mittelman, *Eight Stars to Victory: A History of the Veteran Ninth US Infantry Division* (Ninth Infantry Association, Washington, 1948).

J.H. Morgan, *Assize of Arms: The Disarmament of Germany and Her Rearmament (1919–1939)* (Methuen & Co., London, 1945).

J. Noakes and G. Pridham (eds), *Nazism 1919–1945. 3: Foreign Policy, War and Racial Extermination* (University of Exeter Press, 1991).

P. Oldham, *The Hindenburg Line* (Leo Cooper, London, 2000).

C. Partridge, *Hitler's Atlantic Wall* (DI Publications, Guernsey, Channel Islands, 1976).

G.S. Patton, *War as I Knew it* (Riverside Press, Cambridge, MA, 1947).

N. Prefer, *Patton's Ghost Corps: Cracking the Siegfried Line* (Presidio, Novato, CA 1998).

E.M. Robertson, *Hitler's Pre-War Policy and Military Plans 1933–39* (Longmans, London, 1963).

R. Rolf and P. Saal, *Fortress Europe* (Airlife Publishing, Shrewsbury, 1988).

V. Rowe, *The Great Wall of France: The Triumph of the Maginot Line* (Putnam, London, 1959).

T. Shachtman, *The Phony War 1939–1940* (Harper & Row, New York, 1982).

D. Seck, *Unternehmen Westwall* (Bucherverlag Saarbrücker Zeitung, Saarbrücken, 1980).

M. Shulman, *Defeat in the West* (Secker & Warburg, London, 1986).

H.D. Steward, *Thunderbolt: The History of the Eleventh Armored Division* (Battery Press, Nashville, 1981).

T. Taylor, *Munich: The Price of Peace* (Hodder & Stoughton, London, 1979).

N. Thomas, *Wehrmacht Auxiliary Forces* (Osprey, London, 1992).

H.R. Trevor Roper (ed.), *Hitler's War Directives 1939–45* (Sidgwick & Jackson, London, 1964).

Various, *Wir bauen des Reiches Sicherheit! Mythos und Realität des Westwalls 1938–1945* (Argon Verlag, Berlin, 1992).

R. Weigley, *Eisenhower's Lieutenants: The Campaign of France and Germany 1944–45* (Bloomington, Indiana University Press, 1981).

Gen. W. Warlimont, *Inside Hitler's Headquarters 1939–45* (Presidio Press, Novato, CA, 1964).

I. Werstein, *Betrayal: The Munich Pact of 1938* (Doubleday, New York, 1969).

S. Westphal, *The German Army in the West* (Cassell, London, 1951).

B. Whaley, *Covert German Rearmament, 1919–1939: Deception and Misperception* (University Publications of America, Maryland, 1984).

W.D and S. Whitaker, *Rhineland: The Battle to End the War* (Leo Cooper, London, 1989).

C. Whiting, *The Battle for the German Frontier* (Windrush Press, Moreton-in-Marsh, 2000).

C. Whiting, *West Wall: The Battle for Hitler's Siegfried Line* (Spellmount, Staplehurst, 1999).

C. Whiting, *Bloody Aachen* (Spellmount, Staplehurst, 2000).

C. Whiting, *Siegfried – The Nazis' Last Stand* (Leo Cooper, London, 1983).

W. Willems and H. Koschik, *Der Westwall Vom Denkmalwert des Unterfreulichen* (Rheinland-Verlag, Köln, 1998).

D.G. Williamson, *The British in Germany, 1918–1930: The Reluctant Occupiers* (Berg, Oxford, 1991).
Other Publications
J. Fuhrmeister, *The Westwall in the area of Bad Bergzabern.*
J. Fuhrmeister, *Die Geschichte eines Westwallbunkers an der Saar.*
J. Fuhrmeister and T. Hornig, *Die Halberg – Stellung ein Stück Westwall in Saarbrücken* (1997).
H. Lauer, *Zweibrücken am Westwall* (1989).
F. Wein Festungen Heft 1 'Die Luftverteidigungszone des Westwalls bei Freudenstadt'.
F. Wein Festungen 'Sperrstellen des Westwalls im Schwarzwald' (1998).

ARCHIVAL SOURCES

Public Record Office (London)

Foreign Office Papers
FO1013/2326   Disarmament of Siegfried Line
FO1062/111   Siegfried Line: German proposal for afforestation

War Office Papers
WO 190/829   The Siegfried Line 28 June 1939
WO 190/873   Notes on broadcast about the Siegfried Line 18 October 1939
WO193/157   Siegfried Line: notes on attack on fortified towns. December 1939–May 1940
WO195/6858   Anti-concrete committee: the Siegfried Line 1944
WO195/8366   Anti-concrete committee: control commission experimental demolitions at La Penne and Siegfried Line 1945
WO197/7   Siegfried Line: photographic reconnaissance by RAF September–October 1939
WO208/2151   Notes on the Siegfried Line June 1944
WO208/3184   Development of Organisation Todt 1938–44
WO216/970   Study of German evasions of military provisions of the Treaty of Versailles 1944
WO219/2886   Operation Naples I: Forcing of the Siegfried Line: outline plans September 1944
WO219/2891   Operation Choker I: to assist in attack on the Siegfried Line from rear of Saarbrücken November 1944
WO219/5129   Defences at Brest and breaking the Siegfried Line October 1944
WO219/5131   Report on the Siegfried Line at the Schnee Eifel Ridge: Engineer Technical Intelligence Team January 1945
WO223/99   Staff College Camberley 1947 Course notes on D-Day Landings and ensuing campaigns. 6 Battalion KOSB The Siegfried Line February 1945

Imperial War Museum (London)
89/13/1 Mason, Lieutenant W.E.
88/60/1 Sheldon, Captain D.L.
01/13/1 Skinner, Reverend L.F.
PP/MCR/353 Wingfield, Brigadier A.D.R. DSO, MC

Index